Women and the Making of the Modern House:

A Social and Architectural History

Women and the Making of the Modern House:
A Social and Architectural History

Alice T. Friedman

Harry N. Abrams, Inc., Publishers

EDITOR: Diana Murphy
DESIGNER: Judith Hudson

LIBRARY OF CONGRESS CATALOGING–IN–PUBLICATION DATA
Friedman, Alice T.
 Women and the making of the modern house : a social and
 architectural history / Alice Friedman.
   p.   cm.
 Includes bibliographical references and index.
 ISBN 0–8109–3989–4
 1. Architecture and women. 2. Architects and patrons.
 3. Dwellings—History—20th century. I. Title.
 NA2543.W65F75   1998
 720' .82—dc21   97–23860

Printed and bound in Hong Kong

On the title page: Truus Schröder and her daughter Han at home
(see page 79).

On page 6: Detail from Le Corbusier's preliminary plans for Villa
Stein–de Monzie (see page 113).

The quotation on page 7 is taken from William Maxwell, *Time
Will Darken It* (New York: Harper & Bros., 1948), pp. 7–8.

An earlier version of "No Ordinary House: Frank Lloyd Wright,
Aline Barnsdall, and Hollyhock House" was published as "A House
Is Not a Home: Hollyhock House as 'Art-Theater Garden,'" in *Journal
of the Society of Architectural Historians* 51 (Sept. 1992), 239–60.

An earlier version of "Family Matters: The Schröder House, by
Gerrit Rietveld and Truus Schröder" was published as "Not a Muse:
The Client's Role at the Rietveld Schröder House," in Diana
Agrest, Patricia Conway, and Leslie Kanes Weisman, eds., *The Sex
of Architecture* (New York: Abrams, 1996), 217–32.

An earlier version of "People Who Live in Glass Houses: Edith
Farnsworth, Ludwig Mies van der Rohe, and Philip Johnson" was
published as "Domestic Differences: Mies van der Rohe, Edith
Farnsworth, and the Gendered Body," in Christopher Reed, ed.,
*Not at Home: The Suppression of Domesticity in Modern Art and
Architecture* (London: Thames and Hudson, 1996), 179–92.

Harry N. Abrams, Inc.
100 Fifth Avenue
New York, N.Y. 10011
www.abramsbooks.com

Contents

K —————————— 2/ —————————— S

4½ × 5   2 × 5   4½ ×
Buanderie   Vac.   Calo
                      wc

4½ × 5   Lavabo wc
Séchoir   Entrée
                5×

N

2800 M cubes

2/ 2/
————— M carres
2/ 31

If you happen to be curious about the Indians of Venezuela, you can supply yourself with credentials from the Ministry of Education and letters from various oil companies to their representatives in field camps. With your personal belongings and scientific instruments, including excavating tools for, say, a crew of twelve men – with several hundred sugar bags for specimens, emergency food rations, mosquito netting, and other items essential for carrying on such archaeological work – you can start digging and with luck unearth pottery and skeletons that have lain in the ground since somewhere around A.D. 1000. The very poverty of the evidence will lead you to brilliant and far-reaching hypotheses.

To arrive at some idea of the culture of a certain street in a Middle Western small town shortly before the First World War, is a much more delicate undertaking. For one thing, there are no ruins to guide you. Though the houses are not kept up as well as they once were, they are still standing. Of certain barns and outbuildings that are gone (and with them trellises and trumpet vines) you will find no trace whatever. In every yard a dozen landmarks (here a lilac bush, there a sweet syringa) are missing. There is no telling what became of the hanging fern baskets with American flags in them or of all those red geraniums. The people who live on Elm Street now belong to a different civilization. They can tell you nothing. You will not need mosquito netting or emergency rations, and the only specimens you will find, possibly the only thing that will prove helpful to you, will be a glass marble or a locust shell split up the back and empty.

– William Maxwell, *Time Will Darken It* (1948)

Introduction

When Frank Lloyd Wright sat down to write his autobiography in the late 1920s, he devoted some of his most impassioned and fitful prose to setting the record straight about two women clients – Aline Barnsdall and Alice Millard. Recounting how he had designed and built their homes in the Los Angeles area during the 1920s, Wright explained that the romantic beauty of the California landscape had inspired him to unprecedented flights of artistic imagination. For him Barnsdall's sprawling home on Olive Hill in Hollywood (a courtyard house intended as the centerpiece of a new theatrical community) was "a California Romanza," and he compared its "poetry of form" to a piece of music that offers the musician "free form or freedom to make one's own form." Millard's Pasadena "studio-house" (fig. 1), designed as a home and showroom for her rare book and antique business, he named "La Miniatura," declaring that it was to be "nothing less than a distinctly genuine expression of California in terms of modern industry and American life."[1] These houses set new standards for American architecture, Wright insisted, but there had been serious problems with both – and he wanted to explain why.

As women clients, Wright complained, Barnsdall and Millard were particularly susceptible to the manipulations of builders whose goal was to siphon off their money while undermining their confidence in the architect. Moreover, as women "alone" (Barnsdall was unmarried and Millard was a widow), both clients were surrounded by "friends" and advisers, an "'I told you so' brigade" determined to "protect" them and steal their loyalty away.[2] What was it about a contractor, Wright asked, "that inspires confidence in the client – especially if the client be a woman?"[3] Barnsdall and Millard placed their trust in their builders "as safe insurance against what might prove to be too single-minded devotion to an idea on the part of [the] architect."[4] The last point was particularly hard to take: never mind that the roofs leaked – hadn't these women come to *him* to realize their dreams?[5]

The challenge, as Wright suggested, was to balance the hard realities of program and budget against the runaway fantasies these projects inspired in him. He had invented a new system of concrete block construction

Frank Lloyd Wright. Millard
House (La Miniatura), Pasadena,
California. 1923–24

for La Miniatura and he was determined to make it work, but he had to confess that Millard's friends were probably right: for him, La Miniatura had become "far more than a mere house" – it was "amounting to a passion."[6] He described how he called himself "the Weaver" when he dreamed of it:

Came visions of a new Architecture for a new Life – the life of romantic, beautiful California – the reaction upon a hitherto unawakened people. Other buildings sprang full-born into my mind from that humble beginning in bewildering variety and beauty. Gradually all complications, and needless expense of the treacherous, wasteful building system of a whole country went by the board…. And I might as well admit it – I quite forgot this little building belonged to Alice Millard at all. Palladio! Bramante! Sansovino! Sculptors – all! Here was I, the "Weaver." What might not now grow out of this little commonplace circumstance?[7]

Millard, whom Wright described as having been "lightly but inexorably grasped by the architectural fates and used for high exemplar," clung bravely to her project as the architect and builder did battle around her.[8] Her determination was rewarded: because she had "fought for it and won," Wright concluded, La Miniatura was Millard's "home in more than the ordinary sense."[9]

Wright had a great deal more to say about Barnsdall – the story of her house is told in the first chapter of this book – and it is clear from his autobiography that he had intense and conflicted feelings about her, not just as a client but as a woman. She was, he wrote, "a restless spirit," whose love of the theater kept her far from home for months at a time – she was "as domestic as a shooting star."[10] Yet clearly Wright respected her: she was ambitious and she had a vision, just as he did. Not surprisingly, they clashed at every turn. In the end it was his inability to seize control of Barnsdall's "California Romanza," even after using every tactic in his ample bag of tricks, that galled him the most. He fought back in his autobiography, casting doubt on her identity as a woman: "Miss Barnsdall wanted no ordinary home," Wright declared, "for she was no ordinary woman" – "if she could have denied she was one at all, she might have done so. But the fact claimed and continually got her much to her distress and the confusion of her large aims."[11]

I begin this book with Frank Lloyd Wright and his women clients for a number of reasons. Wright clearly had strong opinions about women (and about clients in general), and because he was so outspoken, his autobiography opens up a range of questions. What, for example, was "an ordinary woman" to Wright, a midwestern man born in 1867 and writing in the late 1920s? What was "an ordinary house" and what was not? Why were struggles over ownership and control – between architect and client, or between architect and builder – so frequent and so bitter? Wright had extensive experience in these matters, having completed dozens of houses during his years in Oak Park and later in California, and he had made a particular study of the single-family home over the course of his career.[12] Moreover, Wright's clients included quite a few strong-willed women: in addition to Millard and Barnsdall, Wright designed houses for Susan Lawrence Dana, Queene Ferry Coonley, Mamah Borthwick Cheney (who would become his companion and lover), and Alma Goetsch and Kathrine Winkler, all of whom had deeply felt beliefs about social reform, domestic life, and new roles for women in American society.[13] These clients came to Wright with their projects because of his reputation as an architect who, like them, placed great value on the home as a force for change in American society.

The houses Wright designed for his women clients are among his most interesting and innovative works. An architect who seized on every new commission as an opportunity to experiment – one thinks immediately of Fallingwater or the Guggenheim Museum – Wright often dreamed up dramatic and original buildings for his clients and was then forced to defend his ideas in the face of skeptical opposition, as he did in the case of the Millard and Barnsdall projects. Inspired by difficult sites and unfamiliar building materials, he was at his best when confronted by new circumstances and seemingly insolvable problems. The challenge of designing houses for unconventional women clients whose programs were hybrids of traditional and unusual domestic activities, though a much rarer occurrence for Wright or any other architect, had a similar effect.

Wright's Susan Lawrence Dana House of 1902–4 in Springfield, Illinois (plate 1; figs. 2, 3) – though not as well known or as well documented as the houses studied in

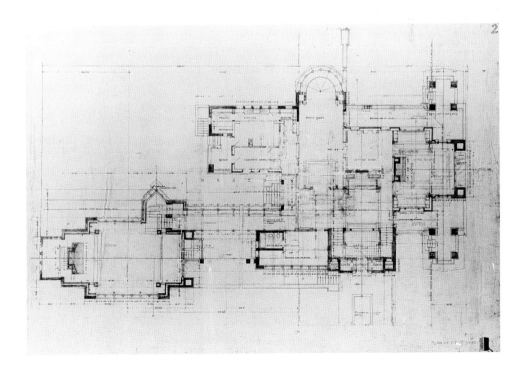

FIGURE 2

Frank Lloyd Wright. Dana House, plan, ground floor

detail in the following chapters – suggests some of the reasons for this phenomenon. Built for a wealthy widow in her early forties, it was "a home designed to accommodate the art collection of its owner and for entertaining extensively," yet it clearly had very little of the conventional home about it.[14] Sprawled out horizontally along a flat site for nearly half a city block, with sheer brick walls and soaring roofs, the Dana House included an art gallery and library, as well as a double-height living hall (plate 2) with a fountain, a double-height dining room with a minstrels' gallery (fig. 4), a living room, and three bedroom suites, occupied by Dana, her mother, and a female cousin. Many of these rooms have the monumental character of public spaces, suggesting a new level of formality and importance for the activities of the women who lived in them.

FIGURE 3

Wright's Dana House under construction, 1902. The walls of the new house encircled the original family home, which was later demolished

PLATE 2

Dana House, entry and living
hall, with Richard Bock's sculpture *Flower in the Crannied Wall*

FIGURE 4

Dana House, dining room

Dana's decision to build her house followed quickly after the deaths of her husband, Edwin, in 1900, and of her father, Rheuna D. Lawrence, in 1901.[15] The house was meant, in part, to serve as a memorial to Lawrence, whose legacy had enabled his daughter to build it and thus to assume a highly visible place in Springfield society as a philanthropist and hostess. A founding member of Springfield's Women's Club and a leader in local charitable organizations, Dana used her home as a showplace for her social activism, entertaining prominent politicians and out-of-town visitors (including a delegation led by Jane Addams, who went to Springfield in 1909 to lobby for women's suffrage) and hosting lavish receptions for local women and children (the latter were encouraged to borrow books from the library).[16] With its numerous level changes, theatrical lighting, long vistas, and open-plan rooms, Wright's design framed and foregrounded Dana's activities, reinforcing her purposes through architectural drama. In this way the Dana House served as a semipublic cultural and community center with Dana as its director, occupying center stage – quite literally, since the gallery could be used as a small theater.

The Dana House focuses attention on questions about gender, cultural assumptions, and architectural conventions that are critical elements in the history and analysis of houses designed and built for women clients. But it also raises a more fundamental question, with which my research for this project began: Why were independent women clients such powerful catalysts for innovation in domestic projects? If one looks not only at Wright's career but also at the work of Le Corbusier, Ludwig Mies van der Rohe, and others, it becomes clear that the houses these architects designed for women heads of households are among their most significant works, and many have become monuments in the history of twentieth-century architecture. Given that women-headed households are atypical in any period, why is it that an

unexpectedly large number of the most significant and original houses built in Europe and America in the twentieth century – houses that stand out not only as examples of modern design but also for their innovative approaches to domestic space – were commissioned by female clients? This book focuses on six of the best-known examples, combining social and architectural history to investigate the roles played by both architects and clients, and to explore the processes of collaboration and negotiation through which decisions about program and design were made.[17]

For the past twenty years architectural historians have been using interdisciplinary approaches to analyze the evolution of domestic architecture in Europe and America in the context of changing social behaviors and values, especially among the middle class. Using letters, handbooks of advice, etiquette books, and other documents as evidence, historians have shown how attitudes about such phenomena as family life, privacy, social behavior, and the education of children have contributed to changes in the design of single-family houses and suburban homes in Europe and the United States.[18] Women's history has been a particular focus in the work of writers like Gwendolyn Wright and Dolores Hayden: because women's roles have traditionally been tied to the domestic realm – and, since the mid-nineteenth century formulation of the "cult of domesticity," to their particular aptitude for their duties as wives, mothers, household managers, and caretakers – these historians have emphasized the importance of housework, home economics, and theories of domestic reform in shaping concepts of the ideal home and family.[19] Given these well-documented connections, it is not unreasonable to expect that a significant shift in thinking about the family, gender, or middle-class women's roles would find expression in the design of houses, nor that some privileged women, given the opportunity to act as clients in their own right, would seek out new architectural solutions to accommodate unconventional ways of living.[20]

Yet there is another explanation for why individual women clients proved to be such effective catalysts for creativity in modern domestic architecture: the conviction shared by modern architects and their women clients that the essence of modernity was the complete alteration of the home – its construction, materials, and interior spaces.[21] Housing was a priority for many modern architects, who were preoccupied by questions of household efficiency, health, standardization, new materials, and technology. The examples described in this book show how the goals of independent women clients were thoroughly entwined with the theories of these designers: not only did women commission avant-garde architects to provide them with houses in which to live out their visions of a new life, but these visions rested on a redefinition of domesticity that was fundamentally spatial and physical. A powerful fusion of feminism with the forces of change in architecture thus propelled these projects into uncharted realms of originality.

Women's focus on the home was grounded in historical experience and in the recognition that, for better or for worse, their power resided there.[22] Although it had become clear well before the end of the nineteenth century that the real seats of economic and political power were the urban offices and boardrooms where men carried out their work, many women recognized that by taking control of the domestic realm – and by claiming expertise in all matters relating to it – they could gain a measure of independence in their own lives. The middle-class home was the stage on which the drama of social differentiation was enacted: organized to display material goods as well as the efficiency and propriety of the household, single-family houses not only concealed domestic labor and family intimacy, but reinforced hierarchies of power by controlling access to private spaces for entertaining and leisure.[23] As guardians of the domestic realm, middle-class women were thus asked to play a difficult and contradictory role: "naturally" suited both to housework and to the refinements of polite society – the former relying upon manual labor and a knowledge of the physical needs of the body, and the latter on delicacy of mind and spirit – they were ultimately confronted with a dilemma that, for many of them, could be resolved only by seeking new roles for women and by redefining the terms of domesticity itself.[24]

These contradictions shaped the course of women's activism between the 1880s and the 1920s in Europe and the United States.[25] Women reformers can be roughly divided into two broad categories. One group dedicated itself to expanding the influence of women by concentrating on the values and pursuits traditionally associated with gentility in the home: through women's clubs, book groups, and charitable work, in small towns, cities, and suburbs, these women came together to share their expertise and develop new skills as readers, public speakers, and organizers.[26] Women's club meetings could be devoted to discussions of cooking, home decorating, or child care, but they might just as easily focus on a lecture on a specialized topic, either presented by an outsider or worked up by one of the women themselves; in this way women educated themselves as homemakers, parents, consumers, and collectors.[27] Moreover, through the activities of women's clubs and charitable organizations – or simply through the expanding networks of female friendship that developed in neighborhoods and communities – middle-class women became increasingly aware of life beyond the home. New urban pursuits – volunteering at a settlement house or school, visiting a museum, shopping, attending lectures, plays, or concerts, or even spending a few hours at the cinema – not only sharpened women's minds but opened up an unfamiliar world of people, places, and experiences.[28]

A second group of reformers, generally a generation younger than the women discussed above, focused on higher education, professional opportunities, and political activism.[29] Seeking greater recognition and economic power, they campaigned for women's suffrage, organized for workers' rights, and pressed for professional advancement in fields such as teaching, medicine, and law. For these women in particular – indeed, for any woman who devoted much of her time and energy to activities outside the home – marriage was difficult or impossible. Since 40 to 60 percent of female college graduates from this period did not marry (compared with only 10 percent of the female population as a whole), and since the divorce rate was increasing in all classes of society, more women began to seek alternatives: new sexual freedoms, improved methods of birth control, and long-term relationships with other women.[30] They also discovered the pleasures and challenges of the city, drifting further and further from women's traditional sphere. For substantial numbers of middle-class women, then, the familiar spaces of home and parlor began to feel constricting, and they looked for new environments in which to live freer, more useful, and more modern lives.

The goals and expectations of the clients discussed in this book were shaped by the broad movement for feminist reform outlined above. Coming of age between 1890 and 1930, these women (whether or not they considered themselves feminists) carried within themselves the categories and contradictions their culture had constructed, and they looked to modern architecture and to architects to provide them with the spaces in which to live out new roles and relationships: architecture, they felt, would literally provide them, and their households, with a place in the modern world. In so doing they confronted two areas of concern. First, they faced the conflict between the expectation of marriage and the independent lives that they had chosen; as women heads of households – whether single, widowed, divorced, les-

bian, or in other sorts of unconventional living arrangements – they redefined domestic space to create room for a range of relationships that crossed boundaries prescribed by age, class, gender, and sexuality. By choosing to build for themselves and their households, they made a radical statement about the value of their lives as independent women. Second, they reexamined the separation between the individual household and the community and replaced traditional divisions with a wider spectrum of alternatives. While this new approach often led to a more fluid exchange between public and private space, and to more communal activities, it is significant that many women clients sought a balance between family and privacy, or chose to live alone.

In each of the houses covered in the following chapters, modern architecture was used to alter the conventions of domestic life in some or all of the following ways: by expanding the definition of home to include various types of work and leisure activities, and shifting the balance between public and private space; by reshaping the composition of the household and accommodating its members in unconventional spaces and/or nontraditional arrangements of rooms; by creating compact, well-designed residential/work spaces for single women, and thus validating the decision not to marry; by foregrounding history and memory, with particular attention to women's roles as family historians and collectors; and by highlighting the importance of spectacle, and of the home as a representation (in stylistic as well as spatial terms) of the activities and values of its occupants.

These themes recur throughout the case studies, linking the houses in unexpected ways. For example, a shift in the balance between public and private activities and spaces was the first priority in most of the projects. Although each client conceptualized this change in an individual way, Barnsdall, Millard, Truus Schröder (the subject of chapter 2), and Constance Perkins (the subject of chapter 5) all emphasized the importance of breaking down the boundaries between their homes and the communities in which they lived, proposing that work activities and persons outside the family be accommodated within the home. For Barnsdall these changes hinged on the decision to make her residence the focal point in a public park and theatrical community; like Dana, she not only viewed her home as a cultural center but provided space for nondomestic activities (theatrical productions, specifically) within the house and on its grounds. For Millard, Schröder, and Perkins the home was intended as a space for work and living, with room for gatherings that were somewhat more informal than conventional business meetings or social engagements. Their houses used such devices as contrasts in scale to differentiate between various functions and employed open planning, sliding partitions, and screens to establish boundaries between areas. The new hybrid domestic types that were created in the process stand out in the history of twentieth-century architecture because of these experiments in design.

Redefinition of the household and its activities is another critical element in many of these projects. For example, Schröder's commitment to a new openness between parents and children – like Vanna Venturi's decision to remain in her own home and to plan for a live-in housekeeper (see chapter 6) – was one of the fundamental ideas behind the concept and design of her house; it necessitated flexibility and layering of spaces for greater access and ease of communication between household members. Moreover, the elimination of conventional hierarchies altered the arrangement of rooms and circulation between areas in innovative ways. This is also particularly evident, as we shall see, in Le Corbusier's Villa Stein–de Monzie (the subject of chapter 3), where the program called for a balance between two bedroom suites, one to be occupied by a couple, Michael and Sarah Stein, and the other intended for their friend and the co-owner of the house, Gabrielle de Monzie, and her daughter.

One of the most unusual new domestic types sought by independent women clients was the home for a group of friends or a female couple. Though not as well known or as architecturally significant as the houses that constitute the main focus of this book, projects responding to this particular redefinition of the household were often innovative designs. These include Eleanor Raymond's renovation of a townhouse at 112 Charles Street in Boston (1923; figs. 5, 6), her Raymond-Kingsbury House (1931; figs. 7–9), and Natalie Hammond Compound in Gloucester, Massachusetts (1941); Rudolph Schindler's Elizabeth Van Patten residence (1934; figs. 10, 11); and Wright's Goetsch-Winkler House (1940; figs. 12, 13).[31]

Though vastly different in social and political meaning, the homes of lesbian couples and of women who lived together as friends were, from the point of view of design, quite similar. This was because of two factors: first, these women were almost always professionals who worked both within and outside the home; and second, their relationships were frequently represented as partnerships of equals requiring both privacy and community. Projects of this type usually included two or more large bedrooms or studios of roughly equal size, a compact kitchen, and a large common living area; private spaces had to be fully enclosed, while common spaces were open and accessible. For example, at 112 Charles Street, which Eleanor Raymond designed as a residence for a group of women (including herself and her partner, Ethel Power), the house was divided into three apartment suites, each with its own bedrooms, kitchenette, and living room; a common area was located in the basement and garden.[32] The Van Patten House follows the same scheme, but on a smaller scale: each of its three bedrooms, stacked on two floors of a hillside house, offers enough private space for work and living, as well as its own balcony and access to a common garden. Here too, as in all the projects of this type, the kitchen is compact and efficient and the dining

FIGURE 5

Eleanor Raymond. Renovation of
112 Charles Street, Boston. 1924

FIGURE 6

112 Charles Street, plans, second
and third floors. The second
floor was occupied by Raymond's
mother; the third floor was
part of a duplex apartment occupied by Raymond, Ethel Power,
and Rachel Raymond

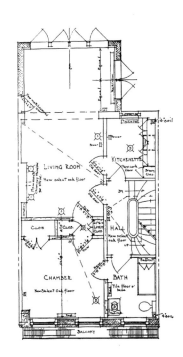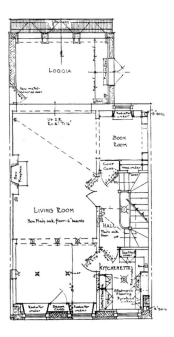

area is minimal. In an article discussing her duplex apartment, published in *House Beautiful* in 1924, Ethel Power explained why this was so:

To appreciate and understand the house, it is necessary to take into account its household which is entirely a non-masculine one.... The needs were very definite and somewhat unusual.... These floors must be planned for the convenience of three women, business women who therefore demanded not only a comfortable and attractive house but one that would be as far as possible, self running.[33]

What the reduction of kitchen and dining space meant, in practice, was not that these women didn't cook – Alma Goetsch, for example, was an enthusiastic chef, and she and Kathrine Winkler emphasized the layout of the kitchen in the program they presented to Wright – but that they ate and entertained informally. This was the essence of the "non-masculine" household: some elements of etiquette and manners, social behaviors so deeply structured by hierarchies of class and gender, could be dispensed with since the women in the households had only themselves and each other to look after, and they did so as equals.

FIGURE 7
Eleanor Raymond. Raymond-Kingsbury House, Belmont, Massachusetts. 1931

FIGURE 8

Raymond-Kingsbury House,
front elevation

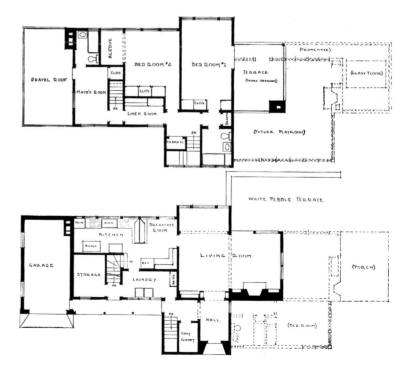

FIGURE 9

Raymond-Kingsbury House,
plans, ground and second floors

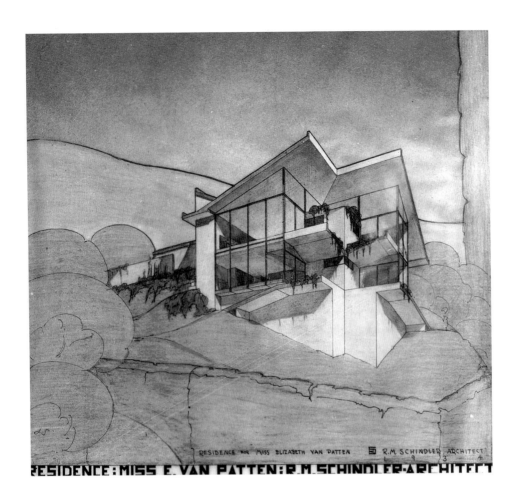

RESIDENCE FOR MISS ELIZABETH VAN PATTEN   R.M.SCHINDLER ARCHITECT 1934

RESIDENCE: MISS E. VAN PATTEN: R.M.SCHINDLER·ARCHITECT

FIGURE 10

Rudolph Schindler. Van Patten
House, Los Angeles. 1934

FIGURE 11

Van Patten House, plans

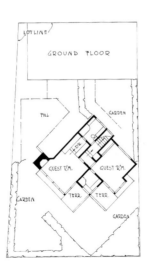

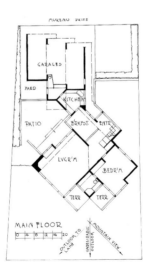

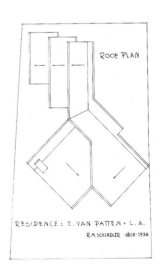

22

FIGURE 12

Frank Lloyd Wright. Goetsch-
Winkler House, Okemos,
Michigan. 1940

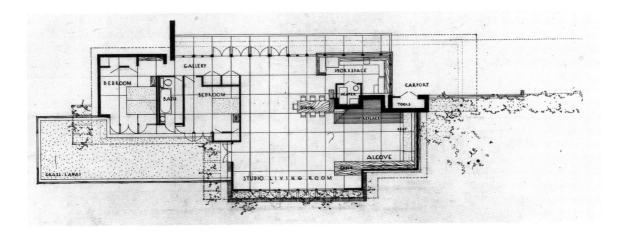

FIGURE 13

Goetsch-Winkler House, plan

In these cases the clients' primary motive for commissioning an architect-designed house was to create an environment in which to live in an unconventional way with other women. But they also had another reason for building modern houses: an identification of their own unconventional lives with architecture that was avant-garde. In the Raymond-Kingsbury house, one of the first International Style buildings in the United States, the choice was particularly daring: though the house was constructed in wood, its blocky forms, large windows, and flat roof immediately marked it, like its owners, as different. In 1931 it was unheard of for two women to set up housekeeping in the suburbs of Boston in a modern house, custom-designed for themselves. Perhaps this is why, when she wrote about her home in *House Beautiful* in 1932, Edith Kingsbury called it "our experiment in the country."[34]

If the expanded definition of the household and its activities is a characteristic feature of many architecturally significant houses built for women, so too is the opposite phenomenon – the narrowing of the domestic program to focus on a dwelling for a single individual. The most extreme and well-known example of this type is the house designed by Mies van der Rohe for Dr. Edith Farnsworth (discussed in chapter 4); because it was a weekend house, its program was reduced and clarified to such an extent that the house became virtually an abstract composition in glass, steel, and open space – much to the dismay of the client who had to live in it. Other examples include Richard Neutra's Perkins House and Eileen Gray's own home, "Tempe à Pailla" (figs. 14–16).[35] Of interest for many reasons, these projects for single clients also shed light on the exceptional nature of Mies's architectural achievement at the Farnsworth House, and underscore the severity of its representation of domesticity.

While Mies's design for the Farnsworth House celebrated modernity unequivocally, a number of clients, including Farnsworth (who insisted on furnishing her new home with antiques and family heirlooms), were ambivalent about making a complete break with the past. Some, such as Barnsdall, explicitly commemorated a parent or other relative; others, like the Steins or Vanna Venturi, used furniture and personal possessions to establish a connection to the past, although this went against one of the basic tenets of modernism. Perhaps the most extreme example is Dana, who maintained a physical and spiritual link with the past by having Wright incorporate into her house a sitting room, complete with marble mantelpiece and antique furniture, from the old Lawrence family home, which had been torn down to clear the site for new construction (see fig. 3). This gesture was not purely symbolic; Dana was a believer in spiritualism and used her house for seances, in which she attempted to contact her husband and father and seek advice on a variety of personal and business matters.[36]

Finally, all of the examples discussed in this book engage the issue of the home as a theater of representation, a place in which physical appearance, social behavior, and personal privacy are displayed and interpreted. One extreme case – in which, however, no modern house was built – dramatizes the scope of the problem and the possible points of conflict between architect and client over the questions of identity, sexuality, and visual pleasure that are entailed in the creation of an image, or images, of domesticity. Much has been written about the house that Adolf Loos designed in 1928 for Josephine Baker, the African-American dancer and star of the Paris stage (figs. 17, 18).[37] By now it is quite clear that the unbuilt project, which exists only in a model and a set of drawings, had everything to do with Loos's desires and nothing to do with Baker's. Having met Baker at "Chez Joséphine," her Paris nightclub, the architect boasted that he could

FIGURE 14

Eileen Gray. Tempe à Pailla,
Castellar, France. 1934

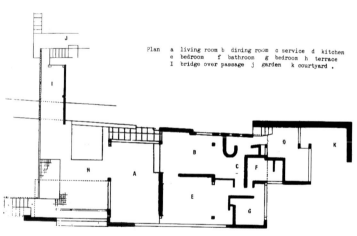

Plan a living room b dining room c service d kitchen
e bedroom f bathroom g bedroom h terrace
I bridge over passage j garden k courtyard .

FIGURE 15

Tempe à Pailla, plan

FIGURE 16

Tempe à Pailla, studio end of the
living room. ca. 1950

Introduction

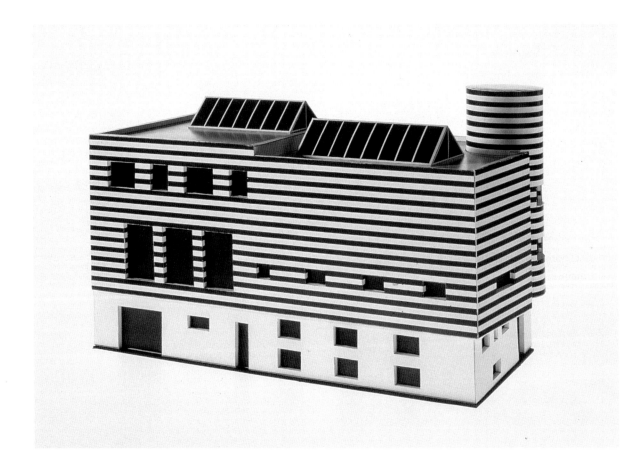

design a beautiful house for her: the result was a passionate displacement of desire, an architectural reverie in
which Loos imagined a series of spaces in which Baker
was displayed for his private entertainment, including
a deep indoor swimming pool with windows below
water level. For Loos the ornamental stripes on the exterior of the house and the dream of Baker's dark body in
the shimmering water were paired images in a fantasy of
racial and sexual superiority; the house and her body
were one – and they were his because he could indulge
his desire to look at and take pleasure in them.

Baker's tastes in architecture were quite different.
She had made her reputation through her genius at creating images of herself that people wanted to see – that,
after all, is how an American black woman born in East
St. Louis could transform herself into a potent symbol
of Africa so convincing that she was named Queen of
the Colonial Exposition in Paris in 1931 – and she knew
that stars lived in enormous mansions stuffed with furniture and objets d'art.[38] Having lived in such a house at
Le Vésinet, a suburb of Paris, during the 1920s, Baker
acquired "Les Milandes," a fifteenth-century château in
the Dordogne (fig. 19) in 1947.[39] In her greatest triumph
as an image maker, she transformed the château into a
combination resort hotel and theme park where she
offered nightly stage shows in the open air.[40] But Baker's
efforts at Les Milandes were not simply show business:
from 1950 on, she turned the house and surrounding
village into a "village du monde" – a center for world fellowship dedicated to the fight against racism (fig. 20).
With her husband, Jo Bouillon, she adopted twelve children from different countries to create her "Rainbow
Tribe," a family that was a vivid visual demonstration of
her principles.[41]

FIGURE 19
Josephine Baker's château,
Les Milandes

According to her biographer Baker had actually discussed her ideas for a model village with Le Corbusier many years before.[42] Like Barnsdall she imagined her home as the focus of an extended community, and like Schröder she had a vision that included a life shared by adults and children. In the end she was to be neither a patron of modern architecture nor an ideal mother. Yet Baker's reform-minded project at Les Milandes reveals that she was truly a daughter of the Progressive Era, and it shows how distant her own image of her life work remained from Loos's dream house of sexual theater. One can only wonder about the architecture that a Baker–Le Corbusier collaboration might have produced.

By focusing on their own homes, women clients sought not only to implement change but also to participate in a creative process. Thus it should be clear that women's special concern for the domestic realm in this century did not come from any essential quality in themselves as women, but was rather a response to the gendered social roles of the culture in which they lived. But what of other sorts of clients who share some of the characteristics of the women discussed above? Married women, for example, or bachelors? Both groups differ in fundamental ways as clients from the independent women described here. Although married women sometimes acted as representatives of their households in working with architects on the design of innovative modern houses – Wright's Coonley House, in Riverside, Illinois (1906–9), or Alvar Aalto's Villa Mairea, in Noormarkku, Finland (1938–41),

FIGURE 20

Josephine Baker, Jo Bouillon, and children of the Rainbow Tribe looking at a poster for the Anti-Racism Conference. January 1957

come to mind – the programs they presented more often than not followed convention in domestic planning, and except in rare cases like that of the Stein–de Monzie household, their houses belonged to their husbands and to a large extent reflected the dominant values and power relations of the broader society. Great works of domestic architecture have been produced in such circumstances, but they fall outside the categories suggested here.

The question of single male clients is even more complex. In the period with which this book is concerned, the social pressures placed on men to marry were as great as or even greater than those confronting women, since the specter of homosexuality was far more threatening for bachelors than for single women.[43] But men not only had more cause to marry, they also had more opportunities, both social and economic, than women did: as independent adults who owned property, worked at productive jobs, and moved freely around the public spaces of cities and towns, men were offered choices that women never were. Unlike women, even when men remained single they were not considered outcasts from the social order. Moreover, without women in their homes, bachelors were typically viewed as exempt from the demands of housework and the rituals of family life.

Men acted as the principal clients for all types of buildings; they were not limited, like women, by their identification with the home. Furthermore, as clients for houses, single men were comparatively rare; men often waited until they married to plan for permanent homes.[44] However, a handful of examples suggest that when single men did hire architects to design their houses they focused on creating spaces for pleasure or entertainment rather than for work, children, or community. Such houses include San Simeon, designed by Julia Morgan for William Randolph Hearst (who was separated from his wife) in San Luis Obispo (1922–30); the villa in Auteuil for Raoul La Roche, which formed half of the double La Roche–Jeanneret House, by Le Corbusier (1924); the Casa Malaparte, on the island of Capri, by Adalberto Libera and Curzio Malaparte (1941); Philip Johnson's Glass House/Guest House complex, in New Canaan, Connecticut (1949; see chapter 4); and John Lautner's Zimmerman House, in Studio City, California (1968).[45] There is a still a great deal to be learned about these remarkable projects – some thematic links are suggested in my analysis of Johnson's Glass House/Guest House and its connection to the Farnsworth House – but the problem as a whole is a subject for another book.

In 1924, just before his house was completed, the banker and art collector Raoul La Roche wrote to his good friend Le Corbusier, "By entrusting you with the construction of my house, I knew that you would produce something wonderful; my hopes have been far surpassed. My independent way of life meant that I left you alone to create this project, and given the result, I praise myself for having done so."[46] As we shall see, it is unlikely that any of the women clients considered here would have written such a letter; even the most independent of them was tied to parents, children, and friends in ways that shaped the design of her home, and none could disengage herself from domestic responsibility in the way that La Roche suggested for himself. Moreover, the idea that they would leave the architect "alone to create," or praise themselves for having done so, ran counter to their goals: as clients rather than patrons of architecture, each of them had a vision of domestic life and saw herself as part of a creative collaboration that would give it form. The convictions that inspired them, and the stories of how their houses came to be built, are the subjects to which we now turn.

1 Frank Lloyd Wright, *An Autobiography*, in Bruce Brooks Pfeiffer, ed., *Frank Lloyd Wright: Collected Writings*, vol. 2 (New York: Rizzoli, 1992), 267–76, 279–89. For La Miniatura, see Neil Levine, *The Architecture of Frank Lloyd Wright* (Princeton, N.J.: Princeton University Press, 1996), 154–56, and Ward Ritchie, "Alice Millard as I Remember Her," *Bookman's Weekly*, Feb. 13, 1995, 648–66. I am grateful to Charles Wood for alerting me to the latter reference.

2 Ibid, 273, 288.

3 Ibid, 284.

4 Ibid.

5 Ibid. Wright wrote that "every idea . . . enters and encounters life, as does a new-born child," and that it was "up to the author of its being to defend it . . . to save its life – continually."

6 Ibid, 285.

7 Ibid.

8 Ibid, 282, 286.

9 Ibid, 288.

10 Ibid, 271.

11 Ibid, 269–70.

12 See Levine, *Frank Lloyd Wright*, chs. 1, 2. For Wright's clients, see Leonard K. Eaton, *Two Chicago Architects and Their Clients: Frank Lloyd Wright and Howard Van Doren Shaw* (Cambridge, Mass.: MIT Press, 1969).

13 For Coonley, see Theodore Turak, "Mr. Wright and Mrs. Coonley," in Richard Guy Wilson and Sidney Robinson, eds., *Modern Architecture in America: Visions and Revisions* (Ames: Iowa State University Press, 1991), 144–63. For Cheney's feminism and her influence on Taliesin, see Anthony Alofsin, *Frank Lloyd Wright: The Lost Years, 1910–1922* (Chicago: The University of Chicago Press, 1993), 26–28, 44–46, 91–100, and Levine, *Frank Lloyd Wright*, ch. 4.

14 Frank Lloyd Wright, *Ausgeführte Bauten und Entwürfe von Frank LLoyd Wright* (Berlin: Wasmuth, 1911), caption to pl. 31, cited in Donald Hoffmann, *Frank Lloyd Wright's Dana House* (Mineola, N.Y.: Dover, 1996), 13–14.

15 For the history of the project, see Hoffmann, *Dana House*, 3–28. None of the office correspondence related to the project survives. See also James R. Allen, Donald P. Hallmark, and Richard S. Taylor, *Dana-Thomas House*, (Springfield, Ill.: Dana-Thomas House Foundation, 1989). For Dana, see Richard S. Taylor, "Susan Lawrence Dana, Feminist," in Mark Heyman and Richard S. Taylor, *Frank Lloyd Wright and Susan Lawrence Dana: Two Lectures* (Springfield, Ill.: Dana-Thomas House Foundation, 1985), 1–17, and Taylor's "Susan Lawrence," unpublished manuscript, Office of Research and Publications, Historic Sites Division, Illinois Department of Conservation, 1982. I am grateful to Richard S. Taylor for making this study available to me.

16 Taylor, "Susan Lawrence Dana, Feminist," 3–4, 10–12, and "Susan Lawrence," 31, 43–44, 52–53, 57–58.

17 One indication of the importance of these houses is the frequency with which they are discussed and illustrated in surveys of modern architecture: see, for example, William R. Curtis, *Modern Architecture Since 1900*, 3rd ed. (New York: Prentice Hall, 1996), where five of the six houses discussed in this book are illustrated; Kenneth Frampton, *Modern Architecture: A Critical History*, 3rd. ed. (New York: Thames and Hudson, 1992), where three are illustrated; and Manfredo Tafuri and Francesco Dal Co, *Modern Architecture*, 2 vols. (New York: Rizzoli, 1986), where three are illustrated and a fourth (the Farnsworth House) is discussed.

18 The best examples of this type are Mark Girouard, *Life in the English Country House: A Social and Architectural History* (New Haven: Yale University Press, 1977), and Clifford Edward Clark, *The American Family Home, 1800–1960* (Chapel Hill: University of North Carolina Press, 1986).

19 See Gwendolyn Wright, *Building the Dream: A Social History of Housing in America* (Cambridge, Mass.: MIT Press, 1981); Dolores Hayden, *Seven American Utopias: The Architecture of Communitarian Socialism, 1790–1975* (Cambridge, Mass.: MIT Press, 1976); Hayden, *The Grand Domestic Revolution: A History of Feminist Designs for American Homes, Neighborhoods and Cities* (Cambridge, Mass.: MIT Press, 1981), and her *Redesigning the American Dream: The Future of Housing, Work and Family Life* (New York: Norton, 1984).

20 For a broad discussion of gender and history, see Joan W. Scott, "Gender: A Useful Category of Historical Analysis" (1986), reprinted in Joan W. Scott, ed., *Feminism and History* (New York: Oxford University Press, 1996), 152–80; for gender and domestic typology, see Alice T. Friedman, "Just Not My Type: Gender, Convention and the Uses of Uncertainty," in Karen A. Franck and Lynda H. Schneekloth, eds., *Ordering Space: Types in Architecture and Design* (New York: Van Nostrand Reinhold, 1994), 331–44.

21 See Peter Rowe, *Modernity and Housing* (Cambridge, Mass.: MIT Press, 1993); William J. R. Curtis, *Le Corbusier: Ideas and Forms* (Oxford, England: Phaidon, 1986); and Richard Pommer and Christian Otto, *Weissenhof 1927 and the Modern Movement in Architecture* (Chicago: University of Chicago Press, 1991).

22 See Nancy F. Cott, *The Bonds of Womanhood: "Women's Sphere" in New England, 1780–1835* (New Haven: Yale University Press, 1977). For the suburban home and the "cult of domesticity," see Gwendolyn Wright, *Moralism and the Model Home: Domestic Architecture and Cultural Conflict in Chicago, 1873–1913* (Chicago: University of Chicago Press, 1980), esp. part 1.

23 For an overview of this subject, see Richard L. Bushman, *The Refinement of America: Persons, Houses, Cities* (New York: Vintage, 1993), chs. 1–4; for women, see pp. 299–312, 440–47.

24 For the history of American feminism, see Nancy F. Cott, *The Grounding of American Feminism* (New Haven: Yale University Press, 1987); Rosalind Rosenberg, *Beyond Separate Spheres: Intellectual Roots of Modern Feminism* (New Haven: Yale University Press, 1982); and John d'Emilio and Estelle Freedman, *Intimate Matters: A History of Sexuality in America* (New York: Harper and Row, 1988), esp. parts 2, 3.

25 For an overview of gender roles in the period, see Peter Gabriel Filene, *Him/ Her/ Self: Sex Roles in Modern America*, 2nd ed. (Baltimore: Johns Hopkins University Press, 1986), 5–39; for Europe, see Bonnie S. Anderson and Judith P. Zinzer, *A History of Their Own: Women in Europe from Prehistory to the Present* (New York: Harper and Row, 1988), vol. 2, 129–96.

26 See Kathleen D. McCarthy, *Women's Culture: American Philanthropy and Art, 1830–1930* (Chicago: University of Chicago Press, 1991), parts 2, 3, and Lois Rudnick, "The New Woman," in Adele Heller and Lois Rucknick, eds., *1915, The Cultural Moment* (New Brunswick: Rutgers University Press, 1991), 69–81.

27 For women's clubs, see Karen J. Blair, *The Clubwoman as Feminist: True Womanhood Redefined, 1868–1914* (New York: Holmes and Meier, 1980), and her *The Torchbearers: Women and the Amateur Arts Associations in America, 1880–1930* (Bloomington: Indiana Unversity Press, 1994); see also Robyn Muncy, *Creating a Female Dominion: American Reform, 1890–1935* (New York: Oxford University Press, 1991).

28 For the importance of cinematic space for women, see Giuliana Bruno, *Streetwalking on a Ruined Map: Cultural Theory and the City Films of Elvira Notari* (Princeton, N.J.: Princeton University Press, 1993); see also Griselda Pollock, "Modernity and the Spaces of Femininity," in her *Vision and Difference: Femininity, Feminism and Histories of Art* (New York: Routledge, 1988), 50–90.

29 Carroll Smith Rosenberg, "The New Woman as Androgyne: Social Disorder and Gender Crisis, 1870–1936," in her *Disorderly Conduct: Visions of Gender in Victorian America* (New York: Oxford University Press, 1985), 245–96.

30 Smith Rosenberg, "The New Woman," 253.

31 Eleanor Raymond's papers are held by the Loeb Library, Graduate School of Design, Harvard University. For Raymond, see Doris Cole, *Eleanor Raymond, Architect* (East Brunswick, N.J.: Associated University Presses, 1981); a recent doctoral dissertation on Raymond by Nancy Gruskin (Boston University) yields further information. A paper on Raymond presented by Lisa Reitzes at a conference on gay and lesbian architects in New York in June 1994 described her career and client network in the context of lesbian subculture; her perspective has been invaluable to me. For Schindler, see David Gebhard, *Schindler* (New York: Viking Press, 1972); correspondence related to the Van Patten House is in the R. M. Schindler Papers, Architectural Collections, University of California at Santa Barbara. For Wright's Goetsch-Winkler House, see Susan J. Bandes, ed., *Affordable Dreams: The Goetsch-Winkler House and Frank Lloyd Wright,* Kresge Art Museum Bulletin 6 (special issue), 1991. A little-known modern house by an African-American woman architect, Amaza Lee Meredith's "Azurest South" (Ettrick, Va; 1939), is described by Charles L. Rosenblum in "Modernism in Black and White: Amaza Lee Meredith's Azurest South," unpublished paper, University of Virginia, 1995.

32 Cole, *Eleanor Raymond*, 23.

33 Ibid.

34 Edith Kingsbury, "Spring Pasture: Our Experiment in the Country," *House Beautiful* (Oct. 1932); quoted by Cole, *Eleanor Raymond*, 46.

35 See Caroline Constant, "Tempe à Pailla," in Caroline Constant and Wilfried Wang, eds., *Eileen Gray: An Architecture for All Senses* (Tübingen: Wasmuth, 1996), 136–45, and her "E.1027: The Non-heroic Modernism of Eileen Gray," *Journal of the Society of Architectural Historians* 53, no. 3, 265–79. The best overview of Gray's work is Peter Adam, *Eileen Gray: Architect/Designer* (New York: Abrams, 1987).

36 Taylor, "Susan Lawrence Dana, Feminist," 5.

37 For the project, see Beatriz Colomina, "The Split Wall: Domestic Voyeurism," in Beatriz Colomina, ed., *Sexuality and Space* (New York: Princeton Architectural Press, 1992), 73–130; Paul Groenendijk and Piet Vollaard, *Adolf Loos: Huis voor Josephine Baker* (Rotterdam: Uitgeverij 010, 1985); and Fares el-Dahdah and Stephen Atkinson, "The Josephine Baker House: For Loos's Pleasure/ A Sequential Reconstruction," *Assemblage* 26 (Apr. 1995), 72–87. For Baker's life, see Jean-Claude Baker and Chris Chase, *Josephine, The Hungry Heart* (New York: Random House, 1993), and Phyllis Rose, *Jazz Cleopatra: Josephine Baker in Her Time* (New York: Doubleday, 1989).

38 For Baker's house at Le Vésinet, see Baker and Chase, *Josephine*, 169–70, 180–81, 185, and Rose, *Jazz Cleopatra*, 152–53.

39 Baker and Chase, *Josephine*, 276.

40 Rose, *Jazz Cleopatra*, 209, 231–41.

41 Baker and Chase, *Josephine*, 327–41, appendix 1. See also Jean-Claude Bonnal, *Josephine Baker et le village des enfants du monde en Périgord* (Le Bugue: PLB Editeur, 1992).

42 Baker and Chase, *Jospehine*, 164.

43 For the "the heterosexual imperative," see George Chauncey, *Gay New York: Gender, Urban Culture and the Making of the Gay Male World, 1890–1940* (New York: Basic Books, 1994), 111–27, and E. Anthony Rotundo, *American Manhood: Transformations in Masculinity from the Revolution to the Modern Era* (New York: Basic Books, 1993). See also Beth L. Bailey, *From Front Porch to Back Seat: Courtship in Twentieth Century America* (Baltimore: Johns Hopkins University Press, 1988).

44 Information on this subject is limited. Some preliminary findings are suggested in "Confirmed Bachelorhood: It May Be a State of Mind," *The New York Times*, Aug. 28, 1991, C: 1, 10.

45 For San Simeon, see Sara Holmes Boutelle, *Julia Morgan, Architect* (New York: Abbeville, 1988), ch.7; for Villa La Roche, see Jacques Sbriglio, *Le Corbusier: Les Villas La Roche–Jeanneret* (Basel: Birkhauser with Fondation Le Corbusier, 1997); for Casa Malaparte, see Marida Talamona, *Casa Malaparte* (New York: Princeton Architectural Press, 1992); for the Zimmerman House and three other houses for single men by Lautner, see Frank Escher, ed., *John Lautner, Architect* (London: Artemis, 1993), 40–47 (Carling), 82–85 (Bergren), 124–29 (Wolff), 144–47 (Zimmerman). Unbuilt projects, such as the Apartment for a Single Person, in the 1931 Berlin exhibition *The Dwelling in Our Time* (see Matilida McQuaid, *Lily Reich: Designer and Architect* [New York: The Museum of Modern Art, 1996], 29–33), and the "bachelor pads" featured in *Playboy* magazine in the 1950s and 1960s (see George Wagner, "The Lair of the Bachelor," in Debra Coleman, Elizabeth Danze, and Carol Henderson, eds., *Architecture and Feminism* [New York: Princeton Architectural Press, 1996], 183–220), should be added to this list.

46 Sbriglio, *Le Corbusier*, 62.

PLATE 1

    Frank Lloyd Wright. Hollyhock
    House, Los Angeles. 1919–21

In the spring of 1916 the American heiress Aline Barnsdall (1882–1946; fig. 1) left Chicago for California in search of a theater where her newly formed company could begin preparations for the coming season's dramatic productions. With a characteristic flurry of activity, she crisscrossed the country, making hasty arrangements to secure the services of the actors, directors, and designers she intended to hire for her new venture. Her list included not only many of the recognized talents of the American stage – people like Irving Pichel, the principal actor and co-director of the Arts and Crafts Theatre in Detroit, and Kirah Markham, the star of the Chicago Little Theatre – but also some who were as yet undiscovered, such as the young playwright and set designer Norman Bel Geddes, who was working as a commercial artist in Detroit.[1] Barnsdall's goal was to pour her considerable experience and vast wealth (rumored to be about $19 million) into the creation of a center for art theater in America that would rival those in the cultural capitals of Europe. She hoped that in California she would find a place to begin her experiment, a distinctively American place, in which the theatrical community she envisioned could grow and prosper. In such a place her architect, Frank Lloyd Wright (1867–1959), could build a theater, a community, and a home that would match her dreams with a boldness and individuality of their own.

The project on which Wright and Barnsdall collaborated between 1915 and 1923 represents one of the most unusual challenges Wright encountered during his long career, since it called for a rethinking of building types and particularly of notions concerning house design,

Aline Barnsdall. ca. 1925

No Ordinary House:

Frank Lloyd Wright, Aline Barnsdall, and Hollyhock House

Barnsdall on the beach. ca. 1923

family life, and domesticity. Barnsdall's Hollyhock House, the most important piece of that project to survive, was a house built not for the private life of a family but as a residential centerpiece in a public garden and theater complex; its large, formal spaces and evident lack of domestic feeling reflect this program. Yet in rejecting the conventions of domestic planning and searching for an unusual hybrid type, architect and client were free to push the boundaries of architecture to new limits, focusing on theatricality, on the experience of monumental form, and on the vividness of the landscape as it was framed and defined by the house. Thus Hollyhock House has a lot to teach us about creativity and about the sorts of new experiences that become possible when conventions of social behavior, program, and planning are challenged.

On May 10, 1916, Barnsdall wrote to the playwright Mary Hunter Austin from Mill Valley, California, describing the profound impact of the visit on her thinking:
Above all California has me by the throat and for a while nothing else could quite be made to appear real. The friend of the Soul of Man seems very close to one out here among these hills and redwoods and I stopped and listened to the earth and "things" and California.…

If only I might have a talk with you after "listening to California." I have changed a number of theories and begin to feel that the dramatic future, out here, is in the open air theatre. And I want to ask you about a new idea of mine. What do you think of Carmal-by-the-Sea [sic] as a place for initial productions? I should think that professional as well as spirited productions could be made there, afterwards playing all over California.… Do you know of any open air theatre where this could be done if Carmal should not prove hospitable to the idea?[2]

This letter was followed by another on June 1:

I spent a couple of days at Carmal, immediately after writing you but saw it would not be practicable to put on the sort of professional things I care about so far from a city. So my present solution is to take a theatre in the old part of town…fit it up simply to create our own atmosphere and run a season for as long as my capital lasts – taking it on the road in repertoire in the spring. If I have not made some appreciable gain in two years I will confine my efforts to one or two big open air performances a year….How thankful I am that I was able to break away and come to California! There is a largeness of spirit here that will even penetrate the souls of the second generation – even tho it be American! The audience has much to learn and last Sunday [when Barnsdall had seen an open air production of William Tell *at the Mountain Theatre] they were not handled well. The hikers were really out of the picture and I had expected so much from that element of the Audience. Most of them could not shed Nature – the human nature of the American office and department store – and open their eyes to Art – possibly because it was not big enough – lets hope so! But I love the spirit of it! It has shown me how far removed my effort must be from the commercial theatre.*[3]

These letters provide the starting point for an inquiry into Barnsdall's ideas about modern drama and theatrical performance, which not only shed new light on the design of Hollyhock House (plates 1, 2; fig. 2), but for the first time provide a context in which to understand the meaning of the open-air theater that forms its core. While the roof terraces and semicircular garden at Hollyhock House have long been recognized as elements in a flexible outdoor theater, it is now possible to show that they grew out of Barnsdall's increasingly well defined and articulated ideas about American theater. Moreover, the theater – as well as broader issues concerning theatri-cality, public life, and spectatorship – became the focus of Wright's response to the hybrid nature of the commission and to Barnsdall as a client. Barnsdall's commitment to theater, and to outdoor theater in particular, filled her with an enduring passion far deeper than anything else in her life could inspire. Her home thus quite literally made room for her greatest love in an unprecedented way.

Although the earliest surviving communications between Wright and Barnsdall (beginning with a letter bearing the notation in Wright's hand "circa: 1915") make no mention of any building other than a theater, by the time Barnsdall finally purchased her site – a full city block in Los Angeles known as Olive Hill – in 1919, her concept of the project had expanded greatly.[4] The theater was now to be the centerpiece of an extensive arts precinct, designed by Wright, which would include a large residence for Barnsdall, houses for her principal associates in the company, houses for visiting directors, studios and apartments for actors, shops, and extensive landscaped grounds.[5] Of these buildings only Hollyhock House, on the crest of the hill, and two other houses, known as Residences A and B, were completed, thus creating the false impression that the houses, rather than the unbuilt theater, were the priority in Barnsdall's commission. Wright fostered this impression in his autobiography, barely mentioning the new theater and focusing instead on Hollyhock House and on the supposed weaknesses in Barnsdall's character, which as he saw it undermined the success of the project. Barnsdall's letters to Austin thus signal the need to reinstate her ideas at the center of the story, ideas that once identified and explored shed new light on the meaning of Hollyhock House not only for her but for Wright as well.

PLATE 2

Hollyhock House, roof terrace

FIGURE 2

Hollyhock House and Olive
Hill, Los Angeles, aerial view.
ca. 1924

Barnsdall and Art Theater

Barnsdall's letters to Austin are charged with energy and enthusiasm, and her comments reveal not only a quasi-spiritual love of nature but also a deep commitment to theater as art and as a form of public education. There is also a developing sense of what it means to be an American patron, on a quest for art forms that respond to the unique American landscape and experience. At the same time, however, these letters reveal Barnsdall's characteristic restlessness, her indecisiveness and snobbery, qualities she herself attributed to her upper-class background. Speaking with a reporter for the *Los Angeles Examiner* in July 1919, a few weeks after finally purchasing Olive Hill, she was explicit about her ambivalence: *I don't want to do it…I know it will take time, agony of spirit and all that liberty which my gypsy soul adores, but it is something I simply have to do. Whether it's a success or a failure, the responsibility of the effort lies with me, and cannot be evaded. Personally I prefer to vagabond through the world amusing myself with my friends, my studies and my love for the out of doors. I have struggled with the inborn conviction without avail. I seem forced to try, at least, to create a domicile fitting for the art which is, I believe, destined to help form the taste and ideals of the world, and I shall put every ounce of energy and experience and thought I have in the doing.*[6]

Barnsdall's grandiose feelings of responsibility for the future of American theater and, indeed, for the future of American culture as a whole, apparently so out of character for a rich and rather spoiled young woman, were the product of two powerful and contradictory influences on her life: the first was her father, Theodore Barnsdall, a wildly prosperous pioneer in the American oil industry (fig. 3), and the second, surprisingly, was Emma Goldman and the world of radical politics, feminism, and avant-garde art theater for which she stood.[7]

FIGURE 3

Theodore Barnsdall. ca. 1890

Born in 1882 in Pittsburgh, Aline Barnsdall attended school there but spent summers in Europe or in the mountains of Colorado, where her father had invested in mines.[8] It is unclear when she first became interested in theater, but by her late twenties she had made a serious commitment to it, traveling to Europe to study acting with Eleanora Duse in 1911–12.[9] According to Bel Geddes, who devoted a number of pages to Barnsdall in his autobiography, *Miracle in the Evening*, the decision to turn from acting to producing was made on the advice of Duse, who "suggested that her love and talent for the theater would be far better expressed in directions other than acting" since she "lacked sufficient control over her emotions to become a dependable actress." Duse had suggested that Barnsdall's good sense about plays and her great wealth would make her particularly suited for a career as a producer; according to Bel Geddes's version of the story (no doubt told to him by Barnsdall herself), "Aline had restrained her tears and gone off to prepare herself."[10]

These "preparations" apparently began with a study tour of the major art theaters of Europe, with a particular focus on Max Reinhardt's productions in Berlin and on the work of Gordon Craig in Florence, and ended in 1913 with her arrival in Chicago to work with the members of the Little Theatre under the direction of Maurice Browne and Ellen van Volkenburg.[11] Chicago was the obvious choice for Barnsdall, as it was for so many other young people with an interest in the arts in the years just before World War I. The city had come to represent, for a small yet growing cohort at least, the hub of the artistic universe, the center of all that was new and progressive in American art, literature, and politics. Chicago was the home of Harriet Monroe's *Poetry Magazine*, of the *Little Review*, founded by Margaret Anderson, and since 1912, of the Little Theatre, which mounted its own productions, hosted lectures on art and drama, and presented plays by touring companies.[12] Much of this activity centered around the Fine Arts Building on Michigan Avenue, which housed a number of theaters, a bookstore, a bustling tea room, and the offices and studios of musicians, writers, artists, and architects – including, in 1908 and 1910–11, Frank Lloyd Wright. In Chicago, Barnsdall also discovered Emma Goldman and was moved by her message that social change could be accomplished not simply through anarchism but, as Goldman's plain-spoken monthly magazine *Mother Earth* repeatedly explained, through feminism, birth control, progressive literature, and art theater.[13] This thinking deeply affected the many young women and men who, like Barnsdall, had come to the city brimming with high ideals and deeply felt emotions in search of Art and Truth.

Barnsdall thrived in this environment. Her restlessness and emotional volatility, noted in every memoir of these years that mentions her (Margaret Anderson described her as "an erratic rich woman with a high temper"[14]), perhaps seemed only an extreme and rather irritating version of the tendency to self-dramatization, which ran rampant in the arts community. And she did indeed begin to put her money and her energy to work in the service of her high ideals. In 1914–15 she collaborated with Arthur Bissel in founding the Players Producing Company, offering a season of new American plays in the ground floor theater of the Fine Arts Building (the Little Theatre was on the eighth floor). The pieces included "social dramas" like Oren Taft's *Conscience* and George Middleton's *Criminals* as well as Alice Gerstenberg's adaptation of *Alice in Wonderland*, which was staged in February 1915 and marked Barnsdall's debut in children's theater. *Alice* was so successful that Barnsdall was able to take it to New York, where it received considerable critical attention and acclaim.[15]

In her autobiography, *Living My Life*, Goldman recalled meeting Barnsdall at one of her Chicago lectures.[16] This encounter may not have taken place until the spring of 1915, at least as Goldman remembered it, because she noted that Barnsdall had already produced a series of plays in Chicago and that they shared a devotion to modern drama. Despite their very different backgrounds, the two women apparently got on quite well and spent "many pleasant hours together." Goldman was impressed (and probably a bit startled) by Barnsdall's commitment to social change, and characterized her as "wide awake to social problems, particularly free motherhood and birth-control." Barnsdall found in Goldman a female friend who felt things as passionately as she did and a model of how to combine high culture, feminism, and politics in a life of activism.

By this time Barnsdall had probably read Goldman's *The Social Significance of Modern Drama* and heard first-hand some of the lectures on which it was based during the author's 1913–14 tour. In the foreword to her book Goldman stated her position with characteristic candor: *Unfortunately, we in America have so far looked upon the theater as a place of amusement only, exclusive of ideas and inspiration. Because the modern drama of Europe has till recently been inaccessible in printed form to the average theater-goer in this country, he has had to content himself with the interpretation, or rather misinterpretation, of our dramatic critics. As a result the social significance of the Modern Drama has well nigh been lost to the general public....*

The Modern Drama, as all modern literature, mirrors the complex struggle of life – the struggle which, whatever its individual or topical expression, ever has its roots in the depth of human nature and social environment, and hence is, to that extent, universal. Such literature, such drama, is at once the reflex and inspiration of mankind in its eternal seeking for things higher and better. Perhaps those who learn the great truths of the social travail in the school of life do not need the message of drama. But there is another class whose number is legion, for whom the message is indispensable. In countries where political oppression affects all classes, the best intellectual element have made common cause with the people, have become their teachers, comrades and spokesmen. But in America political pressure has so far affected only the "common" people. It is they who are thrown into prison; they who are persecuted and mobbed, tarred and deported. Therefore another medium is needed to arouse the intellectuals of this country, to make them realize their relation to the people, to the social unrest permeating the atmosphere.[17]

These sentiments endeared Goldman to the Little Theatre group and to other young artists in Chicago, for she outspokenly described the ways in which the arts could confront the issues with which they themselves were grappling: love, sexuality, marriage, the education of children, poverty, class struggle, and not least, what it meant to be an American.[18] For Barnsdall, who not only dealt with these questions along with the others but who also felt a responsibility to provide leadership through her new career as a producer, Goldman represented a solution, a way in which the pieces of her identity could be pulled together. Through Goldman, Barnsdall grew more and more committed to the view that theater was not simply a serious art but *the* art that, as she said in her 1919 *Los Angeles Examiner* interview, was "destined to help form the taste and ideals of the world."

Yet the lessons she learned went deeper still: she began to take political activism seriously, transmuting the wealth and privilege that had been her father's legacy into a feeling for leadership and a genuine commitment to the rights of the oppressed. As Goldman put it, her "attitude was not mere theory."[19] She became an active supporter of labor organizer Tom Mooney and contributed to his defense fund for many years following his imprisonment in connection with the Preparedness Day bombings of 1916.[20] She was opposed to war, contributed funds to radical groups in Los Angeles, and years later backed Upton Sinclair in his campaign for governor of California. Indeed, unlike many intellectuals, Barnsdall remained a loyal friend of Goldman's long after the enthusiasm for *Modern Drama* had cooled, traveling to Chicago to celebrate her release from prison in 1919 and presenting her with a check for $5,000 to help in her fight against deportation. Barnsdall's generosity cost her her own trip to Europe the following year, when her passport was suspended by the State Department because, as she wrote to Wright, of her "friendship for Emma Goldman."[21]

The Los Angeles Little Theatre

By 1916 Barnsdall had become convinced that her work lay in producing modern drama, in forming a new theater company, and in housing it in her own newly designed theater. She had recently met Frank Lloyd Wright in Chicago through mutual friends and found that they had a great deal in common, not least of all their high hopes for American art and their conviction that they were the ones who could put America on the cultural map.[22] In a letter to Wright of July 27, 1916, she encouraged him to move forward quickly with his designs for her new theater:

Do work on the theatre plans and get them finished as soon as possible for this is the psychological moment and if I do not grip it and build a theatre within the next six months somebody else will. We are looking for land now and I am only waiting for father's very definite consent. He writes constantly that I must wait and have my own theatre, to give out a statement that it is to be built. It must be along the lines of the studio plan and can you tell me roughly what size the lot must be? I want to get the land within the next two months, if possible…so that you may see it when you come out and have the time to build to the best advantage on it.

You will put your freest dreams into it, wont you! For I believe so firmly in your genius that I want to make it the keynote of my work. Can't you give it the grace of the Midway Gardens, with the added lift and color they never achieved? Things done in the theatre will always have a certain lightness, piquancy and grace, so it should have lovely golds that take the sun![23]

During the summer of 1916 Barnsdall rented an auditorium in a downtown Los Angeles building, christened it "The Los Angeles Little Theatre," and began preparations for an ambitious season of new productions. According to Bel Geddes, the first offering was to have been his own *Thunderbird*, a play based on his experi-

ences among the Blackfoot Indians of Montana in the summer of 1912. Bel Geddes's script was to have been accompanied by music written by the American composer Charles Wakefield Cadman, inspired by Native American themes.[24] Twelve boxes of costumes, made from Bel Geddes's designs by his friends on the Blackfoot Reservation, had duly arrived in Los Angeles, much to the delight of the company, among whom interest in Native American culture ran high. Ultimately, however, the production was postponed and eventually canceled because of a string of delays in the schedule, caused at least in part by the realization of both Barnsdall and Bel Geddes that no member of the all-white company could convincingly play the role of a Native American.

Other productions included *Nju*, by Ossip Dimov, which opened on October 31, 1916; *Papa*, by Zoe Akins; and D. H. Lawrence's *The Widowing of Mrs. Holroyd*. All three were American premieres. The season also included a play by Oren Taft, *Conscience* (part of the 1914–15 season in Chicago) and works by Arthur Schnitzler and W. B. Yeats of the sort familiar to Barnsdall and the company from the Little Theatre repertoire and praised by Emma Goldman in her lectures.[25] Through the efforts of a talented professional company these productions achieved a very high standard; those that did not were abruptly canceled.[26] The critics praised in particular Bel Geddes's lighting and sets, the acting of Markham, Pichel, and others, and the direction of both Barnsdall and Richard Ordynski, newly arrived from New York after years with Reinhardt's Berlin Theater and Diaghilev's Ballets Russes. Many years later Barnsdall summed up her efforts: "Any impression that I have made has not been the money I have expended….It has been in my original impulse and discrimination in choosing the right people for the work and in doing something the first time."[27]

Yet this was to be the company's first and only season. It was characteristic of Barnsdall to solicit advice and to surround herself with talented individuals (like Wright, Bel Geddes, or Ordynski), but equally characteristic of her to question her judgment in having done so, thus remaining paralyzed by indecision. This trait would prove to be a major obstacle to the success of her project because it affected not only the design of the theater itself but also every aspect of the life of the company. Barnsdall knew that she wanted to do something innovative and significant for American theater, but she ultimately failed to settle on one advisor or find her own point of view. This weakness, fostered by the rivalries among her associates and their own inability to commit themselves to her, ultimately dealt a blow to the project for which no amount of time, money, or energy could compensate.

Moreover, by the end of February 1917, a number of unexpected changes had taken place: Barnsdall was pregnant by Ordynski, her father had died, she had not yet purchased a site on which to build, and her conversations with Wright about the theater were stalled.[28] Accordingly, she placed her project on hold, intending to pick it up again after the estate was settled, presumably sometime in 1918. Wright was in any case now out of the country, at work on the Imperial Hotel in Tokyo.[29]

OLIVE HILL AS ART-THEATER GARDEN

Examiner artist's drawing of Miss Barnsdall's proposed transformation of Los Angeles' beauty spot, showing site of projected theater, with tropical roof garden, promenades, park and residence grounds at summit.

FIGURE 4

"Olive Hill as Art-Theater Garden." From the *Los Angeles Examiner*, July 6, 1919

Barnsdall and Wright on Olive Hill

As Kathryn Smith has shown in her study of Hollyhock House, both the scope of the project and Barnsdall's financial resources were considerably enlarged by June 1919, when she purchased Olive Hill, a thirty-six-acre tract in Hollywood, California. Wright's office had done very little work on the design for the theater, in any case.[30] Now Barnsdall was ready to move forward with an elaborate plan and, once again, she expected her architect to follow. The principal components of the expanded scheme were outlined in newspaper articles and interviews, in which Barnsdall described her vision to an enthusiastic public. Among the most striking ideas was the notion that the buildings and the garden were to be fully integrated to form an "art park": not only would theater patrons be encouraged to stroll outside during long intermissions, but there would also be a roof garden for "afternoon teas and theatre suppers" and extensive gardens for the use of the public. A sketch made by an artist at the *Los Angeles Examiner* to accompany an article about the project shows the hill as a series of terraced gardens surrounding the theater (near the corner of Sunset Boulevard and fronting on Vermont Avenue) and leading up to Hollyhock House at the crest (fig. 4). The drawing bears the title "Olive Hill as Art-Theater Garden," and the accompanying caption points out the "projected theater, with tropical roof garden, promenades, park and residence grounds at summit." In an interview Barnsdall made clear her intention that the entire site be part of a public recreation complex: "I propose to keep my gardens always open to the public that this sightly spot may be available to those lovers of the beautiful who come here to view sunsets, dawn on the mountains and other spectacles of nature, visible in few other places in the heart of the city."[31]

Among the ideas that were not discussed in the press, however, were Barnsdall's apparent determination never to marry and her decision to raise her infant daughter, Betty (whom she nicknamed "Sugar Top"), by herself in her home on Olive Hill. As a follower of Goldman's whose "attitude was not mere theory," Barnsdall rejected marriage, believing to some degree at least that it was, as Goldman had written, "an institution which makes a parasite of woman, an absolute dependent. It incapacitates her for life's struggle, annihilates her social consciousness, paralyzes her imagination, and then imposes its gracious protection, which is in reality a snare, a travesty on human character."[32]

Barnsdall's feminism and her unwillingness to conform to convention are key factors both in the history of Olive Hill and in the design of Hollyhock House. This is true at three levels: first, at the level of the program, because her household was neither a conventional family nor could its activities be fitted into a conventional home; second, at the symbolic and artistic level, because Wright's interpretation of Barnsdall's commission was colored by his response to her personality and values and by her relationship with him; and third, at what might be called the level of gender politics, because it deeply affected the response of artists (Wright among them), theater people, and others in the community, including public officials, to her ideas and to projects in which she sought to provide leadership. Barnsdall's progressive feminist politics, her beliefs about art, and her uninhibited way of life constituted a challenge to convention that ultimately gave the Olive Hill project its distinctive character, informing Wright's design for Hollyhock House with brilliance and creative energy, while surrounding architect, client, and everyone else involved in an atmosphere of contest and conflict. None of these struggles was foreshadowed in the early days at Olive Hill; indeed,

Barnsdall's only disagreement with her architect then, she said, concerned the color of her house: "'So far,' laughed Miss Barnsdall, 'Mr. Wright and I have differed on only one point. He wants my house to be white, and I think a white house is too glaring for Southern California. So no matter what he says my house will not be white.'"[33]

As he explained at length in his autobiography, Wright saw Hollyhock House as a poetic response to the personality of his eccentric client and to the distinctive qualities of the place in which she chose to build. His characterization of her is memorable: she was "neither neo, quasi nor pseudo…as near American as any Indian – as developed and traveled in appreciation of the beautiful as any European. As domestic as a shooting star."[34] Emphasizing freedom and artistic creativity, he described Hollyhock House as a "California Romanza," an essay in "free form," an artistic "holiday" from the discipline of machine-age architecture:

Hollyhock House was to be a natural house, naturally built; native to the region of California as the house in the Middle West had been native to the Middle West.

Suited to Miss Barnsdall and her purpose, such a house would be sure to be all that "poetry of form" could imply, because any house should be beautiful in California in the way California herself is beautiful.[35]

Wright's ideas about "the sovereignty of the individual" were consistent with hers:

Why should Aline Barnsdall live in a house like Mrs. Alderman Schmutzkopf or even like Mrs. Reggie Plasterbilt's pseudo-Hacienda on the Boulevard-Wilshire. Individuality is the most precious thing in life, after all – isn't it? . . .

In any expression of the human spirit principle is manifest as character that alone endures. And individuality is the true property of such character. No…not one house that possessed genuine character in this sense stands, safe, outside the performance of the passing show.

Hollyhock House is such a house.[36]

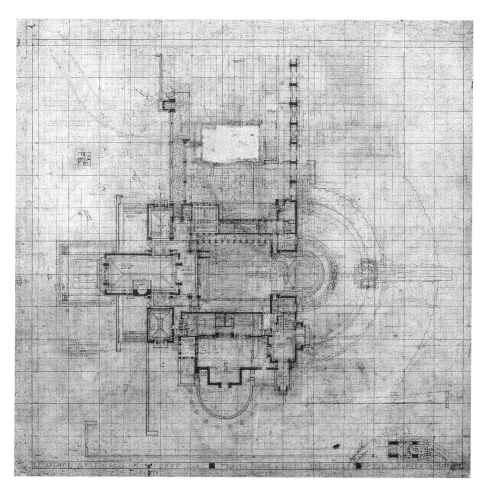

FIGURE 5

Hollyhock House, plan, ground
floor. 1920

Hollyhock House and Its Sources

The earliest surviving plan of Hollyhock House (fig. 5),
dating from January 1920 and differing little from the
house as completed two years later, expresses the meaning and significance of Barnsdall's individuality as Wright
understood it – dominated by her love of theater and her
decision to make her home the center of a new artistic
community – through the strongly articulated imagery of
an open-air theater. Unlike Wright's earlier houses, which
extend outward from a core, Hollyhock House *encloses* an
open courtyard, which is the focus of the design, much as
"the noble ROOM" (as Wright called it) is the real and
symbolic center of Unity Temple or the open light-court
was at the Larkin Company building. Approaching the
house via carefully planned access roads that encircle the
hill, the visitor arrives at a stark, sun-baked motor court

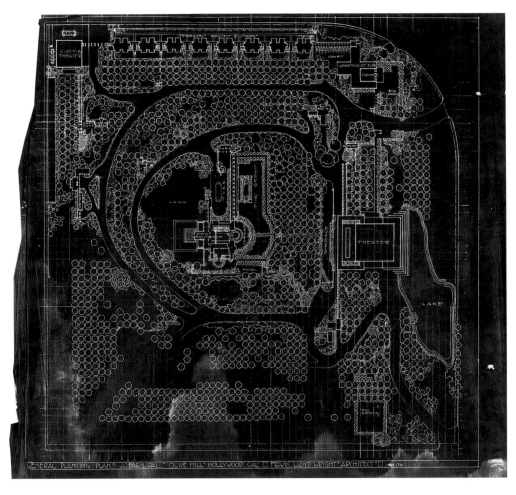

Olive Hill, site plan. 1920

surrounded on three sides by low buildings that served as the garage, rows of pens for pets, and the service entrance to the house (fig. 6). The house itself is entered via a tunnel-like breezeway – low and dark – that projects into the forecourt but, typical of Wright, is otherwise virtually indistinguishable as an entrance. Inside, the rooms are open and filled with shimmering, cool light: whether one looks into the large living room with its immense fireplace, shallow pool of water, and skylight (plate 3; fig. 7), or into the smaller music room or dining room (plate 4) on either side of the entrance foyer, one is struck by the soft, natural light and the contrast with the brightness of the Southern California sun outside. French doors and large windows open out to the rolling lawn and square reflecting pool on the west side of the house and to the grassy courtyard within.

A semicircular exedra shaped by concentric rows of seats (plate 5; fig. 8) encloses the courtyard and contains the view, recalling the distinctive form of an ancient amphitheater with its rising tiers or, perhaps, its modern counterparts, such as John Galen Howard's Hearst Greek Theatre in Berkeley, California, of 1903 (fig. 9). A second-story bridge (which would ultimately accommodate Barnsdall's own room and a guest room) running from north to south forms a sort of *scaena*; below and in front of it, where one would expect to find the stage, is a circular sunken garden, later converted to a reflecting pool. These distinctive forms are conjoined with the rectangular courtyard, flanked on its north side by a loggia and dominated by a strong central axis that runs from the glazed double doors of the living room foyer through the exedra to a semicircular hedge that separates the garden from the park. In the site plan this clearly defined east-west axis extends across the park via a sort of *allée* to the large, freestanding theater. This axial arrangement not only organizes the composition but connects the various parts of the complex symbolically.

FIGURE 7

Hollyhock House, living room.

ca. 1926

PLATE 4

Hollyhock House, dining room
with original table and chairs

PLATE 3

Hollyhock House, living room

PLATE 5

Hollyhock House, garden court

Here again the centrality of the idea of the open-air theater is expressed by the theater's dominant position in the design, since the circular pool at the center of the composition forms a bull's-eye at the very center of the site, exactly where the two principal axes of the house and the site plan intersect.

Although Barnsdall's letter to Austin shows that she had been thinking about producing plays in the open air since 1916, there is no written evidence to suggest that she ever intended to incorporate a working theater into the design of her home. Moreover, her letters and newspaper interviews suggest that by the time the site on Olive Hill was chosen, in 1919, the conception of the theater as a monumental, freestanding, and fully enclosed building seems to have supplanted any ideas about open-air theater in Barnsdall's mind. Yet the outdoor theater at the heart of Hollyhock House clearly has enormous symbolic significance in the project. Although Wright's

FIGURE 9

John Galen Howard. Hearst Greek
Theatre, Berkeley, California,
site plan. 1903. From Sheldon
Cheney, *The Open-Air Theatre*,
1918

FIGURE 8

Hollyhock House, garden court
and exedra. ca. 1927

Barnsdall/Wright

earliest sketches of the site (fig. 10) – made shortly after
the property was purchased, in the summer of 1919 –
were primarily concerned with the massing of the various structures in relation to the contour of the hill, they
nonetheless contain a germ of the theater idea, in the
form of a small sketch of a semicircular plan at the bottom of the east-west perspective. Placed directly below
the point on the drawing where the garden meets the
park at the top of the hill – and clearly differentiated
from the square silhouette of the freestanding theater on
the Vermont Avenue perspective (the middle sketch) –
this small sketch shows that from the very beginning,
the outdoor theater was for Wright the physical and ideological center of the composition. Like the hearth and
chimney in one of his prairie houses, the semicircle at
the core of the theater acts in these designs as a pivot
around which the Olive Hill complex is organized. The
analogy with the hearth can be extended further when
one realizes that just as that form served as the ideological
and spiritual core in Wright's domestic program, providing the warmth, light, and good fellowship by which the
family thrived, here the life of the theatrical community
and its most deeply felt needs are symbolized by the distinctive semicircular form of the amphitheater.

Wright understood that Barnsdall had substituted
emotional ties to her theatrical community for those of a
conventional family. In his autobiography he alluded to
this by pointing out both the essentially nondomestic
nature of the Hollyhock House concept and Barnsdall's
uniquely unfeminine decision to place the theater before
all else:

*Unlike many "patronesses of the arts" Miss Barnsdall
wanted no ordinary home for she was no ordinary woman.
If she could have denied she was one at all, she might have
done so. But the fact claimed and got her continually, much
to her distress and the confusion of her large aims. If any
woman ever hitched her wagon to a star, Aline Barnsdall*

hitched hers thereto. And so far as Hollyhock House and the building of the New Theatre that was to carry her "Art of the Theatre" a generation or two ahead of itself, were concerned – at the moment – she chose her architect as that bright and particular star.[37]

For Wright, Barnsdall's new home represented a fusion of the nondomestic typology of the ancient amphitheater – articulated through the plan, materials, and large scale – with a newly created architectural language that he saw as uniquely appropriate to Southern California. Above all, Barnsdall's new home had to look and feel American, as did the various other buildings that would surround it on Olive Hill. Thus, while its plan contains references to the traditions of European classicism, in its massing and overall appearance Hollyhock House strongly recalls the architecture of the pueblos of the American Southwest. With its jagged profile of stepped and stacked cubes, its smooth plaster walls (Wright had intended them to be concrete), and its tiny window openings, Hollyhock House picks up the most readily recognizable elements of this architecture. The massing and details, such as the frieze of stylized hollyhocks, are also reminiscent of Mayan temples. As a number of scholars have noted, these stylistic devices and motifs pervade Wright's work in the Los Angeles area of the 1920s, expressing his response to the Southern California landscape and his effort to discover the essential forms of a truly American architecture.[38]

For other reasons as well, the peculiarities of the pueblo form made it particularly suited for the Hollyhock House commission. First, its strong connection to the landscape of dry, flat plains and dramatic mesas, apparent, for example, in views of Zuñi Pueblo in New Mexico (fig. 11), may have suggested a resonance with the landscape of Olive Hill, whose distinctive qualities Wright captured in his original massing sketches, discussed above. A number of pueblos that Wright may have known, including Acoma in New Mexico and Walpi at First Mesa, Arizona, were built on top of the mesas, just as Hollyhock House would be built at the top of Olive Hill. This characteristic of the house has always puzzled scholars, given Wright's expressed preference for siting his structures on the "brow" of the hill (as at Taliesin, for instance), but the example of the hilltop pueblos may provide the clue in this case.

A second feature of the pueblos that may have influenced Wright's thinking is the peculiarly theatrical quality of the interior plazas, a feature that was exploited during ceremonies, which spectators would watch from the rooftop terraces. For Wright, and perhaps for Barnsdall, the pueblos represented an ideal model on which to base the concept for the house of an American involved in the theater, a person who, like Wright, was not only highly theatrical herself but also committed to the idea of community, to American art, and to the expression of the power and beauty of the Southern California landscape. Yet, as Wright explained in his autobiography, she was also a world traveler and a sophisticated upper-class woman who knew European culture very well – indeed, she was among the first such clients of his practice.[39] Thus, his design for her house is deeply connected to American traditions, to nature itself, and to the ground on which it stood, while it incorporates in the plan elements of a sophisticated language of theater architecture drawn from antiquity. It is a *theatrum mundi* for a sophisticated American: "Like it or leave it. There stands Hollyhock House in Hollywood – conceived and desired as a California Romanza. No not so domestic as the popular neo-Spanish of the region. But comfortable to live in well, with all its true pride in itself. Yes, a very proud house is Hollyhock House."[40]

While no evidence survives to show whether or not Barnsdall ever made use of the various stages and dramatic settings in and around the house, it is clear from her commitment to open-air productions that they could not have been intended simply as symbolic elements in the design.[41] The scope and variety of outdoor productions as Barnsdall and her friends knew them, as well as the theory behind the energetic open-air theater revival in the early twentieth century, are spelled out in Sheldon Cheney's *The Open-Air Theatre*, a book that, according to its preface, was largely completed by 1915 (it was published three years later). This date has considerable relevance to our understanding of the Olive Hill project since Cheney began a lively correspondence with Barnsdall in the fall of 1916, following his first meeting with her and the members of her troupe in Los Angeles.[42] Cheney had just founded a new magazine called *Theatre Arts*, based at the Arts and Crafts Theatre in Detroit, which would quickly become the principal clearinghouse for new ideas in American art theater. Barnsdall looked to Cheney for advice on her project just as she did to her other "experts."

In the opening chapter of *The Open-Air Theatre*, Cheney traced the history of the genre and outlined its social significance in his own time:

In the whole history of dramatic art there is no more illuminating truth than this: always when the drama has been simplest, most genuine, and lit up most brightly by the joy of living, and always when the drama has been closest to the life of the people, it has had its setting in the open. . . .

The current revival is a spontaneous growth, arising on the one hand from a rediscovery of the value of the out-of-doors as a corrective to an overcitified and artificial life, and on the other, from a new spirit of dramatic experiment, and protest against the over-sophisticated stage.[43]

Viewed as a branch of the art theater movement, open-air theater was a particularly apt choice for Barnsdall. Cheney's emphasis on its socially beneficial aspects was clearly influential in her thinking, and it is evident from their correspondence that the two genuinely shared their devotion to the form, drawing on common values and ideals. Cheney even cited Eleanora Duse, Barnsdall's mentor, to support his enthusiasm: "'To save the theatre, the theatre must be destroyed; the actors and actresses must all die of the plague. They poison the air, they make art impossible. . . . We should return to the Greeks, play in the open air; the drama dies of stalls and boxes and evening dress, and people who come to digest their dinner.'"[44] Cheney's opinions also echo sentiments found in the writings of Goldman that emphasize the importance of bringing drama to the people, the power of its message when presented simply, and the sense of community that grows as a result of common goals and achievements.

In *The Open-Air Theatre*, Barnsdall, and perhaps Wright, found a handbook of theories and a how-to guide for putting these into practice through architecture. Cheney described the different types of open-air theater at length and provided illustrations of the most important examples. Among these are two that bear directly

FIGURE 11
Zuñi Pueblo, New Mexico.
In the background is the
Taaiyalone mesa

on the design of Hollyhock House: the Cranbrook Greek Theatre, in Bloomfield Hills, Michigan, by Marcus R. Burrowes (fig. 12), and the "Roman Theatre according to Vitruvius" reproduced from the first English translation of *De architectura* (*The Ten Books on Architecture*), published by Harvard University Press in 1914 (fig. 13). Both are described in detail in the book's appendices, which were intended "to be of use to architects and others who may be charged with the actual creation of an open-air playhouse."[45]

The unresolved quality of the Hollyhock House design, underscored by its awkwardness as an open-air theater, appears symptomatic of Wright's ambivalence concerning the overall concept for the project. Neither the model provided by Cranbrook nor that of Vitruvius's Roman Theatre has been followed consistently, yet aspects of each have been employed to evoke an idea in a bold and visually accessible language. A third type, apparently drawn from Cheney's examples for garden theaters, has also been incorporated here, for, as Smith has shown, it would have been possible to use the rear part of the semi-circular clearing as a greensward stage with the tall evergreens behind it as a backdrop.[46] The cumulative effect of this apparent piling up of pieces from various schemes is a design that is highly evocative of theater imagery and, indeed, of the idea of theatricality, yet never entirely satisfactory as a place for theatrical presentations.

The explanation for Wright's uncharacteristic reliance on preexisting prototypes would appear to stem from two circumstances: first, his absence from Los Angeles during most of the design phase of the project, which left his son Lloyd Wright and Rudolph Schindler in charge; and second, the close association of a number of theater experts with Barnsdall as a client and with the project architects themselves. Although Wright worked on the project sporadically between 1916 and 1920, he seems never to have given it the consistent attention through which both the program and his conception of it would have grown and developed. While the original design was Wright's own and reflected his interpretation of the commission, it is evident that the development of key elements – the arrangement of the spaces within the overall plan and the detailing of the interior, for example – was left to his assistants, notably Schindler, or was a reworked elaboration of themes set out in Wright's own previous projects.[47] Wright was certainly sympathetic to much that Barnsdall believed and, as mentioned above, was himself engaged in the search for an American, and specifically Southern Californian, aesthetic. Though he was loath to admit it, however, the design that he produced for her relied heavily on the contributions of others.[48]

Wright and Theater Architecture

Despite the problems outlined above, Wright did bring a number of original ideas to the Barnsdall commission. His fascination with the shapes of ancient amphitheaters is evident both at Hollyhock House and in other projects associated with Olive Hill, including the Community Playhouse or Little Dipper School. Although perhaps originally introduced to this subject by his client, Wright became deeply committed to the idea of outdoor theater early in their partnership and stubbornly insisted on designing not only Hollyhock House but also the freestanding theater as a sort of amphitheater in which the audience and the players were not separated by a proscenium.[49] One project for the theater at Olive Hill, published in *Theatre Arts* magazine, even used a skylighted ceiling treatment to contribute to the impression that the auditorium was open to the sky (fig. 14). From the evidence of photographs, plaster models (fig. 15), and a number of surviving sketches related to the project, it is clear that the image of the ancient amphitheater remained a dominant theme in Wright's thinking and that he struggled to find an original response to it in his designs.

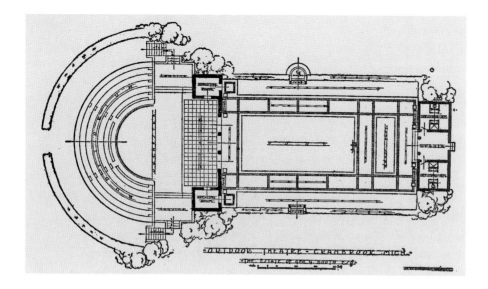

Yet given the importance of theater design for the
professionals associated with Barnsdall, and Wright's
apparent unwillingness to work with them on the project,
it is not at all surprising that no mutually acceptable
approach could be found. Bel Geddes, who clearly viewed
Wright as a capricious braggart and a bully, recalled with
dismay the architect's comments on the theater: "'It isn't
necessary for me to see other theaters to design better
ones.…We can't learn anything from Europe. They have
to learn from us. Europe is a dying civilization. The theater in Europe died in Athens in 500 B.C.'" And later:
"'Aline, the true theater is an architectural structure…I
have improved the forms of churches and houses and
office buildings, and if left alone I will give you the finest
theater in the world. If you are unable to leave me alone,
I will not waste my time going any further with it.'"[50]
Though Bel Geddes was clearly presenting his own version
of events – and he blamed Wright for the fact that the
theater was never built – it is evident that Wright cared

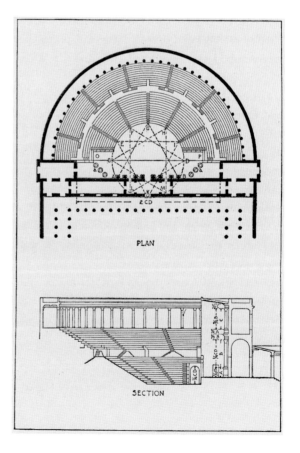

PLAN

SECTION

very deeply about recovering the fundamental elements of ancient theater architecture – community, simplicity, contact with nature – and bringing them back to life.

These concerns surface again in the designs for the Little Dipper, a building intended as a playhouse and school for Barnsdall's daughter and her friends. The structure was to be built on a site adjacent to the house. Music and movement were the focus of the lessons, which were to be taught according to the theories of Emile Jaques-Dalcroze, a Swiss musician and teacher whose work Barnsdall had first encountered in Europe.[51] The Dalcroze method, based on a system known as "eurythmics," was also popular in the avant-garde theater community. An article by Elizabeth S. Allen entitled "Eurythmics for the Theatre" appeared in *Theatre Arts* magazine in November 1919; in it Allen described the ways in which simple rhythmic movement and gesture could add expressive power to dramatic action.[52] Barnsdall had demonstrated her own commitment to children's theater earlier with her production of *Alice in Wonderland*; characteristically, the school was both a timely response to her need to provide for her daughter's education and an outgrowth of her effort to bring the newest and best art forms to Los Angeles.

The Little Dipper was divided into two parts: a raised stage and an open-air sandpit surrounded by tiered seats arrayed in concentric circles around a small pool (fig. 16). Both areas could be used for music lessons and other sorts of children's play activities. The round bowl of the sand-pit would have provided the children with a mini-amphitheater in which to perform plays for their friends.

Barnsdall's "Gifts" to the People of Los Angeles

Unfortunately this remarkable building would never see the light of day. Although construction began in 1923, Barnsdall had by then given up hope of achieving her ambitious plans for Olive Hill. Her struggles with Wright over the design of the theater continued with little progress and scant hope of resolution. More damaging still was the fact that she had lost her hold on the key members of her company: people like Bel Geddes and Markham had already deserted Los Angeles for New York.[53] Without them, her theatrical community would come to nothing; without the community, she herself had no reason to occupy Hollyhock House, the building she and Wright conceived as its centerpiece.

Planning for the theater continued, but Barnsdall began thinking about new uses for Hollyhock House and, in spring of 1923, she commissioned Wright to design a new house for her on a twenty-four-acre site in Beverly Hills.[54] In December 1923 Barnsdall met with representatives of the city to discuss a plan in which Hollyhock House would serve as a city-run library and community center; she intended to make the house and ten acres of surrounding land her gift to the people of Los Angeles. A portion of the Olive Hill site was to be offered up for sale, the proceeds from which would finance Barnsdall's various ongoing projects. When these negotiations fell through, however, all building activities on the site were halted. Still in possession of Olive Hill at the end of 1924, Barnsdall abandoned the Little Dipper and ordered the existing foundations demolished.

Perhaps to console herself for these disappointments, Barnsdall took an active interest in open-air musical and dramatic productions at the Hollywood Bowl, a privately sponsored open-air amphitheater for public concerts and performances under construction in the Hollywood Hills. Barnsdall's support for the Hollywood Bowl took a number of forms, including a pledge of $5,000 to the

FIGURE 14

Frank Lloyd Wright. Barnsdall
Theater, interior perspective.
From *Theatre Arts,* August
1926

FIGURE 15

Frank Lloyd Wright. Barnsdall
Theater, model. 1920. From
Theatre Arts, August 1926

board of directors in 1923 to help purchase the property and the offer of a prize, also of $5,000, the following year for a new design "for the permanent improvement of the Hollywood Bowl."[55] Very likely it was through her influence that Lloyd Wright became involved in the project, proposing and building various acoustic shells for the amphitheater in the 1920s.[56] Though a far cry from the lavish splendors of Olive Hill as she originally imagined them, the Hollywood Bowl was for Barnsdall an important American monument, a place where the public could come into contact with art and nature through open-air theater.

In a letter to Cheney written on August 8, 1923, on the eve of her departure for Europe, Barnsdall tried to explain the ideals that motivated her many projects: *I believe that Mr. Wright will never do an "interior" for me. He is too much the architect and not enough the man of the theatre. But as an architect he is bigger than any man in the theatre at present. We are building a little school for Sugar Top and fifteen other children in which Paul Swan the dancer and sculptor is going to teach a combination of sculpture, painting, dancing, costume making and drama to young children as part of a school program and Mr Wright's plan is a joy. We call it "The Little Dipper" unofficially.... It includes a tiny childs amphitheatre too delightful for words. I too hope that something definite for next summer in Hollywood Bowl may be worked out between Norman and me.... The Bowl Concerts have been a great success and I have sat evening after evening and planned and dreamed of things I might do there surrounded by the magic of those southern California nights. I add California because it is one of the drawbacks as well as urges – especially in the Hollywood valley it comes so close to being too cold for out of door performances. As to productions: one by an American and a classic beginning with the Greek classics and coming down through the ages. The*

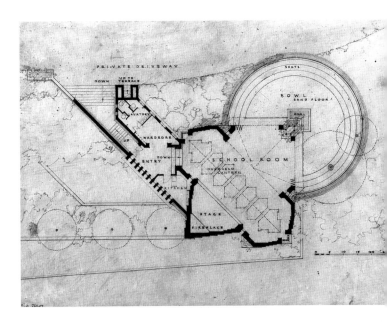

academic aspect of this may make you smile – but I have the touching memory of that hoard from Iowa, Kansas and Wisconsin – and incidentally from the farms of New York and Ill. . . . sitting in that circle of light night after night – they sit in heavy coats and a kind of spirit of earnestness pervades the place in so far as their response to the music is concerned. . . . They pioneer once more – from their ugly Kansas towns but this time for a touch of beauty – everything is comparative you know. Unceasing are the arguments Wright and I have on this. For after all he is one of the great provincials like those men who have done so much for literary and artistic France. He loves America and the tragedy is that he has had to make his greatest effort in Japan.[57]

This passage reveals that, as a group, Barnsdall's disparate Los Angeles projects reflected a consistent set of goals, inspired by her commitment to American culture and public education. In later years she would refer to Olive Hill as part of her "quest for Arcadia in the U.S.A."[58] Spurred by these ideals, her continuing interest in making Hollyhock House part of a gift to the city makes a great deal of sense, and it is not surprising that she rejoiced when, in 1927, her gift was finally accepted as a headquarters for the California Art Club. Her statement at the official opening of the house in August of that year, reprinted in *California Art Club Bulletin*, a copy of which she sent to Wright, makes her intentions clear:

I would like this gift to grow like our own California oak – slowly, with its separate branches each reaching from the same trunk – the Art Club, the Recreation Center and finally my own theatre. In giving the park I have thought of my father, of the happiness of children and young people with Olive Hill as a place to work and play, a background for their dreams and memories and my reluctance to see a building and landscaping of great beauty destroyed. . . .

So we have the fitting background for a group of artists reaching out for newer, fresher expression, children, the potential force of the future handled with kindness

and understanding and allowed that same creative freedom in their play that the artists have in their more serious work, the trial of a great music method that creates future musicians and audiences and much more and eventually a theatre that will draw people together, I hope, in sympathy with the life and art of other races and a joy in the development of their own drama.

No country can be great until the least of its citizens has been touched by beauty, truth and freedom; unless all three radiate from this little hill it is as nothing.[59]

Despite her earnest efforts to bridge the gap created by class and money, Barnsdall's motives and her projects were often misunderstood, obstructed, or thwarted by others because of her all-too-apparent wealth, her left-wing politics (Wright wrote that some called her a "Parlor Bolshevik"), her gender, and her own inability to concentrate on people or places for very long. Indeed, in the letter to Cheney of August 8, 1923, she revealed the deep conflict she felt about her own philanthropic impulses and the problems money created in her relationships with others:

But more and more I come to believe I do a harmful thing to my own nature to give money where I do not also give an idea. There seems to be something unhealthy in the after relation of a gift. . . . I give spontaneously and when I can't a second time I am treated as tho I had deprived them of their rights. . . . This has been one of the big disillusionments of life to me that one must be clever *in giving. I can't be clever and I don't think it right* for me *to give any longer unless I give my self with it to stand for an idea as well as a gift. . . . Some of us children of the last generation of easy going rich men have had a terrible heritage to fight. They took early from our rich resources and gave grandly and could for their generation. We resist the temptation or try to and know that we must give of ourselves. To put it in every day English I'll be damned if I want to give anything to anybody.*[60]

Wright, one of the principal beneficiaries of her patronage, was deeply ambivalent about her, and it is he, through his autobiography, who is responsible for creating the image of her as self-indulgent and irresponsible. Though Wright, perhaps more than anyone else, was aware of her ambitions for Olive Hill and, as such, surely understood her reasons for abandoning Hollyhock House, he nonetheless saw fit to represent her to his readers as a rich woman who gave up her house for mysterious personal reasons. Moreover, he insisted on the notion that Barnsdall's house was built for her private enjoyment – "Up there on Olive Hill…the daughter of one of America's pioneers had constructed a little principality, her very own, free to live as a queen"– and that she, a woman alone, had begun to feel lonely there, "more lonely because of it than she had felt without it."[61]

In print Wright consistently attempted to lay the entire blame for the failure of the Olive Hill project on Barnsdall's feminine susceptibility to "advice," presenting his own inability to see the construction of Hollyhock House through to the end as a desperate attempt to protect the integrity of his masterwork from these meddlers: "Now, *the* penalty (one of the many, probably) for being feminine, with extremely small hands and feet, rich, alone and mundane, is to have an entourage of dear 'friends.' …Collectively this insurance-brigade knew about as much about this building, Hollyhock House, as Sodom knew of Sanctity."[62] In their private correspondence, however – a correspondence that lasted until her death in 1946 – Wright could acknowledge not only his fondness for Barnsdall but also the fact that their problems went far deeper than his published account would ever suggest. As he put it in a letter from Taliesin dated June 27, 1921:
And then beside all else there has been so much in this attempt on our own part that has been irrelevant and adverse to the real matter in hand. Instead of reasoning logically about the features as they arose, the flea-bites of personal rancour would often goad us into tangents that left the scheme and went wide of the mark: And too – I would often go bang or go hang against flat walls that no logic nor any power I had could pierce. Those walls were particular recollections, preferences or prejudices you had preconceived, perhaps not germane to the case at all, but nevertheless irrevocable. You confounded these idiosyncracies with individuality and defended them.[63]

Barnsdall, however, saw the picture very differently, as she explained to him in a letter of February 4, 1926:
I thought it best not to answer your letter [a letter written by Wright some time before this date, which does not survive] until our disagreement was settled one way or another and now that it is settled I hope that we may not consider each other enemies and that we may never attempt to work together again. It cant be done. We are both too much of the same mold – egotistical, dictatorial and creative.… In one thing you are gravely mistaken and you will never know me if you don't get this right [and] also realize there is a new kind of woman in the world today. Haven't you read your Bernard Shaw? You write "And there is a third woman. A wistful, lonely one, none too sure of anyone, or anything about her – she having ventured too far into the 'unchartered' than fortified by her knowledge of life or circumstances, driven sometimes to cover her fear by defiance and to buttress her woman weakness with a willfulness beyond parallel!" You will never know me if you dont come to realize that I have never known fear in that or any other moral sense, that I am only at home and interested on unchartered seas. My willfulness I was born with. I hav'nt [sic] that old fashioned thing called "womans weakness" and I doubt if any woman ever really had it. Rather they projected it to flatter the ego of men. I have nothing in my life I need to buttress knowing that the position I take is because I have a fine, more forward feeling for life and love than most women. As for men they have nothing they can give in their present stage of development in relation to love

– they may be fairly civilized in other ways.... You judge me by a deep rooted conventionality within your self. You are free in your art but not in your relation to life; you consider aspects of people and their little conventions, created for safety, more important than they are.[64]

This wasn't the last word on the subject – the two would continue exchanging barbs and sharing insights for the next twenty years – but it does shed a great deal of light both on the relationship and on Wright's highly charged artistic and personal response to his client. For Wright, whose conflicting notions of womanhood were tautly strung between the two poles represented by his first wife, Catherine Wright, and Oak Park, Illinois, on the one hand and Mamah Borthwick Cheney, his companion and lover, and the capitals of Europe on the other, Barnsdall represented an irreconcilable paradox. He tenuously resolved it by emphasizing the American, the primitive, and the elemental in his architectural language of "otherness" on Olive Hill. Wright's recurrent emphasis on the theme of untamed or uncivilized forces enabled him to come to terms with the gap between the domestic and the public and theatrical at Hollyhock House.

Though Wright and Barnsdall would continue to squabble over money and control, accusing one another of deception and dishonesty (a struggle that ultimately led to Wright's bringing suit in 1926), planning for the theater continued until 1927 with Wright as architect. An announcement in the *Los Angeles Times* on January 21, 1927, reported on a plan to build a "Greek Theatre" on Olive Hill, noting that Barnsdall had met with members of the city planning association and presented them with a plaster model of an open-air Greek theater, which she planned to erect at Barnsdall Park at a cost of $2 million.[65] A letter to Wright of November 16, 1927, makes it clear that although she and her architect were still at odds over the details of the design, Barnsdall expected to go ahead with it. Nevertheless, she let Wright know that she would be unable to do anything further until most of

Olive Hill could be sold. Ultimately, Barnsdall came to recognize that even the last surviving part of the project – ironically, the part with which she had begun – would never materialize. Nothing further was reported in the press concerning the plans for the Greek theater after the initial announcement, and there is no evidence that Barnsdall pursued the project in 1928. Ultimately it too was abandoned.

Barnsdall remained connected to Olive Hill in one way or another until her death, in December 1946. Over the years her efforts to put the land and buildings to use would include such ideas as a recreation center for young women employed as nursemaids and housekeepers, a senior citizens' center, a "radical center," a home for soldiers, and an art museum.[66] None of these schemes was realized. Her own house, always intended as just one semipublic element in an extensive "art park," remained the focus of artistic activities on Olive Hill, the one part of the project that truly thrived in the wake of Barnsdall's departure and for fifteen years thereafter. Despite her failure as an impresario on the grand scale, Barnsdall remained true to her belief in the power of the arts to change lives and minds. It is in this spirit that the Olive Hill project should be remembered, as a monument to a period in American cultural history when it was possible for one woman to bring feminism, socialism, experimental theater, and new American architecture together in a single far-reaching project intended primarily not for her own private enjoyment but for the public good. Thus it is fitting that Hollyhock House should become, and remain to this day, the centerpiece of a public park rather than a private retreat, for she never saw it as a "little principality" where she "was free to live as a queen," as Wright and others suggested. A failure of neither her character nor her vision of the central role of the arts in public life, the house and its ongoing use by the public should be counted among Barnsdall's successes.

1 For Bel Geddes, see Bruce Bliven, "Norman Bel Geddes: His Art and Ideas," *Theatre Arts* 3 (July 1919), 179–90, and Norman Bel Geddes, *Miracle in the Evening*, ed. William Kelley (Garden City, N.Y.: Doubleday, 1960).

2 Barnsdall, letter to Mary Hunter Austin, May 10, 1916, Mary Hunter Austin Collection, Au 1346, Huntington Library, San Marino, Calif. In my citations of Barnsdall's letters I have preserved her distinctive style and spelling as much as possible; I have changed some punctuation in the interest of clarity.

3 Barnsdall, letter to Mary Hunter Austin, June 1, 1916, Mary Hunter Austin Collection, Au 1347. The letterhead says "1025 No. Negley Ave. Pittsburgh," Barnsdall's family home.

4 Unless otherwise noted, letters written by Barnsdall or Wright cited in this chapter are in the collection of the Frank Lloyd Wright Foundation, Taliesin West, Scottsdale, Ariz. Hollyhock House and the Olive Hill projects are discussed in detail by Kathryn Smith in her *Frank Lloyd Wright, Hollyhock House and Olive Hill: Buildings and Projects for Aline Barnsdall* (New York: Rizzoli, 1992), and her "Frank Lloyd Wright, Hollyhock House and Olive Hill, 1914–1924," *Journal of the Society of Architectural Historians* 38 (Mar. 1979), 15–33. See also Neil Levine, *The Architecture of Frank Lloyd Wright* (Princeton: Princeton University Press, 1996), and his "Hollyhock House and the Romance of Southern California," *Art in America* (Sept. 1983), 150–64. I am indebted to both authors for sharing their research and expertise with me. A third monograph, by Donald Hoffmann, *Frank Lloyd Wright's Hollyhock House* (New York: Dover Press, 1992), is also very helpful. An earlier version of this chapter, entitled "A House Is Not a Home: Hollyhock House as 'Art Theater Garden,'" was published in the *Journal of the Society of Architectural Historians* 51 (Sept. 1992), 239–60.

5 A list of "Drawings Promised," enclosed in a letter from Barnsdall to Wright dated Sept. 24, 1919, includes a "Motion Picture House" in addition to "my home" and other buildings.

6 Flora Lawrence, "Eminence to Be Made Rare Beauty Spot," *Los Angeles Examiner*, July 6, 1919, 5.

7 For Theodore N. Barnsdall, see the *Pittsburgh Bulletin*, Mar. 3, 1917, 14, and the *New York Times*, Feb. 28, 1917, 2: 6.

8 For a biography of Barnsdall, see Norman M. and Dorothy K. Karasick, *The Oilman's Daughter: A Biography of Aline Barnsdall* (Encino, Calif.: Carleston Publishing, 1993). In a letter to Wright of Oct. 29, 1933, Aline wrote from Switzerland: "We have a good deal to talk about when I eventually see you. Have come to conclusion that what I want is a self supporting farm or small ranch and my mind turns to Colorado. It has the high light air I must live in to be at my best; I spent many happy summers there when I was a girl, and the soil can be so flush red and beautiful." On July 30, 1942, she wrote to him again, from Grand Lake, Colo.: "This is the region which taught me to like the USA. Father had a mine here and we came to it for a number of summers." Barnsdall's father also had close ties to Oklahoma. He maintained a friendship and business relationship with Chief Bigheart of the Osage nation, which ultimately led to Barnsdall's lucrative development of oil resources on Osage land; see *The Chronicles of Oklahoma* 32 (1954), 389. These ties may have contributed to Aline's lifelong interest in the culture of the Plains Indians; see Barnsdall to Wright, Nov. 22, 1932, and June 4, 1946.

9 Bel Geddes, *Miracle*, 173.

10 Ibid.

11 See Sheldon Cheney, *The New Movement in the Theatre* (New York: M. Kennerley, 1914), and his *The Art Theatre* (New York: M. Kennerley, 1914). For a glimpse of Barnsdall's European experience and early years in Chicago, see Lawrence Langner, *The Magic Curtain* (New York: Dutton, 1951), 56–84.

12 For the Chicago Renaissance, see Dale Kramer, *The Chicago Renaissance: The Literary Life of the Midwest* (New York: Appleton-Century, 1966), and Jackson Robert Bryer, "A Trial-Track for Racers: Margaret Anderson and the Little Review" (Ph.D. diss., University of Wisconsin, 1965).

13 *Mother Earth* was started in New York in 1905; Goldman was frequently on lecture tours but established offices and significant followings in both New York and Chicago. In New York her circle included Charlotte Perkins Gilman, Mabel Dodge, and Margaret Sanger. For Goldman, see Alice Wexler, *Emma Goldman: An Intimate Life* (New York: Pantheon, 1984), and Candace Falk, *Love, Anarchy and Emma Goldman* (New York: Holt, Rinehart & Winston, 1984).

14 Margaret Anderson, *My Thirty Years War* (London: Knopf, 1930), 107. Recalling Barnsdall's visit to the offices of the *Little Review* and their subsequent meetings, Anderson referred to her simply as "Nineteen Millions" or "N.M."; it was only in reply to a question from Dale Kramer in June 1964 that Anderson made it clear that this was Aline Barnsdall; Kramer Notebook 3, Special Collections, Newberry Library, Chicago. See also Bryer, "Trial-Track," 201–3.

15 See Alice Gerstenberg, "Hope of the Little Theater in Chicago," *Townsfolk* (Feb. 1948), 16. The history of Chicago theater in these years is described in letters written by Gerstenberg and others to Dale Kramer in 1960; Kramer Notebooks, esp. nos. 3, 4, 5. According to Gerstenberg, the play was first produced on Feb. 11, 1915, and moved to the Booth Theater in New York in March; *Alice in Wonderland* (New York: Longmans Green, 1929). Excerpts from positive reviews in Chicago and New York papers appear on pp. xi–xii.

16 Emma Goldman, *Living My Life* (New York: Knopf, 1931), 707–8.

17 Emma Goldman, *The Social Significance of Modern Drama* (Boston: R. G. Badger, 1914), 5–7.

18 The challenge facing American artists was summed up in a book by Waldo Frank

entitled *Our America* (New York: Boni & Liveright, 1919), which Barnsdall knew and admired (as is clear from her letter to Sheldon Cheney of August 8, 1923, discussed below). Like Barnsdall and Wright, Frank wrote about American culture both as a mission of the younger generation and as a response to the drama of the landscape itself: "But America was intense before the white man came. America is a land with a shrieking rhythm. And whatever you would understand of our weakness and our strength you must interpret in this key.... Even our climate is an excitant.... America is vivid and vibrant beyond the scales of temperate Europe"; *Our America*, 22–23.

19 Goldman, *Living My Life*, 707.

20 Curt Gentry, *Frame Up: The Incredible Case of Tom Mooney and Warren Billings* (New York: Norton, 1967), 143, 329, 352, 374ff.

21 Barnsdall to Wright, May 30, 1920.

22 Wright described his ideas about American architecture in a number of published and unpublished texts, including "The Sovereignty of the Individual," published as the preface to the *Ausgeführte Bauten und Entwürfe von Frank Lloyd Wright* (Berlin: Wasmuth, 1910) and reprinted in Edgar Kaufmann, Jr., and Ben Raeburn, eds., *Frank Lloyd Wright: Selected Writings and Buildings* (New York: Meridian Books, 1960). For Wright's description of his first meeting with Barnsdall, see Smith, *Hollyhock House*, 15. In a letter of June 4, 1946, Barnsdall presented still another version, alluding to their first meeting "that evening in Mrs. Potter Palmer's garage."

23 Barnsdall to Wright, July 27, 1916, from Mill Valley, Calif. The letterhead is from the Players Producing Co.

24 Bel Geddes, *Miracle*, 98–114, 152–54, 165–67.

25 See Constance d'Arcy Mackay, *The Little Theatre in the United States* (New York: H. Holt, 1917), 156–58, and Bel Geddes, *Miracle*, 166–71.

26 An early letter from Wright to Barnsdall, dated Oct. 27, 1916, refers to a note he had received from his son Lloyd (already a member of Barnsdall's circle and soon to be married to the actress Kirah Markham) "applauding you [Barnsdall] for the spirit you manifested, your real nerve in calling off the venture before the opening night."

27 Barnsdall to Wright, Nov. 16, 1927. For Ordynski, see Bel Geddes, *Miracle*, 166, and Barnsdall, letter to Austin, May 10, 1916.

28 Bel Geddes described a series of tense meetings between Wright, Barnsdall, and himself in 1916 and 1917 in which Wright flatly refused to take any advice on the design. Barnsdall apparently knew that his project was unworkable and refused to go ahead with it in the form he suggested; the result was a deadlock. *Miracle*, 161–64.

29 See Smith, *Hollyhock House*, ch. 3, esp. 34–35.

30 Ibid., ch. 5.

31 Lawrence, "Eminence," 5.

32 Emma Goldman, "Marriage and Love," in her *Anarchism and Other Essays* (New York: Mother Earth Publishing Assn., 1910), 233–45, esp. 241. In a letter of Nov. 16, 1927, Barnsdall wrote to Wright: "Instead of my facing the power of money in the old sense let us face the fact that the world must work toward a cleaner relation between money and art – and *no exchange of money* where there is love. Too great a stench has been created by it. The finest future types of women want something different. Every now and then you hear of some woman refusing alimony – in principle. Sooner or later, counting in thousands of years, the stench will be cleared away."

33 Lawrence, "Eminence," 5.

34 Frank Lloyd Wright, *An Autobiography* (New York: Longmans Green, 1932), 228. Reprinted in Bruce Brooks Pfeiffer, ed., *Frank Lloyd Wright: Collected Writings*, vol. 2, (New York: Rizzoli, 1992), 271.

35 Ibid., 270. Various drafts of the section of the manuscript dealing with Hollyhock House are in the Frank Lloyd Wright Archives at Taliesin West.

36 Ibid., 274–75.

37 Ibid., 269–70.

38 Wright described these as "primitive American Architecture...long slumbering remains of lost cultures; mighty primitive abstractions of man's nature"; Kaufmann and Raeburn, *Frank Lloyd Wright*, 21, quoted from Wright, *A Testament* (New York: Horizon Press, 1957). See Vincent Scully, *Frank Lloyd Wright* (New York: Braziller, 1960), 24–25, and his *American Architecture and Urbanism* (New York: Holt, Rinehart & Winston, 1969), 155–56; Dimitri Tselos, "Exotic Influences in the Architecture of Frank Lloyd Wright," *Magazine of Art* 47 (Apr. 1953), 160–69, and his "Frank Lloyd Wright and World Architecture," *Journal of the Society of Architectural Historians* 28 (Mar. 1969), 58–72; and Levine, *The Architecture of Frank Lloyd Wright*, 140 and n. 76.

39 For Wright's clients before World War I, see Leonard K. Eaton, *Two Chicago Architects and Their Clients: Frank Lloyd Wright and Howard Van Doren Shaw* (Cambridge, Mass.: MIT Press, 1969).

40 Wright, *An Autobiography*, 274.

41 The open-air theater is discussed by Smith in "Hollyhock," 27. She cites evidence that it was used by the California Art Club as a theater after 1927; Frank W. Vreeland, "A New Art Centre for the Pacific Coast," *Arts and Decoration* 28 (1927), 64–65. Levine first suggested the connection between the treatment of the open-air theater in the house and the design of the Barnsdall Theater; Smith, "Hollyhock," 158.

42 Sheldon Cheney Papers, Roll 3497, Archives of American Art, Smithsonian Institution. The first letter is dated Sept. 4, 1916. Bel Geddes says that Cheney, "a young, lanky, intently talking writer," appeared at the stage door of the Los Angeles Little Theatre and said that he was "leaving for Detroit where he intended to start a magazine he would call *Theatre Arts Magazine*"; *Miracle*, 160.

43 Sheldon Cheney, *The Open-Air Theatre* (New York: M. Kennerley, 1918), 1, 5.

44 Ibid., 8.

45 Ibid., 134. For Cranbrook, see Eileen L. Roberts, "Ionic Order Restored," *Inland Architect* 45 (July–Aug. 1991), 21–25. For Marcus R. Burrowes, see *Michigan Society of Architects Monthly Bulletin* (Sept. 1953), 38.

46 Smith, "Hollyhock," 27–28.

47 For Lloyd Wright, see David Gebhard and Harriette Von Breton, *Lloyd Wright, Architect* (Santa Barbara: University of California at Santa Barbara, 1971), esp. 23–28. For Schindler, see Esther McCoy, *Vienna to Los Angeles: Two Journeys* (Santa Monica: Arts and Architecture Press, 1979), esp. 34–38.

48 For further evidence, see Barnsdall to Wright, Jan. 29, 1920, which contains a reference to Lloyd Wright's designs for the interior.

49 See also Wendell Cole, "The Theatre Projects of Frank Lloyd Wright," *Educational Theatre Journal* 12 (1960), 86–93. The model and an interior perspective were published in *Theatre Arts* 10 (Aug. 1926), 534–37, having appeared in *Wendigen* a few years before.

50 Bel Geddes, *Miracle*, 156, 162. Later in the book Bel Geddes describes a letter he wrote to Wright after seeing the model for the theater in 1922: "Your attitude forces me to believe you are obsessed with founding a FLW style of staging which would inevitably result from being forced to work within the architectural limitations imposed by your design"; 269.

51 Barnsdall sent Cheney a copy of the program for a "lecture demonstration" given by Dalcroze at Wigmore Hall in London in 1922, on which she had written: "This was given me in Geneva. It may help you to know what I mean. I am anxious to bring a teacher out here and start a class of children on the hill. Will build a hall later and help it develop." Sheldon Cheney Papers, Roll 3947.

52 Elizabeth S. Allen, "Eurythmics for the Theatre", *Theatre Arts* 3 (Nov. 1919), 42–50.

53 See Bel Geddes, *Miracle*, 268–73, 276–81, where he discusses his role in the failure of the project. In a letter of Sept. 1, 1923, to Sheldon Cheney, Barnsdall blamed herself; Sheldon Cheney Papers, Roll 3947.

54 The history of Barnsdall's various gifts to the city of Los Angeles is discussed by Norman Karasick in "Art, Politics and Hollyhock House" (master's thesis, University of California at Dominguez Hills, 1982). For the Beverly Hills house, see Smith, *Hollyhock House*, 166–71. Barnsdall also had Schindler design a house for her in 1927, the "Translucent House," to be built at Palos Verdes; see David Gebhard, *Schindler* (New York: Viking, 1980), 102–4. In 1939 she wrote to Richard Neutra, asking him to build her "a house like von Sternberg's" of 1935 and reporting that "one reason I left Olive Hill was because I always felt heavy and under vitalized there." The letter of Feb. 15, 1939, in the Neutra Archive at UCLA, is quoted by Thomas S. Hines in *Richard Neutra and the Search for Modern Architecture* (New York: Oxford University Press, 1982), 137–38.

55 Barnsdall, letter to Dr. Percival Gerson, May 8, 1923, Gerson Collection, UCLA; *Southwest Builder and Contractor*, June 6, 1924, 47.

56 Gebhard, *Lloyd Wright*, 25–26, 43–45.

57 Barnsdall, letter to Cheney, Aug. 8, 1923, Sheldon Cheney Papers, Roll 3947.

58 Barnsdall to Wright, Aug. 9, 1943.

59 *California Art Club Bulletin* 11 (Aug. 1927). Barnsdall sent a copy of the flyer to Wright and wrote next to her statement, "This gift has become the pet of the newspapers"; Frank Lloyd Wright Archives.

60 Barnsdall to Cheney, Sheldon Cheney Papers, Roll 3947.

61 Wright, *An Autobiography*, 275.

62 Ibid., 273. See also the manuscript of this section, Frank Lloyd Wright Archives, 2401.035, 8–9.

63 Wright to Barnsdall, June 27, 1921.

64 Barnsdall to Wright, Feb. 4, 1926.

65 "Art Theater To Be Built," *Los Angeles Times*, Jan. 21, 1927. For the Greek theater, see Karasick, "Art, Politics and Hollyhock House," 38 n. 3, and *Los Angeles Times*, Dec. 23, 1926, 2: 1.

66 Some of these ideas are discussed in Karasick, "Art, Politics and Hollyhock House," esp. 17–35, 40–44. In a letter to Wright of July 28, 1929, Barnsdall mentioned that she had a "tentative plan for building an Art Gallery on the south slope of Olive Hill." Wright responded on Aug. 10 with enthusiasm, but the idea came to nothing. A letter from Barnsdall to Wright of Nov. 5, 1930, says, "I am still living in Residence 'B' but it may become a girls club for the city recreation. They are thinking of taking over the whole hill." In this letter she also mentions Schindler's renovation work at Hollyhock House.

PLATE 1

Gerrit Rietveld and Truus
Schröder. Schröder House, Utrecht,
the Netherlands. 1923–24

No matter how many times one has visited the Schröder
House in Utrecht, the Netherlands (plate 1), the sight
of it at the end of Prins Hendriklaan is always a happy
surprise.[1] Compared to its somber neighbors, dark brick
row houses that line the street in an orderly series of doors
and windows, the Schröder House seems fresh, playful,
and filled with the promise of new discoveries, as if it
had been assembled from the parts of a child's building
toy. Metal strips, lengths of wood, and bits of tubular
steel painted bright red, blue, yellow, and black provide a
sort of framework for the roof, walls, and windows, thin
planes that never meet at the corners but appear to be
propped together in an elegant yet strangely precarious
composition. The Schröder House has often been compared to the paintings of Piet Mondrian (plate 2), but
the similarity remains on the surface, for when it is
experienced in person, the house seems to share little of
the painter's patient and cerebral investigation of form.
With its smooth, bright walls (maintained in pristine
condition since the house was renovated and opened to
the public, in 1987), colorful touches, and handcrafted
appearance, the Schröder House seems instead the very
embodiment of an impulsive, joyful, and confident
modernity. Despite its age, the house Gerrit Rietveld
(1888–1964) and Truus Schröder designed in 1923–24
is eternally young.[2]

    Yet there is also something self-conscious and didac-
tic about the place; one quickly senses that the parts of
this building toy were deliberately shaped and colored
to provide us with a learning experience. Indeed, the
Schröder House, like so many architect-designed buildings of the 1920s, has its polemical side, expressing new

Truus Schröder. ca. 1925

Family Matters:

The Schröder House, by Gerrit Rietveld and Truus Schröder

with Maristella Casciato

ideas not only about the nature of modern materials and architectural design, but also about a philosophy of progressive education: Mrs. Schröder was a young widow with three children, aged twelve, eleven, and six, when the family moved in, and she had a vision of family life in the modern world. The house's double personality – playful and carefree on the one hand, yet disciplined and even moralistic on the other – reflects the complex personalities of architect and client, and the unique nature of the collaboration between Rietveld, who had never built a building before, and Schröder, a well-to-do woman with strong ideas about how and where she wanted to live.[3] Passionate about art and about each other, both saw the house as an opportunity to create a totally modern environment, free of the repressive traditions and rules – both social and architectural – that kept them

Piet Mondrian. *Tableau 2*. 1922.
Oil on canvas, 21⅛ x 21⅛ in.
Solomon R. Guggenheim
Museum, New York, 51.1309

from new experiences and the expression of emotions. Their commitment to this partnership was long-standing: they would continue working together on a number of important domestic and other design projects, particularly during the 1920s and 1930s.[4]

Entering the house via the front door, the visitor is greeted by the orderly (and small-scale) world of the schoolhouse. A narrow hallway, fitted with both adult- and child-size cupboards for coats and shoes, is surrounded by what appear to be four rather ordinary-looking rooms. Directly opposite the door is the stair and a landing, on which there is a bench, telephone shelf, and a row of small drawers.

The experience of this pleasant, unremarkable foyer offers no warning of the extraordinary environment that lies above (plate 3). Having climbed the stairs, the visitor emerges into another realm entirely, a large, open space filled with light and color. On the floor and walls, shiny rectangles of red, blue, yellow, black, gray, and white play off the clear light of the windows, creating in effect a grid of shifting, two-dimensional planes in a three-dimensional composition. Large expanses of glass dematerialize the boundary between interior and exterior and offer changing views of the neighboring buildings on Prins Hendriklaan and of the garden. (A highway constructed next to the house in 1963 destroyed the view from the front window, which originally opened onto unspoiled countryside.) Retractable wooden partitions, deployed along yellow, blue, and red tracks in the ceiling, make it possible to subdivide the open room, creating a constellation of smaller spaces that serve as the living/ dining area and rooms for the children. These rooms are sparsely furnished with tables, cupboards, beds, and chairs designed by Rietveld.[5]

This unprecedented assemblage of brightly colored elements produces an environment imbued with a sense of freedom and choice. There is a new attention to the

PLATE 3

Schröder House, upper floor,
looking toward the boy's and
girls' rooms

additive processes of design and construction, reflected and reiterated through the day-to-day experience of dwelling. The interior of the upper floor is literally animate; its folding partitions and movable walls (particularly in the corner where the bathroom and Mrs. Schröder's bedroom are located) slide, pivot, click, and lock into place like the smooth wooden parts of a giant magic box in which a coin is made to disappear and reappear at will. Like the exterior, the interior has a serendipitous, playful quality, but it also makes its message clear: one must construct an environment as one constructs a way of life – thoughtfully and deliberately.

In this strange, malleable space all things seem possible. The human body, a living organism in a man-made environment, takes on new importance, just as Rietveld's chairs and other furniture become focal points of attention, demanding to be analyzed, disassembled, and reassembled. In this way the house "stages" individual experiences and interpersonal relationships, heightening awareness of movement, of sight and sound, and awakening a deep appreciation of the complexity of domestic life. Despite its own extraordinary vitality, then, the interior is strangely contemplative, eliminating unnecessary motion by focusing on ritually repeated actions like the folding and unfolding of the partition walls. In this way the house makes room for new thoughts and experiences.

What Rietveld and Schröder shared was an exuberant confidence in the present and in their own ability to make art that was both beautiful and liberating. In 1918 Rietveld had revolutionized furniture design with the first unpainted versions of his Red-Blue Chair (fig. 1; he added the colors in 1923). By reexamining the posture of the human body in a sitting position, Rietveld had been able to identify and isolate the chair's component parts; these he brought together in an elegant three-dimensional composition that was both functional (though hardly

comfortable) and decorative.[6] For him the process of making architecture, like that of constructing a piece of furniture, itself represented a quintessential modern activity, one in which new machine technology led the way: design was a matter of *assembling* a kit of parts – sections of flat wall, thin metal or wooden supports, windows of various sizes, pegs, hinges, and metal fastenings – with a specific purpose in mind, thereby creating new forms and dynamic spaces. As he wrote in 1932, in an article entitled "New Functionalism in Dutch Architecture":

It is a sign of progress that the huge monumental edifices will belong to the past and that we now also take an interest in small practical houses. Our pieces of furniture too are no longer heavy immobile objects. They are no longer exclusively intended for a single purpose nor, in fact, made for exceptional surroundings. They are beginning to consist of small, light sections that can be assembled, so that one can construct a sort of framework as large as one wants; a piece of furniture consisting of supporting surfaces, in combination with open and closed boxes, drawers and so on; not just for the welcome variety provided by new materials…. The aim is to preserve a free, light and unbroken space, that gives clarity to our lives and contributes to a new sense of life."[7]

The work Rietveld and Schröder did together was intended not simply to communicate this "new sense of life" but literally to guide body and mind toward clearer and more natural actions and thoughts. In 1921 Schröder and her husband had hired Rietveld to renovate a room in their house as a private sitting room/study for her; Mrs. Schröder's new room had to look "modern" as well as to communicate something of the feeling of modernity to its users. Their ideas about living in a "free, light and unbroken space," as Rietveld wrote, were bound up with a fierce commitment to a new openness about relationships within their own families and to truth in

FIGURE 1

Gerrit Rietveld, seated on an
early version of his Red-Blue
Chair, and co-workers in front
of his furniture-making workshop in Utrecht. 1918

their emotional lives. Bourgeois notions of respectability
and propriety, with their emphasis on discipline, hierar-
chy, and containment, would be eliminated through
architectural design that countered each of these aspects
in a conscious and systematic way. They saw their next
project, the Schröder House of 1923–24, as an opportunity to pursue their goals on a larger scale, exploring the
ways in which the parts of a building could be shaped
into a spatial environment that would stimulate people
to live and even to think differently.

Rietveld and Schröder were not only professional
partners but also friends and lovers; he was often in the
house and appeared at art events and social gatherings
with her, despite the fact that his own wife and six children also lived in Utrecht. The Schröder House was their
laboratory, and they studied its effects on themselves
and on the children. Truus Schröder lived there for some

sixty years; Rietveld kept an office in the house in the early years (1924–32) and even lived there himself at the end of his life, from the time of his wife's death, in 1958, until his own, in 1964.[8] While they speculated about the broader implications and possible applications of their experiments to housing design (for example, in the two apartment houses near the Schröder House on Prins Hendriklaan and around the corner on Erasmuslaan, erected in 1931 and 1935), it is clear that for both Rietveld and Schröder the house and its meaning were intensely personal. It is hardly surprising, then, to discover that it remains unique in the history of architecture: beloved, wondered at, intensely studied – but never imitated.[9]

Truus and An Schräder. ca. 1910

Truus Schröder

In a series of interviews conducted in 1982, Truus Schröder described her life and the circumstances that shaped the design of her home.[10] Born in Deventer in 1889 to an upper-middle-class Catholic family (her maiden name was Schräder), she received a first-rate education, developing a taste for books and ideas as well as a sharp critical sense about matters of religion, philosophy, and the arts. Her mother died when she was a small child, and when she was a teenager she was sent to a convent boarding school. The experience shaped her emotionally as well as intellectually; throughout her life her closest relationship was with her older sister An (figs. 2, 3), whose intelligence, avant-garde tastes, and left-wing politics she admired. Trained as a pharmacist, Truus seems never to have practiced but instead immersed herself in reading, concentrating on literature, philosophy, art, and architecture, interests she shared with her sister.[11]

In 1911 Truus married Frits Schröder, a lawyer, and they settled in Utrecht.[12] The couple had two children, a boy and a girl, born in 1912 and 1913; a third child, a girl, followed in 1918 (figs. 4, 5). The family lived in a comfortable apartment above Mr. Schröder's offices at 135, Biltstraat, but it was apparent that Truus and her husband had major differences about the way in which they wanted to live and bring up their children. In a letter to Truus of June 11, 1914, Frits Schröder outlined their problems. He loved her, he wrote, but "[their] differences manifest themselves in all [their] interests." He was more practical and saw things as they were, while she was more theoretical and saw things "as they ought to be"; his views were the result of experience, whereas hers came from reading books. If they were to follow her ideas about education, he wrote, then the children might very well be better people and experience beauty more profoundly, but they would very likely be unfit for the harsh realities of society; this, he feared, would ultimately "destroy" them. Moreover, he continued, he deeply disapproved of her sister An's lifestyle and influence on her. The last point was certain to anger Truus, whose love and admiration for her sister were unshakable.[13]

An Harrenstein-Schräder, a writer and art critic, was married to a doctor and lived in Amsterdam. Through her Truus was introduced to a circle of artists who held far greater interest for her than the bourgeois Utrecht society in which she lived. This group included Jacob Bendien (who lived with the Harrensteins for many years and was, in all probability, An's lover), Paul Citroen (Bendien's brother-in-law), Charley Toorop, Theo van Doesburg, and other members of the De Stijl circle, as well as visit-

ing artists such as Bruno Taut and Kurt Schwitters, and left-wing politicians and members of the Dutch Communist party.[14] Their interests stretched beyond art and politics to include spirituality (in particular, Theosophy), meditation, free love, and women's rights. These were the people to whom Truus Schröder looked for intellectual and artistic stimulation, but theirs was a world far removed from Utrecht and the Biltstraat apartment, with its heavy, dark furniture and high-ceilinged, formal rooms, in which she spent her days as the wife of a successful lawyer. In contrast, Frits Schröder's support for the local arts community was expressed through membership in such organizations as Kunstliefde (Love of Art) and Voor de Kunst (For Art), to which he and Truus belonged from 1918 on; these affiliations could hardly have offered his discontented wife much consolation, if any.[15]

This unhappy state of affairs dragged on through the First World War and continued in the years that followed. In 1921 Frits Schröder suggested that Truus redesign and furnish a room in their home for her use alone. Frits had been introduced to the work of Gerrit Rietveld by a business associate, and he suggested that she consider him as her architect. Mrs. Schröder was easily convinced. She commissioned Rietveld to design a private study, complete with a built-in daybed and armchair, a table, and some chairs (fig. 6).[16] Mrs. Schröder saw the new room as a place to which she could escape and where she could live as she liked:

I hardly met any people who had a feeling for what was modern. Not through my husband. My husband was eleven years my senior; he had a very busy practice and a great many acquaintances, some of his family lived in Utrecht, and they weren't at all interested in that sort of thing. It was only through my sister that ideas came in from the outside. We would discuss such things in my room, and then it was mine, only mine. And once or twice Rietveld visited me.[17]

FIGURE 3

Truus and An. ca. 1925

FIGURE 4

Frits and Truus Schröder. ca. 1911

FIGURE 5

Truus Schröder with her mother-
in-law and two of her children,
Marjan and Binnert. 1923

The room represented more than a retreat; it was a place in which a new way of life could be discussed and experienced. The love affair between Truus Schröder and Gerrit Rietveld, which began about this time, gathered force as the couple talked together about their lives, their relationships, and the meaning of art for each of them: *When I first got to know Rietveld, he, like myself, had been through a lot of unpleasantness. We had a deep understanding of each other's problems with the social norms of our times, which were strongly present. At that time, Rietveld really had to break free from the strict Protestant beliefs with which he had been brought up. And because I had just broken free from religious conventions myself…I think I encouraged this in him…but I think that talking with me helped him sort things out. For a while we were deeply involved with each other's problems and helped each other to develop further.*[18]

In his design for the room Rietveld lowered the ceilings and pared the furniture and lighting fixtures down to essentials, rejecting the rich fabrics, ornament, and heavy forms of conventional upper-class interiors.[19] His own ideas about form and color, shaped in part by his contact with the artists of the De Stijl movement, were channeled and challenged by Schröder's critique. This mutual respect and exchange would shape their relationship for a period of more than forty years.

FIGURE 6

Gerrit Rietveld and Truus Schröder. The study at 135, Biltstraat, Utrecht. 1921

The Schröder House

When her husband died, in 1923, Mrs. Schröder again looked to Rietveld for help in designing her home. Her first idea was to find an apartment that he could remodel; her plan was to remain in Utrecht for only the next six years, until the children were out of school, and then to move to Amsterdam.[20] Nevertheless, having discovered a suitable lot at the end of a row of brick houses on the edge of the town, Schröder and Rietveld set about designing a new house for her family. Although she had a comfortable income from her husband's estate, her budget was limited; the final cost of the house was approximately the same as for a small, semidetached dwelling at that time.[21]

The site Schröder and Rietveld chose permitted them to experiment with a new hybrid type as well as a new style. The site on Prins Hendriklaan was surrounded on three sides by open space (fig. 7) and faced directly onto fields and open countryside. Accordingly, Schröder and Rietveld designed the house to have two principal fronts, a narrow one facing the street, which responded to the scale of its neighbors, and a broad one with a more formal, central entrance, which was approached via an enclosed garden (plate 4). Viewed from the garden side the house resembled a freestanding suburban villa of the type in which the Schräder family lived when Truus was growing up.[22] Looking out from the garden with one's back to the house or from inside through the large windows of the principal living areas (fig. 8), one had the sensation of having left the city behind, of being in the more contemplative and peaceful environment of the country. This mixing of urban, suburban, and rural types at the Schröder House offered flexibility and a choice of experiences in daily life; throughout the house there are other design elements, such as the use of both fixed walls and movable partitions, that free the occupants to make choices among various ways of living. The fact that the house is both literally and figuratively open-ended is one of its most distinctive qualities, and it provides a richer, more complex definition of what the architect and the client thought modern living was all about.

When Schröder described her program to Rietveld, she emphasized her need for a home in which parents and children would be brought together in an open space, where conversations could be wide-ranging, and where focused activities, including the children's schoolwork, might also be carried out: "I thought it was very good for the children to live in an atmosphere like that, also to have Rietveld often around. To have that experience. To hear those conversations, including those with people who disagreed. In fact, to take part in that exchange of ideas. I was very pleased that the children could share in that."[23] Schröder described the design process, which was guided as much by the client's ideas about family life as by aesthetic or architectural considerations:

We didn't make preliminary plans…Rietveld made a sketch of the plot of land, showing the measurements. The next question was: how do you want to live? Well, I was absolutely set against living downstairs. I've never lived this way, I found the idea very restricting. Rietveld was delighted about this, particularly because of the magnificent view. So we started to map out the upper floor, because you can't do without bedrooms. A room for the two girls and a room for the boy – in fact, that's how we started, with rooms. And where should we put them. All of us together, of course; the children had missed so much.[24]

The result was a small house (21 x 30 feet) with a studio, library, workroom (originally a maid's room), and eat-in kitchen on the ground floor; Truus's room, the children's bedrooms, and a large living and dining area on the second floor (figs. 9, 10). While the downstairs rooms are small and separated by traditional fixed walls, the upper

PLATE 4

Schröder House, on Prins
Hendriklaan

"rooms" are actually one large space that can be partitioned by thin, sliding panels. On the plans submitted to the building department, the upper floor was labeled "attic" to circumvent the local building regulations.[25]

Truus's concept of open space had been forged throughout the difficult years of her marriage to Frits Schröder:

You see, I'd left my husband on three occasions because I disagreed with him so strongly about the children's upbringing. Each time, they were looked after by a housemaid, but still I thought it was horrible for them. And after my husband died and I had full custody of the children, I thought a lot about how we should live together.

So when Rietveld had made a sketch of the rooms, I asked, "Can those walls go too?" To which he answered, "With pleasure, away with those walls!" I can still hear myself asking, can those walls go, and that's how we ended up with the one large space.[26]

FIGURE 7

Schröder House. ca. 1925

FIGURE 8
Schröder House, living/dining
area. ca. 1925

Although Truus's own bedroom, located in the corner of the upper floor, is separated from the principal
living area by fixed walls, it is in no way as prominent or
large as a traditional parents' bedroom. Her goal was to
live her life in close association with her children, to be a
part of their daily lives (fig. 11). A low shelf along the wall
in the main living area was intended to be used as a desk
where they could do their homework together; in practice, the older children often found the privacy of the small
library on the ground floor more appealing. Adults and
children were constantly together in the large living/
dining room, and the children were encouraged to learn
from the frequent discussions among visiting artists and
intellectuals. In the end this was one of the most lasting
contributions to Schröder's life and to that of her family:

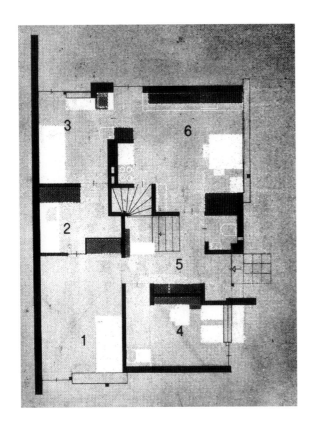

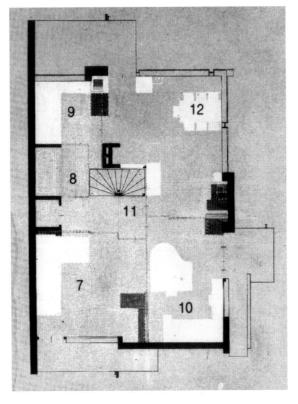

I wanted a real exchange of ideas in this house. That was one of my aims. I wanted to have people here that you could discuss with. People with a critical attitude, all sorts of people. The criticism was less than I had expected, but what there was, was more tangible. Different from cultural evenings, when you come home bubbling with ideas, which have disappeared after a couple of days because you have moved on to the next subject. Actually the discussions here were always on the same topic. But in fact I liked it that way. Not so much a question of a famous house, but something to do with the essentials…that someone really feels spoken to. That someone who comes here takes something away that he or she can ponder over, and maybe reconsider.[27]

In addition to its educational advantages, living in the house provided opportunities for play that neither Rietveld nor Schröder anticipated. She recalled:

There used to be a wide white stripe [on the floor], near the stairwell. And when the children came home from school, I would call, "Look out, the floor's clean." Then they'd have to jump over the white part, because otherwise it was always getting grubby. And I didn't like having to say that. That was something I really disliked. The children told me later that they didn't mind at all. They thought it was quite fun, having a floor that you had to jump over. I thought it was educationally wrong.[28]

FIGURE 9

    Schröder House, plan, ground floor. 1. Studio 2. Workroom (darkroom) 3. Workroom (originally maid's room) 4. Library 5. Entry 6. Kitchen

FIGURE 10

    Schröder House, plan, second floor. 7. Girls' room 8. Bathroom 9. Truus Schröder's room 10. Boy's room 11. Stair landing 12. Living/dining area

FIGURE 11

Truus and daughter Han
(sitting in the Berlin Chair).
ca. 1925

Nevertheless, living in the house was sometimes a strain for the children:

In the weekends crowds would come to have a gawp.... It wasn't so nice for the children. On one occasion my daughter Hanneke came home from school quite scarlet in the face, crying her eyes out, so I asked her what was the matter. She sobbed, "I told a lie, because they said to me, 'You live in that loony house' and I said that I didn't live in that loony house." Something like that was very hard for a child to cope with.[29]

While Mrs. Schröder's theories about early childhood development, open space, and modern family life contributed greatly to the project, in practice the design of the house was left to Rietveld. He was the acknowledged expert, and it was "his personal vision," his sense of form and color, and his excitement about the potential for change in the world of art that attracted her in the first place: "Rietveld experienced life through his senses, and that 'abstract' manner was nothing for him. The only thing of which you can be certain, is what you apprehend and can digest through your senses. That was your reality. I found that of the essence, it spoke to me at the deepest level."[30]

For the previous four or five years Rietveld had been experimenting with wooden furniture in which the component parts were isolated and articulated through the use of cantilevered planes and overlapping supports as well as bright colors. Working with a vocabulary of frame and plane, he created and defined a new sense of space, one in which mass and enclosure were replaced by flat surfaces and displaced grids that allowed a continuous flow of space through and around an object. At the Schröder House, Rietveld's evolving artistic language found expression in the creation of a total environment, where architecture and furniture shared an emphasis on the isolated and brightly colored elements of constructed form. Through such devices as the displaced corner of the living/dining area (see fig. 8), which effectively dematerializes the supporting frame of the building, or the glazed transoms and continuous ceilings on the ground floor, which permit the space of one room to flow into another, Rietveld pushed architectural thinking with the same imagination and originality he had brought to furniture design.

Both Rietveld and Schröder were committed to incorporating the most up-to-date thinking and devices into the design of the house. The original plans included a garage in place of the studio on the Prins Hendriklaan side, reflecting Mrs. Schröder's assumption (unfounded, as it happened) that she, and everyone else, would eventually own a car. Moreover, each "room" on the upper floor had storage cupboards, a washbasin, and an electrical outlet, which Mrs. Schröder felt were important to allow individuals to cook for themselves if they wanted.[31] For the main living space, Rietveld designed a cabinet with modular storage compartments for sewing supplies,

stationery, a phonograph, and a movie projector. This unusual addition to the house's modern "equipment" (fig. 12) was used for showing the latest art films, including those of Soviet filmmakers banned in the Netherlands, and reflected Rietveld's and Mrs. Schröder's commitment (shared by the Harrensteins and their Amsterdam circle) to film as an experimental art medium and as a vehicle for progressive social commentary.[32]

Ultimately, the most lasting benefits of living in the house came from the physical and emotional excitement of the environment. Mrs. Schröder summarized:

This house exudes a strong sense of joy, of real joyousness. That's something in my nature, but here in this house it's stimulated. And that's absolutely a question of the proportions, and also of the light; the light in the house and the light outside. I find it very important that a house has an invigorating atmosphere; that it inspires and supports joie de vivre.[33]

In his 1932 article Rietveld emphasized this commitment to changing the emotional life of the occupant through design:

The greatest change that architecture has gone through in recent times has been its liberation, its separation from the plastic dimension.... Architecture becomes an environment and nothing more. The result is that architecture has become less weighty, but at the same time much more functional and human. The building is no longer a thing that exists in itself or that stands for something; rather it is in active relationship to human beings and human beings will then have to adopt an active attitude towards it in order to be able to experience its qualities.[34]

The Schröder House was an intensely modern architectural environment; it provided an entirely new kind of space in which individuals – women, men, and children – could make choices about how they wanted to live. Offering a variety of alternatives, from the privacy of the small rooms on the ground floor to the open communal space of the light-filled living area upstairs, and containing unique flexibility within itself, the Schröder House was not only a creative work of architectural design but offered its users a new environment in which to redefine family life, women's rights, and the responsibilities of individuals to themselves and to each other. Further, by creating opportunities for these individuals to focus on the rituals of daily life (by opening and closing the partitions, for example) and by making them acutely aware of their surroundings and of the conditions in which they lived, the Schröder House helped to create a modern consciousness, a sense that daily life and values were *staged* and enacted in a work of architecture that was designed and built with a larger purpose in mind. These ideas and experiences were directly related to Truus Schröder's broad social and intellectual goals. Thus, as a client, as a designer, and as a feminist, Schröder helped to shape and define the course of modern architecture.

FIGURE 12

View of the main living area, showing modular cabinet and projector. ca. 1925

Rietveld and De Stijl

Although Rietveld was not a formally educated man (he left school at age eleven), he was entirely familiar with the art movements and theories of his time. He seems to have found numerous ways to keep abreast of the latest thinking, taking evening courses in Utrecht and studying the work of other artists, such as his teacher, the architect and designer P. J. C. Klaarhamer. His friendship with Robert van't Hoff, an architect strongly influenced by the work of Frank Lloyd Wright, proved to be especially important for Rietveld's development, as it led to commissions to study and copy some of Wright's furniture designs.[35] His membership in the arts society Voor de Kunst provided him with opportunities to meet other artists and prospective clients, among them Frits Schröder and Dr. A. M. Hartog, a doctor whose office in Maarssen he renovated in 1922.[36]

Rietveld's connection to the artist Theo van Doesburg, the driving force behind both the *De Stijl* journal and the movement of the same name, had an especially dramatic impact on his career in the late 1910s and early 1920s by bringing him into contact with numerous painters and architects, among them Piet Mondrian, Vilmos Huszár, Jan Wils, and Cornelis van Eesteren, whose experiments with abstract form and color helped Rietveld achieve a new level of sophistication in his own work.[37] Through *De Stijl*, which published photographs of Rietveld's Child's Chair of 1918 and the unpainted version of the Red-Blue Chair of the same year, Rietveld's furniture and new construction techniques reached a broader audience. This exposure led in turn to further contacts and collaborations, among them an important project, ultimately realized, in which his furniture became an integral part of an experimental interior designed by van Doesburg (fig. 13); it was first published in *De Stijl* in 1920 under the title *Example of Coloristic*

Composition in an Interior (a retouched color illustration was published in *L'Architecture vivante* in 1925).[38] With its floating planes, fragmented grids, and protruding edges, Rietveld's furniture of the late 1910s already revealed a marked affinity with the art of De Stijl, and the work drew van Doesburg and others to him.

According to Yve-Alain Bois the art of De Stijl can be understood as the product of two "operations" that control the manipulation of abstract form: "*Elementarization*, that is, the analysis of each practice into discrete components and the reduction of these components to a few irreducible elements. *Integration*, that is, the exhaustive articulation of these elements into a syntactically indivisible, non-hierarchical whole."[39] In Rietveld's furniture, for example (and at the Schröder House), there is not only an emphasis on revealing the process of construction but also a celebration of the integral relationship and apparent balance between the component parts and the overall composition. This unity is achieved through an approach to design in which color, form, and space are treated as equal elements, so that the resulting three-dimensional composition says as much about spatial limits and the absence of mass as it does about the relationship between the forms themselves.

In 1924 van Doesburg published an article entitled "Towards a Plastic Architecture," which clearly outlines his views on the subject. Although it appeared when the Schröder House was already under construction (it is unlikely that Rietveld or Mrs. Schröder had seen the text before it was published), the essay describes the new approach to architectural form that the Schröder House achieved. According to van Doesburg it was the experience of free and open space, realized through "mobile" planes, movable walls and screens, that gave the new architecture its distinctive character. Opening up walls and enlarging windows eliminated the distinction between interior and exterior space, creating what he called the "hovering" aspect of architecture and challenging "the force of gravity in nature." Moreover, the new architecture was "anti-cubic" and asymmetrical, active rather than passive, with no "dead spaces" or repetitions. Color played an integral part in the design: used "organically" rather than decoratively, color contributed to the creation of a harmonic whole, an aesthetic composition conceived "without prejudice to utilitarian demands."[40]

Rietveld's furniture and the Schröder House incorporate and resolve these artistic challenges far more successfully than the De Stijl works of architecture and interior design that predate them. For example, the well-known drawings and models for three small houses by van Doesburg and van Eesteren shown at the Galerie de l'Effort Moderne in Paris in 1923 place much greater emphasis on the composition of boxlike components and the pattern of window openings than on the articulation of the relationship between plane and grid; contrary to van Doesburg's theories, they display a marked heaviness of form and a distinct separation between outside and inside space.[41] Even in Rietveld and Huszár's *Spatial Color Composition for an Exhibition*, shown in Berlin in 1923 and published in color in *L'Architecture vivante* the following autumn (plate 5), there is a reliance on the conventional relationship of floor, walls, and ceiling

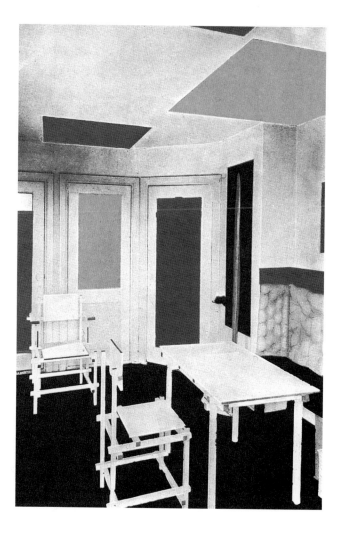

FIGURE 13

Theo van Doesburg. *Example of Coloristic Composition in an Interior*. 1920. From *L'Architecture vivante*, 1925

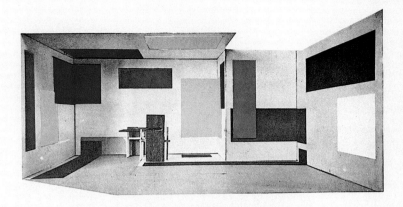

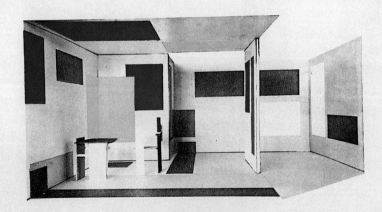

MAQUETTE

V. HUSZAR
INTÉRIEUR. 1924

Editions Albert Morancé
Copyright 1924

as enclosing elements; blocks of color are applied to these planes in an effort to fragment them visually, but the project is architectonically conservative. Planes predictably meet at the corners of the composition, although the use of primary colors tends to break up surfaces and unify the composition three-dimensionally. While it is possible that in this case Rietveld was responsible for only the furniture (the famous black and white Berlin Chair, an example of which was in the Schröder House), it is significant that the project exhibits few of the qualities that make his other work distinctive.[42]

It is not surprising, then, that the Schröder House was greeted with such enthusiasm. Photographs were immediately published in *De Stijl*; in 1925 van Doesburg wrote to a friend to say that the house seemed to be the very embodiment of their "most recent principles."[43] For many critics the house was a milestone in the progress of modern architecture: it represented a real break with the past, a celebration of color and abstract form. Though some commentators focused on its use of materials, mistakenly assuming that concrete had been used to build the walls (they are actually made of brick faced with plaster), it was the huge windows, thin walls, open space, and extraordinary colors that seized the imaginations of the majority of architects, critics, and the public.[44] The house thus catapulted Rietveld and Schröder into the public eye, drawing crowds to Prins Hendriklaan and focusing attention on the innovative approach of both the architect and the client.[45]

PLATE 5

Gerrit Rietveld and Vilmos Huszár. *Spatial Color Composition for an Exhibition.* 1923. From *L'Architecture vivante*, Autumn 1924

Dutch Feminism and Modern Design

The Schröder House was an extraordinary achievement, a unique and defining moment in the lives of its creators. After it was built Rietveld and Schröder pursued a number of design projects together, collaborating most successfully on interior designs that drew equally on the expertise and experience of each – his in dealing with form, color, and design (in architecture, increasingly), hers in thinking about modern convenience and new ways of living, especially for women and families. Their work included the design of a new living room and bedroom for An Harrenstein's Amsterdam home, completed in 1926 and widely published (fig. 14), which incorporated many of the ideas used at the Schröder House – built-ins, blocks of bold color, and vertical and horizontal partitions.[46]

In 1930 Harrenstein, with a group of other feminists, founded a women's magazine, *De werkende vrouw* (The Working Woman), to which both Schröder and Rietveld contributed articles on architecture and design.[47] The goal of the journal, as stated in its first editorial (presumably written by Harrenstein, who served as editor-in-chief), was to publish articles on the full range of women's work experience, including work in the home. This agenda would expose readers to a wide range of topics, from women's unions to legal and financial issues, sports, hygiene, clothing, and of course art, architecture, literature, and "the plastic arts." The new magazine thus played an important (though all too brief – it survived for only two years) role as a clearinghouse for ideas in the middle-class feminist movement in Holland between the wars. It presented an image of the "modern woman" to which a number of readers could relate: she was well educated, economically comfortable, and concerned with questions about work, home, and family. Although it dealt with the problems of working women generally, *De werkende vrouw* was clearly aimed

FIGURE 14
Gerrit Rietveld and Truus
Schröder. Harrenstein House,
Amsterdam, living room. 1926

at the interests of bourgeois intellectuals; as such, the magazine represents the significant broadening of Dutch feminism outward from the small circle of working women and upper-class academics and other experts who had dominated the movement through the First World War.[48] That women like Truus Schröder, her sister, and their friends were not only interested in reading the journal but also willing and able to contribute to it is a marker of their own commitment to feminist ideas and of the importance of feminism in intellectual and left-wing circles in the late 1920s and early 1930s.

Schröder's interest in progressive interior design, and specifically her emphasis on women's work at home, were clearly of a professional nature, and the articles she wrote for the journal reflect her research.[49] They include two pieces that appeared in the earliest issues: an overview and description of the Frankfurt Kitchen, designed by Grete Schütte-Lihotsky and Ernst May in 1926, and a theoretical article on interior design.[50]

In her article on interior design Schröder clearly and succinctly introduced contemporary Dutch architectural theory to a general audience. She described architecture as "space-making," pointing out that the use of planes rather than masses in architectural design enhances consciousness of spatial relations and proportions. Moreover, she continued, this consciousness of space is an active rather than a passive experience and can serve as a stimulus to thought and pleasure for "the tired worker." Bourgeois respectability and luxury have nothing to do with real architecture; on the contrary, this new sort of architectural design, based on the interplay of planar forms, and on the appreciation of relationships of scale, is far superior to "the so-called artistic interior," with its emphasis on coziness and warmth. The piece is illustrated with two photographs of the bedroom she and Rietveld designed for the Harrensteins in 1926, and in the captions both of them are credited.[51]

It is possible to situate Truus Schröder's feminism and her goals for her house within the broad movement of Dutch and European feminism in the early twentieth century. Although *De werkende vrouw* was published for only a short period, its contributors included a number of distinguished feminist philosophers and theorists; as mentioned above, its readers were middle-class intellectuals more interested in art, family, and educational theory than in women's rights in the workplace. Truus herself never held a job outside the home, and her position as a widow with three children stimulated her to take a greater interest in household labor and child care than she might have otherwise.

Like many of her contemporaries, Schröder was broadly influenced by the writings of the Swedish feminist Ellen Key, whose ideas on women's maternal gifts and their special role in the home, explained in a series of books published between the late 1890s and World War I, were particularly well known in Holland and Germany.[52] Key urged feminists to shift their attention away from the workplace and women's equality *outside* the home to focus on women's unique abilities to nurture and guide their families within it. Moreover, Key believed that marriage was unduly restrictive of women's emotional, spiritual, and sexual life, and she thus campaigned for "free love," birth-control, and state support of single mothers. Such ideas had an impact on feminists like Truus Schröder, who sought greater equality for women in all aspects of their lives and who were particularly concerned with creating a more independent and respected role for women within the family.

Although never politically active, Schröder took a strong interest in housing design. In 1930 she and Rietveld collaborated on a project for a block of dwellings to be built across from the Schröder House on Erasmuslaan, on a plot of land that Schröder herself originally owned.[53] The first block of four row houses was completed in 1931, and a model interior was open to the public. The furniture makers Metz & Co. planned to put some of Rietveld's designs into production if the display proved popular.[54] A second group of houses, four two-story flats with an ingenious interlocking vertical section, were completed in 1935. These projects were realized during Rietveld's most active and professionally prominent years, when he enjoyed both local and international attention.[55]

Perhaps the most unusual commission on which Rietveld and Schröder collaborated was the conversion of a large house in Haarlem into fifteen studio apartments for single working women, in 1937–38.[56] Sponsored by the Flatstichting voor vrouwen door vrouwen (The Foundation for Flats for Women by Women), the project sought to make modern amenities and design available to the occupants; built-in furniture and appliances rendered the small spaces highly efficient, and sliding panels gave them an unusual flexibility for use as both bedrooms and sitting rooms.

Motivated by her strong belief in women's rights, Schröder sought to respond to the needs of nontraditional households.[57] Her own house is testimony to her ambitious goals and to her concern for broad social and artistic change; her personal circumstances and struggles reinforced that commitment and pushed her to new levels of creativity in problem solving. The Schröder House not only broke down boundaries between generations and redefined social relations through unconventional design; it also contested the structure of the traditional family. It went beyond the familiar type of the artist's studio to suggest a new model for a small family house and workshop. Through her architecture and design Schröder was thus able to integrate feminist ideas into the modernist program, using her house as a laboratory in which to test, through experience, new architectural forms, new approaches to daily life, and a new vision of women's role in society.

The Schröder House celebrates collaboration while remaining firmly tied to the vision of one woman. The client's contribution was unusually significant in this case: not only did Schröder act as patron and partner, but she created both the program and the opportunity to realize it in built form. Moreover, the Schröder House would not have been built or even conceived without a series of radical breaks with gender convention, each of which was due to the sheer force of Schröder's personality: her financial independence and authority as a client; her ability to act as a spokesperson for her own ideas; Rietveld's respect for her as a collaborator and equal in matters of design; her decision to change the way in which she lived with her family; and her eloquence and commitment to her house and to modern architecture.

Nevertheless, it must be emphasized that the unique design of the house is especially due to Rietveld, to his talent as an architect, and to his own commitment to change in the world of art and architecture. Rietveld, too, had a vision, and it drew Schröder to him and kept her attention over the course of their long life together. Through their passion and commitment, the Schröder House took shape in 1923–24 as a unique, modern building, a home in which the challenges of living in the present were celebrated with energy and exuberance.

1   This chapter is based on research conducted in collaboration with Maristella Casciato in Holland and the U.S. during 1994 and 1995; I could not have undertaken this project, in particular the archival research dealing with documents in Dutch, without her. I have also benefitted greatly from her knowledge of Dutch architecture and from her own previous work on Rietveld: see her "Gerrit Thomas Rietveld, Truus Schröder-Schräder: Casa unifamiliare, Utrecht, 1924," *Domus*, no. 686 (Sept. 1987), 40–49, and "Models of Domesticity in Twentieth-Century Dwelling: The Case of the Schröder House (1924)" (unpublished paper). For the Schröder House, see Paul Overy et al., *The Rietveld Schröder House* (Cambridge, Mass.: MIT Press, 1988); this volume includes original material drawn from interviews with Truus Schröder conducted by Lenneke Büller and Frank den Oudsten in 1982, first published in *Lotus International* 60 (1988), 33–57. For Rietveld, see Theodore M. Brown, *The Work of G. Rietveld, Architect* (Utrecht: A. W. Bruna, 1958), G. H. Rodijk, *De Huizen van Rietveld* (Zwolle: Waanders Uitgevers, 1991), Marijke Küper and Ida van Zijl, eds., *Gerrit Th. Rietveld: The Complete Works* (Utrecht: Centraal Museum, 1992), and Bertus Mulder, *Gerrit Thomas Rietveld: Leven, Denken, Werken* (Nijmegen: Sun, 1994). Rietveld's drawings are held by the Rietveld-Schröder Archive, Centraal Museum, Utrecht (hereinafter referred to as Rietveld-Schröder Archive); a small number of other drawings and documents, including early sketches for the Schröder House and the drawings for the two apartment buildings in Utrecht, is held by the Netherlands Architectural Institute, Rotterdam. I am grateful to both institutions, in particular to Jaap Oosterhoff, curator of the Rietveld-Schröder Archive, for their help with my research.

2   In *Painting as Model* (Cambridge, Mass.: MIT Press, 1990), 121, Yve-Alain Bois describes Rietveld as having "substituted the functionalist ethic" of modernism with something closer to what Baudelaire called the "Ethic of Toys : 'Everything is deployed in such a way as to flatter our intellectual desire to dismantle his pieces of furniture or architecture into their component parts.'"

3   Schröder's contribution was noted by Jean Badovici in *L'Architecture vivante*, where she is named with Rietveld as the architect of the house. Jean Badovici, "Maison à Utrecht par T. Schraeder et G. Rietveld," *L'Architecture vivante* (Autumn–Winter 1925), 28–29, pls. 31–33.

4   See Küper and van Zijl, *Complete Works*, cat. nos. 87, 96, 102, 107, 108, 126, 131, 164, 212, 248, 259, 275, 381, 383.

5   Ibid., cat. no. 85.

6   Ibid., cat. no. 35.

7   Gerrit Rietveld, "Nieuwe zakelijkheid in de Nederlandsche architectuur," *De vrije bladen* 9, issue 7 (1932), 1–27; English trans. in Küper and van Zijl, *Complete Works*, 33–39. The quotation appears on p. 39.

8   Overy, *Rietveld Schröder House*, 17. Truus Schröder died in 1985.

9   For Rietveld's involvement in the modern housing movement, see Richard Pommer and Christian F. Otto, *Weissenhof 1927 and the Modern Movement in Architecture* (Chicago and London: University of Chicago Press, 1991), esp. 150–51. For the apartment house projects in Utrecht, see Küper and van Zijl, *Complete Works*, 130–34, 157.

10 Mrs. Schröder's contribution was also the subject of a short book, *Tr. Schröder-Schräder, Bewoonster van het Rietveld Schröderhuis* (Utrecht: Impress, 1987) written by Corrie Nagtegaal, who lived in the house as a tenant/companion in the last years of Schröder's life. I am very grateful to Ms. Nagtegaal for her willingness to share her research and experiences with us in July 1995.

11 Although the majority of the holdings in Truus Schröder's personal library were distributed to family members and sold at auction after her death, the remaining collection (about three hundred volumes), housed in the Rietveld-Schröder Archive, reveals the wide range of her interests in art, poetry, aesthetics, domestic architecture, and psychology. It is worth noting that in addition to the Bauhausbücher, a series of short books on art and design issued by the Bauhaus, she also owned a number of publications of the Department of Architecture at The Museum of Modern Art, New York. Schröder's handwritten diaries and her scrapbooks of newspaper clippings and other miscellaneous texts, also in the Rietveld-Schröder Archive, suggest an ongoing interest in women's issues, literature, fashion, and household management.

12 Overy, *Rietveld Schröder House*, 21.

13 Frits Schröder, letter to Truus Schröder (hereinafter referred as T. Schröder), June 11, 1914, Rietveld-Schröder Archive. I am grateful to Nancy Stieber for her help in translating this text. See also Nagtegaal, *Tr. Schröder-Schräder*, 8, and Lenneke Büller and Frank den Oudsten, "Interview with Truus Schröder" (hereinafter referred to as "Interview"), in Overy, *Rietveld Schröder House* 43 n. 2.

14 Paul Overy, *De Stijl* (London: Thames and Hudson, 1991), 33. In 1933 Bendien and Harrenstein published a book on contemporary painting, *Richtingen in de heedendaagse schilderkunst* (Rotterdam: Brusse, 1933). For Bendien, see the exhibition catalogue *Jacob Bendien, 1890–1933* (Leewarden and Utrecht: Fries Museum and Centraal Museum, 1985). For Citroen, see Herbert van Rheedan et al., *Paul Citroen: Kunstenaar, docent, verzamelaar* (Zwolle: Waanders Uitgevers, 1994), esp. 82–87. In 1940 Citroen edited a collection of Bendien's writings, *Jacob Bendien, 1890–1933: Een herrinneringsboek* (Rotterdam: Brusse, 1940). The articles on Bendien and Citroen in the *Dictionary of Art* (London: Macmillan, 1996) are also helpful.

15 Frits was a member of Kunstliefde from 1913 to 1916 (Rietveld had joined in 1911). See Marijke Küper, "Gerrit Rietveld," in Carel Blotkamp et al., *De Stijl: The Formative Years, 1917–1922*, trans. Charlotte I. Loeb and Arthur Loeb (Cambridge, Mass.: MIT Press, 1982), 259–80, esp. 260, 278 n. 25.

Schröder / Rietveld and Schröder

16 "Interview," 46.

17 Ibid., 47.

18 Ibid., 90, 92.

19 See Küper and van Zijl, *Complete Works*, cat. nos. 51, 84.

20 "Interview," 52.

21 The house cost somewhere between 6,000 (Mrs. Schröder's recollection in "Interview," 78) and 11,000 guilders (Overy, *Rietveld Schröder House*, 22, after Brown, *The Work of G. Th. Rietveld*, 155 n. 38). Küper and van Zijl cite, without a source, a figure of 9,000 guilders (*Complete Works*, 101).

22 A postcard dated 1901 (Rietveld-Schröder Archive, 993) provides an illustration of the Schräders' home, a substantial, freestanding Italianate villa.

23 "Interview," 93.

24 Ibid., 56.

25 Schröder also recalled that she had visited a friend who lived in "one large empty attic room," and that she had wondered what living in such a place would be like. "Interview," 52. See also Overy, *De Stijl*, 114.

26 "Interview," 56.

27 Ibid., 96, 102.

28 Ibid., 71.

29 Ibid., 78.

30 Ibid., 61, 89.

31 Ibid., 30, 60.

32 During the 1920s Rietveld was the secretary of the Utrecht branch of Filmliga, the radical film society, and both he and Mrs. Schröder were fascinated by the artistic potential of film; Overy, *De Stijl*, 33. In her autobiography, Han Schröder mentions that she met "modern artists and avant-garde moviemakers" at the home of her aunt in Amsterdam as well; Han Schröder, "Curriculum vitae," typescript, International Archive of Women in Architecture, Virginia Polytechnic Institute, Blacksburg, Va., 4.

33 "Interview," 93.

34 Küper and van Zijl, *Complete Works*, 37.

35 Overy, *De Stijl*, 75.

36 Küper and van Zijl, *Complete Works*, cat. no. 57.

37 For van Doesburg, see Joost Baljeu, *Theo van Doesburg* (New York: Macmillan, 1974); this volume includes English translations of van Doesburg's key writings.

38 *De Stijl* 3, no. 12 (Nov. 1920), 12; *L'Architecture vivante* 3, no. 9 (1925), special issue on De Stijl. See Bois, *Painting as Model*, 111–12. For an overview of relevant De Stijl projects, see Overy, *De Stijl*, chs. 6, 7, and Nancy Troy, *The De Stijl Environment* (Cambridge, Mass.: MIT Press, 1984), esp. ch. 4.

39 Bois, *Painting as Model*, 103.

40 "Towards a Plastic Architecture," *De Stijl* 12, no. 6–7 (1924), 78–83, reprinted in Baljeu, *Theo van Doesburg*, 142–47; the quotation is on pp. 144–47.

41 See Nancy Troy and Yve-Alain Bois, "De Stijl et l'architecture à Paris," in Bois and Bruno Reichlin, eds., *De Stijl et l'architecture en France* (Liège: Pierre Mardaga, 1985), 25–90. Van Doesburg's own axonometric drawings and "counter-constructions" of the same year begin to display greater fragmentation and elemental construction; see Bois, *Painting as Model*, 118.

42 Troy, *The De Stijl Environment*, 129ff.

43 *De Stijl* 6, nos. 10–11 (1924–25), 160 (exterior); *De Stijl* 6, no. 12 (1924–25), 140 (interior). For the letter to César Domela, see Troy, in Bois and Reichlin, *De Stijl et l'architecture en France*, 46.

44 See Walter Gropius, *Internationale Architektur*, Bauhausbücher 1 (Munich, 1925), 76–77, where a caption notes that the house was made of "concrete, iron, glass"; and Jean Badovici, "Maison à Utrecht."

45 Rietveld and Schröder's designs were included in an exhibition at the Stedelijk Museum in Amsterdam in 1929; J. J. P. Oud and J. Duiker were the other featured architects.

46 Küper and van Zijl, *Complete Works*, cat. nos. 107, 110–11; the bedroom was bought by the Stedelijk Museum in Amsterdam when the house was demolished, in 1971. A doctor's office and guest room were completed in 1930 (cat. no. 156).

47 Truus Schröder-Schräder, "Wat men door normalisatie in den woningbouw te Frankfurt a/d Main heeft bereikt" (What Has Been Achieved by the Standardization of Housing in Frankfurt a/d Main) 1, no. 1–2 (1930), 12–14, and "Een inliedend woord tot binnenarchitectuur" (An Introductory Note on Interior Design) 1, no. 3 (1930), 93–94. Gerrit Rietveld, "De stoel" (Chairs) 1, no. 9 (1930), 244, and "Architectuur" (Architecture) 1, no. 11–12 (1930), 316–18. *De werkende vrouw* was published only until Sept. 1931 and copies of it are extremely rare; a complete run of the journal is held by the Internationaal informatiecentrum en archief voor de vrouwen beweging (International Information Center and Archives for the Women's Movement), in Amsterdam.

48 One such specialist, who acted as a bridge between the first and second feminist movements in Holland, was the psychologist and women's rights advocate Ana Polak (1874–1939), author of *De vrouwenbeweging in Nederland 1898–1923* (The Women's Movement in the Netherlands), 1923. The head of the National Bureau for Women's Work, she contributed an article to *De werkende vrouw* on the differences between men's and women's work (see 1, nos. 1–2 [Jan.–Feb. 1930]); a later article focused on the question of whether housewifery was a profession (see 1, no. 10 [Oct. 1930]).

49 Truus Schröder's scrapbooks in the Rietveld-Schröder Archive show that she was constantly clipping articles and photographs from newspapers and journals; these clippings range from articles on energy-saving kitchen design to illlustrations of modern appliances.

50 See *De werkende vrouw* 1, no. 1 (1930), 12–14, and 1, no. 3 (1930), 93–94. For the Frankfurt Kitchen, see Susan R. Henderson, "A Revolution in the Woman's Sphere: Grete Lihotzky and the Frankfurt Kitchen," in Debra Coleman, Elizabeth Danze, and Carol Henderson, eds., *Architecture and Feminism* (New York: Princeton Architectural Press, 1996), 221–53; Peter Noever,

ed., *Die Frankfurter Küche von Margaret Schütte-Lihotsky* (Berlin: Ernst und Sohn, 1991); and Nicholas Bullock, "First the Kitchen – Then the Facade," *AA Files*, no. 6 (May 1984), 58–67.

51 I am grateful to Nancy Stieber for her help with the translation of this text.

52 For Key's influence, see Richard J. Evans, *The Feminist Movement in Germany, 1894–1933* (London: Sage Publications, 1976), and Katharine S. Anthony, *Feminism in Germany and Scandinavia* (New York: H. Holt, 1915). See also Kay Goodman, "Motherhood and Work: The Concept of the Misuse of Women's Energy, 1895–1905," in Ruth-Ellen Joeres and Mary Jo Maynes, eds., *German Women in the Eighteenth and Nineteenth Centuries* (Bloomington: Indiana University Press, 1986), 110–27. Key's works influenced Frank Lloyd Wright, and Wright's lover Mamah Borthwick Cheney was designated as Key's official English translator in 1909. See Anthony Alofsin, *Frank Lloyd Wright: The Lost Years, 1910–1922 – A Study of Influence* (Cambridge, Mass.: MIT Press, 1994), and his "Taliesin: To Fashion Worlds in Little," in Narciso G. Menocal, ed., *Wright Studies* 1 (Carbondale: Southern Illinois University Press, 1992), 44–65.

53 Küper and van Zijl, *Complete Works*, cat. nos. 154, 163, 164.

54 Rietveld worked for Metz & Co. from 1927 until the 1950s. See Küper and van Zijl, *Collected Works*, cat. nos. 119, 146–48, 155, 162, 189, 192, 258, 306, 423, 432.

55 Rietveld's other multi-unit projects included a block of apartment dwellings at the Wienerwerkbund Siedlung, in Vienna, of 1929–32, and a group of houses on Robert Schumannstraat in Utrecht, built in 1931–32; see Küper and van Zijl, *Complete Works*, cat. nos. 172, 175.

56 Küper and van Zijl, *Complete Works*, cat. no. 275.

57 According to Corrie Nagtegaal (interview with Alice Friedman and Maristella Casciato, July 1995), Truus Schröder had been influenced by the work of Clara Wichmann (1885–1922), a prominent feminist theorist whose articles on women's rights and jurisprudence appeared in *De groene Amsterdamer*, an Amsterdam newspaper of politics. Schröder was also an avid reader of the romance novels of Cary van Bruggen (1881–1932).

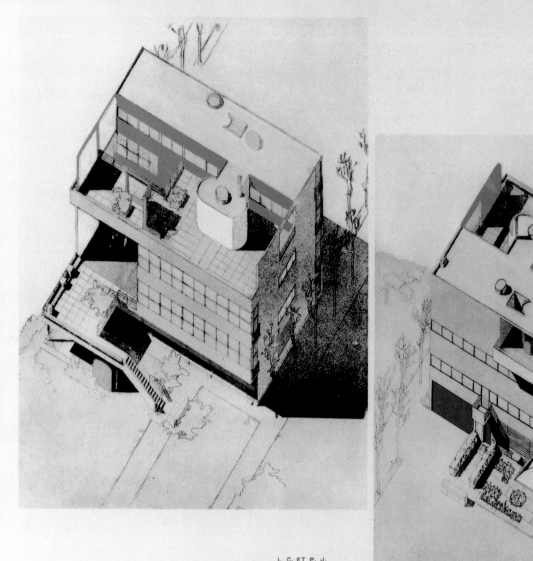

L'ARCHITECTURE VIVANTE
PRINTEMPS M CM XXIX
ÉDITIONS ALBERT MORANCÉ

15

PLATE 1

Le Corbusier. Villa Stein–
de Monzie, Garches, France,
axonometric views. 1926–28.
From *L'Architecture vivante*,
1929

Talk. Talk. And more talk. Nothing stopped with the fact.
Nothing just was. Was it this? Or was it that? Might it not
be something else? Nothing so simple but that it was divided
and subdivided. Nothing so slight but that it warranted
consideration. It was all like that.

Harriet Levy, "Recollections"

Gabrielle de Monzie. ca.1918

Looking back on her life in Paris with the famous Steins,
their friend Harriet Levy, a fellow Californian, remembered the sound of people talking. The four Steins (fig.
1) – Michael (1865–1938), his wife Sarah (née Samuels,
1870–1953, known as Sally), Leo (1872–1947), and
Gertrude (1874–1946) – all loved to talk, and they talked
(and wrote) incessantly – about art, about books, about
themselves, their feelings, their lives. Cut off, albeit by
choice, from San Francisco's close-knit, voluble Jewish
community, they talked to each other, to their friends, to
their neighbors, to anyone who would listen. The Steins
were curious, confident, and bookish, and they seized
on new ideas about art, literature, and life with a single-
minded passion and an intense pleasure in knowing that
they were on the cutting edge of change.

Sarah Stein. 1916

They were also at pains to explain their discoveries
to friends and acquaintances. Their energetic, pioneering
efforts as collectors and connoisseurs of modern painting and sculpture, especially the works of Cézanne, Picasso,
and Matisse, are well known.[1] From 1905 until the First
World War, the open, airy rooms at 27, rue de Fleurus – the
home of Leo and Gertrude – and the large salon around
the corner at 58, rue Madame – the home of Michael,
Sarah, and their young son, Allan – were recognized as
centers of contemporary art in Paris, informal galleries
where friends and acquaintances could come to look at
the pictures and listen to the Steins talk about art.

Michael Stein. 1916

Being Modern Together:

Le Corbusier's Villa Stein–de Monzie

At times it seems that as much as the loquacious Steins said and wrote in their own lifetimes, that mountain of words has since been exceeded a thousand-fold by the outpouring of verbiage generated by their admirers. The Stein era in Paris came to an end with the outbreak of World War I, but since the 1930s curiosity about Gertrude Stein's colorful life, her lifelong lesbian relationship with Alice B. Toklas, and her inscrutable, modernist writing has spawned a virtual cottage industry of studies and biographies, aided no doubt by Gertrude's relentless self-promotion. Yet despite the enormous literature that already exists about this influential family, there is still much more to tell, particularly about Michael and Sarah. Their activities as patrons of art and architecture bear the distinct stamp of Sarah's vibrant personality, her reform-mindedness, her spiritualism, and her proselytizing tendencies. Her commitment to the art of Henri Matisse – as a collector of his work, and as his student

and friend – was unshakable and resulted in the formation of not only the Steins' own art collection but also that of their friends Etta and Claribel Cone in Baltimore, for whom she and Michael acquired numerous pictures.[2]

Far less well known is the pivotal role the Steins played as patrons of the architect Le Corbusier (1887–1965). One of his largest and most important houses, the villa "Les Terrasses" at Garches (plate 1; fig. 2), outside Paris, was built for them and their longtime friend Gabrielle Colaço-Osorio de Monzie (1882–1961) between 1926 and 1928. This house, which Le Corbusier himself viewed as the culmination of his early career, was immediately praised as a milestone in the development of modern architecture, and it has long been recognized as one of the most significant buildings of the twentieth century.[3] For the Steins and their friend, a threesome who lived together as a family from the early 1920s until Michael Stein's death, in 1938, and for their architect, the house represented a watershed, the realization of many of the aspirations and ideals of their years in Paris. Yet very little has been published about the contribution of the Steins and Madame de Monzie as clients, or as participants in the process of building this remarkable work of architecture.

The Villa Stein–de Monzie (figs. 3, 4) is the largest and most luxurious house that Le Corbusier designed in the 1920s. Set far back on its site and approached via a long, straight driveway that ends at the door of an ample garage, the house's pristine white walls and crisp ribbon windows give it the appearance of a modern-day Palladian villa set in a landscape of dark trees. The flatness of the facade and its unified form heighten the sense of imposing monumentality, particularly when the house is viewed from a distance. The gate-lodge at the front of the property underscores the impression of old-world luxury updated with modern conveniences. On the gar-

FIGURE 1

The Steins: from left, Leo, Allan, Gertrude, Therese Ehrman, Sarah, Michael. 1904

FIGURE 2

Le Corbusier. Villa Stein–
de Monzie, Garches, France.
1926–28

den front the walls open up to form a series of wide
terraces accessible from the interior and from the garden itself. A roof terrace, complete with a solarium and
lookout tower, provides additional outdoor space for
sunbathing and exercise, as though it were the upper deck
of a large ocean-liner and the inhabitants of the house
passengers on a long sea voyage.

Because it was built for a household that included a
married couple – and because the man in that couple,
Michael Stein, took such an active role in the planning
process – Les Terrasses would not appear to fit easily into
the broad categories outlined in the introduction to this
book. Yet it is included here for several reasons: first,
because the complexity of the household group that commissioned it called conventional family structure and
gender relations into question; second, because the relationships among the people who were part of that
household challenged the clients and their architect to

Villa Stein–de Monzie, view
from the gate-lodge. From
L'Architecture vivante, 1929

conceive of domestic space in a new way; and third, because the house that resulted not only was an unprecedented work of modern architecture but also, like so many of the houses discussed in this book, represented a creative breakthrough for its architect. While the history of the project certainly focuses our attention on the key roles played by women, the story of Les Terrasses is more properly understood as a case in which women and men negotiated their relationships in an unusual way, and sought to represent themselves architecturally in a project that had significant implications for the history of architecture. While the client of record was Gabrielle de Monzie, what is most fascinating about the house is the unconventional balance of power among the three adults who entered into the project as equals and the ways in which Le Corbusier interpreted this relationship in his design.

As James Ward revealed in his 1984 study of Les Terrasses, it was Christian Science that brought Sarah Stein and Gabrielle de Monzie together some ten years before they met Le Corbusier, and the bond forged by their deep commitment to each other motivated them to form a single household.[4] Nevertheless, it was Michael Stein who kept the household together, playing the role not only of Sarah Stein's husband but also of friend, banker, advisor, and caretaker for both women. The relationship between Michael and Gabrielle was in many ways like that of a brother and sister, recapitulating the close family ties of the Stein siblings, Michael, Leo, and Gertrude. Many things between the Steins and Madame de Monzie were shared, but their private lives remained separate. When it came to the design of their new country house, the household demanded a completely original response, one that simultaneously accommodated intimacy and privacy within a balanced and equal allocation of space.

Le Corbusier experimented with various solutions, arriving at a design of unusual complexity, particularly in the plan and section, where the tension between bilateral symmetry and open, abstract form yields a new approach to the configuration of the domestic interior. (I will discuss this point more fully below.) While the architect had struggled with such questions throughout the 1920s, Les Terrasses represents a turning point and a resolution, the penultimate step in a process that would eventually result in the "classic" design of the better-known Villa Savoye at Poissy in 1929–30. The boldness and success of the Les Terrasses design were the result of the unique combination of circumstances arising from Le Corbusier's own evolution as an architect and the challenges (and opportunities) presented by the Stein–de Monzie household as a client group.

As Tim Benton suggested in *The Villas of Le Corbusier*, one of the main things that the house is "about" in terms of design is the "continual struggle" on the part of the architect "to arrange the lopsided functions of the brief (two bedrooms for Madame de Monzie and her daughter, one large bedroom for the Steins), while preserving

FIGURE 4

Villa Stein–de Monzie, garden facade. From *L'Architecture vivante*, 1929 some degree of privacy for the two."[5] We are now in a position to go much further with this analysis, and to show how the unique structure of the household, combined with the clients' commitment to modern architecture, art, and religion, created a framework within which Le Corbusier could develop a new approach to domestic architecture. The Steins and their friends were great letter writers as well as talkers, and the hundreds of documents that survive create a detailed picture of their daily lives and the concerns that preoccupied them and their friend Gabrielle de Monzie. Thus, while none of Madame de Monzie's own letters survive, the Steins' volubility and frequent communications – Michael Stein was a particularly loyal correspondent, even when he only had time to send a postcard – enable us to place her, and them, in a social and intellectual milieu in Paris during the 1910s and 1920s. Similarly, although Le Corbusier's office made very few notes about the project after Sarah Stein's initial phone call in 1926 (meetings between the architect and the clients were conducted face-to-face in the office or on site), we can document the process of design development and construction based on Michael's comments; these, plus other evidence, reveal that the house was viewed by the clients and their architect as a progressive alternative to the prevailing norms for art, architecture, and family life.[6] What emerges is an image of a way of life shaped by a nexus of ideas and values, a life deliberately and self-consciously constructed in response to the challenges of the modern world. The Stein–de Monzie household clearly shared many of Le Corbusier's convictions about modern art, about the latest health and exercise regimens, and about the importance of new technology for the improvement of their own lives and those of others in contemporary society. Thanks to their extraordinary partnership, Les Terrasses became a three-dimensional demonstration of what modern architecture could achieve.

The Four Steins

Unlike Gertrude and Leo, who considered themselves the creative equals of their artist friends and set out to break new ground in their chosen fields of literature and art criticism, respectively, Michael and Sarah saw themselves as patrons with a special gift for recognizing and fostering the talents of others. Their passionate commitment to patronage gave them an unusual gift for friendship and kept them connected to a large and loving circle of friends – a group that included the Cone sisters, Henri and Amélie Matisse, and many others, particularly women, who came and went as houseguests, companions, and hangers-on. As collectors, Michael and Sarah concentrated almost exclusively on the work of Matisse, beginning with their first purchase (with Leo and Gertrude) of *The Woman with a Hat* at the Salon d'Automne in 1905.

FIGURE 5

Sculpture class at the Académie
Matisse, Hôtel Biron, Paris.
ca. 1909. From left: Jean Heiberg,
an unidentified woman, Sarah
Stein, Henri Matisse, Patrick
Henry Bruce. Photograph cour-
tesy The Museum of Modern
Art, New York

They also actively promoted his career: in 1908, for example, with Michael's financial backing, Sarah persuaded
Matisse to open a school of painting. She attended classes
herself (fig. 5) and diligently transcribed the master's
words of wisdom to his students; her notes remain one
of the best records of his ideas in this period.[7]

The popular Saturday evening gatherings held at 58,
rue Madame, the remodeled parish house into which the
elder Steins moved soon after their arrival in Paris (fig.
6), provided Sarah with a captive audience for her disquisi-
tions on Matisse's genius. As Harriet described the scene:
*The crowds who came to her home on Saturday night to view
the paintings were received and entertained by a woman
beautifully gowned in original costumes [and] antique
jewelry. A hostess who sat upon a couch and did not leave
it, who explained the paintings on the walls, the greatness
of Matisse, his unique position in the world of art.... She
seemed to receive joy from the paintings.*[8]
Like her brother- and sister-in-law, Sarah Stein used the
open houses as a forum in which to talk about art and
ideas, but unlike Leo and Gertrude, who disdained the
role of teacher, Sarah was unfailingly didactic, bossy,
and insistent that others follow her lead. She demanded

FIGURE 6

The salon at 58, rue Madame.
ca. 1909

Stein–de Monzie/Le Corbusier

absolute allegiance and angrily ridiculed any opinion that conflicted with her own. Her friends both adored and hated her – Harriet confessed to having had such a profound desire to murder her after one particularly heated exchange that she was forced to spend an entire day alone in the Luxembourg Gardens calming herself down – but Sarah always kept the upper hand. Michael, by contrast, tended to let others do the talking and struggling, quietly buying and selling pictures, and diligently managing the family finances.

In the early years in Paris especially, the four Steins constantly exchanged ideas and pictures, and they all used similar language to describe the qualities they valued. According to Leo, the acknowledged expert, artists were to be praised for "the elimination of the inessential," and he taught Gertrude, Sarah, and Michael to focus on matters of style, such as form, color, and composition, in the manner of Bernard Berenson, the art historian, whom the Steins had met in Florence some years before.[9] Yet as each one cultivated a distinctive personality as a collector – Leo favored Cézanne, Gertrude cast her lot with Picasso, and Sarah (followed by Michael) supported Matisse – each developed a set of characteristic critical values and a vocabulary of his or her own.

The Steins shared their love of art, but they also had in common a fondness for the latest theories on health and fitness, and took up stringent new diets and exercise regimens with enthusiasm. Leo and Sarah in particular were convinced that the way to be free of the depressions and anxieties that troubled them was through rigorous physical self-discipline; Gertrude and Michael, though clearly interested, seemed far more content to take life in stride. By 1908 Sarah had embraced the teachings of Christian Science with the same conviction and single-mindedness that Leo reserved for "Fletcherizing" (chewing food repeatedly) and fasting, and both were eager to share their discoveries with the others. Gertrude satirized this tendency in the prose portrait of Leo and Sarah enti-

tled "Two," written around 1912, when she noted that "sound is coming out of him" and "sound is coming out of her."[10] Yet Gertrude had her own peculiar enthusiasms: having read and discussed Freud with Leo, she remained devoted to Otto Weininger's misogynist and anti-Semitic treatise *Sex and Character*, which appeared in 1903, and she devised a system for understanding individual character and sexuality based on Weininger's theories.[11] Like the others, Gertrude insisted that this new discovery (and each one she subsequently embraced) represented a major breakthrough in modern thought.

According to Harriet, none of the Steins was exempt from a vexing tendency toward self-importance: *Everything that Gertrude did was important. Importance was attached to all kinds of things in Paris that were without significance in California…. What was it that made things that happened to Steins important? Was it just because they happened to Steins? Or was it because they happened to Steins in Paris? Couldn't they have happened to other people? In that case, would they still be important?*[12]

While the four Steins would inevitably drift apart following Leo's departure from 27, rue de Fleurus, in 1914 and the advent of World War I, their letters show that Gertrude, Leo, and Sarah each remained unshakable in the conviction that their individual passions were paramount: Gertrude was consumed with a need to prove her genius as a writer and by her relationship with Alice; Leo – who made it clear that he was disgusted by Gertrude's homosexuality – pulled away and immersed himself in art criticism and self-analysis; and Sarah became a Christian Science "practitioner" or healer.[13] For each, the failure of the others to share his or her enthusiasm was an affront that contributed to the widening distance between them. As the First World War came and went, the incessant sound of conversation, so characteristic of the early years in Paris, was stilled by their growing frustration with one another.

The Steins, Matisse, and Christian Science

Sarah and Michael Stein's career as patrons and promoters of the arts began modestly enough in San Francisco in the 1890s.[14] Following the death of Daniel Stein in 1891, Michael, his eldest child, took over responsibility for managing the family's inheritance and began working in his father's business, the Omnibus Cable Company. When Leo and Gertrude went East to college, Michael remained in San Francisco, marrying Sarah Samuels, the outspoken and academically successful daughter of a wealthy German Jewish merchant, in March 1894. By 1895, the year their son was born, Michael had been promoted to the position of superintendent in the newly formed Market Street Railway company.

The young couple was well off, educated, and up-to-date. They collected art and tried to keep abreast of the latest trends in education, health, and philosophy. Sarah, who described herself in a letter of October 30, 1899, as having "salon-lady propensities," took courses in Italian art, comparative literature, and music, and avidly amassed reproductions of works by Botticelli, Leonardo, and Dürer. In the late 1890s she and Michael began acquiring Chinese paintings and bronzes, and they wrote to Gertrude – who was then a student at Radcliffe College – to ask whether Leo might "have any books on Japan that he no longer cares for…as [they] are so much interested in Japanese Art and naturally in the country itself." They enclosed a snapshot of their "modest collection" with the letter, noting that they "recently added a pair of bronzes that are superb." Ever anxious to impress the younger siblings, they could not resist the temptation to brag, adding, "We bought 'em cheap."[15]

The Steins also took an interest in psychology and medicine, and Sarah in particular followed her sister-in-law's progress at Radcliffe (where she studied with the psychologists Hugo Munsterberg and William James)

and later at Johns Hopkins Medical School, with intense curiosity. Her letters from San Francisco are full of questions about Gertrude's course work, news about her own health (troubles with backache and "nervous depression") and descriptions of homeopathic remedies that had been passed on to her by a friend.[16] She was hungry for information and insecure about her own lack of knowledge: in one letter, probably written in November 1896, she begged Gertrude to "Please send Munsterberg's toys right along as I am anxious to experiment on the kid!"; in another, dated August 27, 1899, she noted that she had gone "to a lecture by Professor [William] James," adding, "I only wish I knew a little philosophy!" She was plagued by anxieties about her child's health and yet unsure about the right thing to do as a good parent. She wrote to Gertrude on November 11, 1899:

Oh Gertrude, I'd give anything to be a Hottentot lady with a few naked babies provided the babies were all O.K. – I am so sick of being a modern mother and particularly a quasi-medical mother who knows enough about collapses and hemorrhages and all kinds of pleasant things to make her hair turn gray and yet be no earthy good to anybody.[17] Given these persistent doubts, it comes as no surprise to discover that Sarah would be drawn to the reassuring certainties of Christian Science, nor does it seem odd that she would eventually turn her attention to the work of Le Corbusier, an architect dedicated to healthy living through modern design.

Michael Stein shared his wife's preoccupation with health and diet, and like her, he was anxious to pass on the latest information to friends and family. He wrote to Gertrude on January 12, 1901:

Don't forget the importance of the Haig diet in connection with affections of the brain and nervous system. I have just received a new book by him "Diet and food in relation to strength and power of endurance." The diet has cured the wife of a friend of mine who had hysteria induced by womb trouble and migraines at the same time, wiping out the two complaints; and Sally [that is, Sarah] is now as tough as a trooper without a sign of nervousness.[18]

The Steins had a great deal to talk about, and they were overjoyed when they were reunited as a family in Paris in 1904. Initially Leo took the lead in all things pertaining to art, but Sarah was never far behind. The first signs of her growing independence from the others began to appear in 1906, when she and Michael, anxious to see how their real estate holdings had fared in the San Francisco earthquake, returned home from Paris carrying with them two Matisse paintings, including the *Portrait of Mme Matisse*, which they nicknamed "The Green Stripe."[19] They clearly delighted in their role as advocates for the new style: in a letter of October 1906, Sarah described how "Mikey sprang the Matisses on one [friend] just for fun." With Leo and Gertrude safely back in Paris, Sarah could claim authority without having to share center stage.[20]

Moreover, ever enthusiastic about the latest new cure, Sarah became interested in Christian Science at about this time. The new religion was becoming increasingly popular among educated, progressive women like herself, particularly well-to-do Reform Jews.[21] There had been numerous Jewish converts in San Francisco, and there would be many more, drawn by promises of assimilation into "American society" and by the patina of respectability conferred by scientific-sounding doctrine. By the time she returned to Paris later in the year, Sarah Stein had found her new cause.

Christian Science was the discovery of Mary Baker Eddy, whose own spiritual awakening during the last decades of the nineteenth century became the foundation for a religious movement dedicated to individualism, positive thinking, and spiritual renewal. Through her lectures and writings – notably *Science and Health with a Key to the Scriptures* (1875) – Mrs. Eddy preached

a combination of self-help and mind cure that had an uncanny ability to attract converts. Five characteristics of Mrs. Eddy's new religion contributed to its immense popularity with women like Sarah Stein. First, she promised to empower her followers by giving them the tools to cure themselves through their own mental efforts. Second, she invoked the authority of science to give her theories credibility among educated women and men, emphasizing participation through an activity that was both familiar and comfortable to middle-class people, that is, reading daily selections from the Bible and *Science and Health*. Third, she soft-pedaled questions of Christian dogma, referring to Jesus as a great teacher and leader and, more important, never insisting on the divinity of Christ. This approach gave her writings a modern, pragmatic tone and made it possible for Jewish converts to embrace Christian Science and still feel that they had remained Jewish. She presented an ambiguous, open-ended image of God, who is referred to in her writings only as Mind, Supreme Being, and Principle. Fourth, and of particular importance for progressive women, was Eddy's insistence that God was both male and female.[22] Thus, she emphasized the role of women in the church, insisting that each service be jointly led by a male and a female Reader. Fifth, she stressed the relationship between the individual and the community, advocating that her followers attend weekly meetings where they could derive inspiration from testimonials to faith and healing and talk to other people about their experiences.[23]

Sarah Stein possessed a number of qualities that predisposed her to embrace Christian Science: she was anxious about her health and that of her family, open to spiritual and aesthetic experiences, and – like the rest of the Steins – self-willed and sure of her own opinions. Sarah could also be a good listener and a sympathetic advisor (as in the case of Matisse, but also to her many women friends), two qualities that were essential for a Christian Science practitioner. Her biggest challenge was convincing the ever-cynical members of her own family.[24]

Gertrude and Leo remained dubious about their sister-in-law's conversion, to say the least, but with typical Stein panache Sarah began to proselytize and offer advice. One of her first patients was Harriet herself, who had been troubled not only with soreness in her shoulder but also by persistent lameness. During the summer of 1908, when the Steins rented the Villa Bardi in Fiesole, leaving their former summer residence, the Casa Ricci, to Harriet and Alice Toklas, Sarah undertook to cure Harriet through the teachings of Mrs. Eddy; to everyone's surprise she was successful. Two days later Harriet had a relapse and came to Sarah with the bad news. She remembered the incident well:

Sarah was red with rage. She looked at me as at one who had betrayed her and said "Nothing like that. You walk. For the first time I have convinced Gertrude and Leo of the Truth of Christian Science Healing. The first time they have had any confidence in me as a practitioner. Don't you dare to go back on me. Now walk!" she said and pushed me out of the house. I walked home and have been walking ever since.[25]

Harriet became convinced (and she would eventually persuade many members of her family back in San Francisco to join her in Christian Science), but Gertrude and Leo remained unmoved – they had enthusiasms of their own.

Christian Science and Matisse's art became Sarah's twin creeds. For her the two were connected, and it is not difficult to see how: they were both modern, accessible, and optimistic. According to Harriet, for Sarah Stein, Matisse "became…and remained…the one great artist" (she added wryly, "Mike listened to Sarah").[26] Matisse's painting, with its bright colors and "untroubling" subject matter, offered just the sort of positive vision of the world Christian Scientists sought. Indeed, the text of one of Matisse's most famous statements, written in about 1908,

suggests strong affinities with Christian Science teachings: "What I dream of is an art of balance, or purity and serenity, devoid of troubling or depressing subject matter, an art which could be for every mental worker, for the business man as well as the man of letters, for example, a soothing, calming influence on the mind, something like a good armchair which provides relaxation from physical fatigue."[27] In *Science and Health*, Mrs. Eddy had advised her followers to "relinquish all theories based on sense-testimony" and to "give up imperfect models and illusive ideals." She urged them to "form perfect models in thought and look at them continually…[and] let unselfishness, goodness, mercy, justice, health, holiness, love – the kingdom of heaven – reign within us, and sin, disease, and death will diminish until they finally disappear." She continued, "The recipe for beauty is to have less illusion and more soul, to retreat from the belief of pain or pleasure in the body into the unchanging calm and glorious freedom of spiritual harmony."[28] Similarly, Matisse wrote that he tried "to put serenity into [his] pictures," and to represent the truer, more essential character of things "underlying this succession of moments which constitutes the superficial existence of beings and things."[29] Matisse was not a Christian Scientist, but such statements enabled Sarah Stein to integrate her spiritual and artistic convictions.

For Sarah and a small circle of friends who gathered around her (including, by 1914, Gabrielle de Monzie) modern art and Christian Science offered two means to the same ends: spiritual enlightenment and relief from the distress of daily life. They embraced abstract art as a simplified image of beauty, using paintings and meditation to transcend physical and psychic pain. Matisse's bold forms and bright colors in particular came to represent an optimistic alternative to the confusion and powerlessness they experienced in the world. Much as the De Stijl artists would link their work to Theosophy, emphasizing the redemptive value of "pure" form and spiritual clarity in the modern, urban environment, so Stein and her circle found in Christian Science a contemporary philosophy that resonated with, and reinforced, the freshness and clarity of the art they loved.[30] Industrial technology had ushered in a new era in the twentieth century by applying principles of engineering to age-old problems, and Christian Science – like modern art, Freudian psychoanalysis or the latest healthy diet – was promoted as a comparable cure: a pragmatic, logical system that would uncover and explain essential truths. Modern architecture could be discussed in the same terms: in the writings of Le Corbusier, for example, the connection between new materials, simple, abstract shapes and good health was made explicit. (I will return to his writings later in this chapter.) Replacing old habits and misconceptions with positive new ways of thinking and living, these discoveries and the radical changes they promised bore the hallmark of modernism.

For the next decade she would immerse herself in the life of the expatriate Christian Science community.[31] The bohemian world she and Michael had shared with Gertrude and Leo and their artist friends was behind her now, replaced by a far more respectable social whirl of dinners, tea parties, visits to galleries and concerts, attendance at church and at weekly testimonial meetings, and holidays in Brittany and the south of France. In October 1912 Harriet once again assumed her place in the Stein circle, accompanied by her niece Sylvia Salinger (fig. 7), a recent convert to the religion.[32] Sylvia's letters from this period, preserved in their entirety, offer a wonderfully detailed view of their daily lives. Now the Steins' "at homes" were attended by English and American Christian Scientists who, like Sylvia herself, peered long and hard at the pictures, trying "to see beauty" in them. When their guests stayed for supper, the talk seldom turned to art. Sylvia had been advised by Sarah to

"rejoice" as a cure for her migraines, and she and the other young people Sarah had taken under her wing preferred to listen to Mike's impressive collection of Victrola records than to do almost anything else. Shopping, eating, and drinking (wine was served despite Mrs. Eddy's advice against it) occupied a good deal of time and attention. A Sunday afternoon excursion to an automobile show was as likely as a visit to a gallery.[33] Though Sylvia described her aunt Harriet, in an intriguing rehash of Leo's old dictum, as wishing only for "an elimination of the non-essential" at Christmas, it is clear that enjoyment of the world and of the material pleasures it had to offer vied with intellectual soul-searching in the circle around the Michael Steins. Gertrude, Alice, and even Leo continue to make appearances in the letters, but they remain at the edge of the picture.

Although he never converted to Christian Science, Michael Stein was naturally inclined to cheerfulness and to a love of material things, and he embraced all that life in and around Paris had to offer. Postcards and letters he wrote to Gertrude and Alice, who were in Spain in the spring and early summer of 1912, reveal his continued preoccupation with physical exercise, which included swimming, hiking, bicycling, tennis, and even horseback riding on the outskirts of Paris. On one occasion in 1912 he and his son were accompanied by Matisse, and another time by Leo (fig. 8). The summers were particularly action packed: photographs taken at Agay, on the Riviera, in 1913 and 1914 show the Steins surrounded by a group of young friends, swimming, diving, and clowning around (fig. 9). In many ways Michael Stein would come to represent the ideal modern man as envisioned by Le Corbusier and other theorists of the time: devoted to art and physical exercise, to motor cars and new technologies of every kind, and rich enough to support the latest offerings of the Paris merchants, artists, and architects.

Harriet Levy, Sarah Stein,
and Sylvia Salinger in Paris.
Winter 1912–13

Michael, Leo, and Allan on
horseback in Paris. 1912

Michael and Sarah Stein at
Agay. 1913

During the 1920s the Steins and their friend Gabrielle de Monzie would embrace modern architecture in this optimistic spirit, building an enormous new country house that was as distinctive for its celebration of industrial technology – cars, steamships, steel beams, concrete, plate glass – as it was for its extraordinary, stripped-down appearance. Although as Christian Scientists the two women had no particular reason to prefer one style over another – the church seemed to take no position on the matter – like Michael, they were predisposed to embrace the promises of modern architecture.[34] Indeed, the constellation of unconventional ideas about art, spirituality, health, gender, and family life that they brought to the project not only overlapped with Le Corbusier's own ideas but also helped define the concept of their house as it took shape in his mind.

Gabrielle de Monzie and Le Corbusier

The Steins' decision to hire Le Corbusier is intimately tied to their friendship with Gabrielle de Monzie (fig. 10). She remains an elusive figure, despite the fact that she was part of the Christian Science circle in Paris and played a central role in the Steins' lives over a period of many years. She is mentioned infrequently in their letters, appears in very few photos, and left no written records or letters of her own. Nevertheless, the outlines of her biography are clear. Like the Steins, she was Jewish and well-to-do. She was married to the progressive politician Anatole de Monzie and owned a number of châteaux in the south of France; her close relationship with the Steins seems to have been based at first on her compatibility with their life of leisure and culture, and on her friendship with Sarah, but after her separation and divorce from her husband she increasingly relied on Michael for guidance and business advice.[35] Between 1917 and 1922 Madame de Monzie and the Steins traveled and lived together for extended periods; later she became a permanent member of their household, along with her adopted daughter, Jacqueline. In 1923 they began looking for a country house to share; three years later they joined forces to commission Le Corbusier to design the villa that would become known as Les Terrasses. This extraordinary household, in which women played such a decisive role, would remain intact until Michael's death, in 1938; indeed, the two women would continue living together for some years thereafter, although by the time of Sarah's death, in 1953, Madame de Monzie had moved to her own home in San Francisco.[36]

World War I was a turning point in all their lives. Having vacationed in Agay in the summer of 1914, the Steins stayed on through the winter of 1915, after war was declared. They considered returning to California but instead remained in France, spending much of the war in resort hotels and country houses far from Paris and the threat of attack by the Germans. The portraits Matisse painted of the couple in Paris in 1916 (plates 2, 3) reveal that they were in the city for at least some of the time and that they kept in touch with the artist. Yet for months on end they lived in the country; whenever they were in one place for any length of time, Madame de Monzie visited Sarah, who probably acted as her practitioner. They also benefitted from Madame de Monzie's hospitality: during the summer of 1918, for example, the Steins lived at the château "La Taillade," near Cahors;[37] from there Michael wrote to Gertrude that it was "just like Bardi, only bigger."[38] He seems to have enjoyed the memory of their happy summers in the Italian countryside. A city dweller all his life, Michael took up gardening and wrote frequent, anxious letters to his sister inquiring about her activities and the welfare of their collections.

By the war's end the Steins were increasingly distressed about life in the city, and they preferred the quiet and relaxation of the country. Visits to Paris, where their son, Allan, had taken a job as a captain in the Red Cross, proved disappointing: "Paris is crowded and unspeakably expensive," Michael wrote in the fall of 1918, "Neither Sally nor I have been well since we are here. I guess we have passed our city days for good." By the following spring it was clear that they would not return to 58, rue Madame: "Paris is more crowded than ever," Michael lamented, "and the price of apartments is something extraordinary."[39] Although they eventually found a place to rent in Passy, on the western edge of Paris, and lived there between 1922 and 1924, the Stein–de Monzie household was frequently on the move, driving long distances in Michael's new Hudson (Allan had become a car dealer after the war), staying at one or another of Madame de Monzie's châteaux, or touring the countryside in search of a villa to buy in the south of France.[40]

Gradually it dawned on them that they might not have to travel quite so far to find the sort of life they were seeking. With a car and chauffeur at their disposal, and frequent train service from the Gare Saint-Lazare between Paris and the far western suburbs, it would be possible to enjoy the pleasures of the garden and good country air without having to give up occasional day trips to the city. In the suburbs they could build a home that was custom-designed to suit them, in a style consistent with their tastes in art and their concerns about healthy living. Thus they turned to Le Corbusier, a young architect with just the sort of approach they found appealing.

It is not difficult to explain how the Steins and Madame de Monzie became aware of Le Corbusier's work or why they chose him as their architect. Their interests and worlds overlapped in numerous ways. Since his arrival in Paris in the winter of 1916–17, Charles-Edouard Jeanneret (he adopted his new name, Le Corbusier, in 1920) had lived and worked as an artist and writer in a milieu the Steins knew well. While Michael and Sarah no longer had strong ties to bohemian Paris, Michael in particular kept abreast of the art market after the war, frequenting the galleries and the salons, acquiring and selling pictures (mostly on behalf of the Cones), and reading the latest art books and journals.[41] Perhaps the Steins knew Jeanneret and Amédée Ozenfant's *Après le cubisme* of 1918 or took an interest in the Purist paintings (their own works and those of Fernand Léger) they exhibited and wrote about. Perhaps they had seen the two young artists at the four auctions (held in June and November 1921, July 1922, and May 1923) of the confiscated collection of their old friend Daniel-Henry Kahnweiler, bidding for Cubist paintings on behalf of a competitor, the wealthy Swiss banker Raoul La Roche.[42] Indeed, in 1923, when La Roche commissioned Le Corbusier to build a double house where his collection

PLATE 2

Henri Matisse. *Portrait of Sarah
Stein*. 1916. Oil on canvas,
28½ x 22¼ in. San Francisco
Museum of Modern Art. Sarah
and Michael Stein Memorial
Collection, Gift of Elise S. Haas

Stein–de Monzie / Le Corbusier

could be displayed (Le Corbusier's brother, Albert, and sister-in-law, Lotti Raaf, lived in the other half) not far from where the Steins and Madame de Monzie were living, they may well have gone over to have a look.

There were other opportunities to notice the architect. Le Corbusier had exhibited a model of his Maison Citrohan, a prototype for a mass-production house, at the Salon d'Automne of 1922, and Michael, who had earlier invested in apartment houses in San Francisco, would have found it particularly interesting. Ten years before, at the Salon d'Automne of 1912, he had reportedly been impressed by Raymond Duchamp-Villon's model for a Cubist House because "he saw in it important solutions for the problem of building with cement."[43]

More important, the Steins almost certainly knew *L'Esprit nouveau*, the journal Jeanneret and Ozenfant founded in 1920 and published until 1925; they would certainly have been drawn to it because of its modern approach. It contained articles on many subjects that interested them: art, architecture, construction and building materials, sports, physical fitness, cars, plumbing, household equipment, and so on.[44] The optimistic, authoritative tone of the articles, the focus on health, and the spirit of progressive social reform embodied in *L'Esprit nouveau* all suggest strong affinities with the holistic and aesthetic interests brought together by Sarah Stein and espoused by her husband and friends.

Two major events associated with the journal would have spurred their interest in Le Corbusier's work. The first was the publication, in 1923, of *Vers une architecture*, a highly readable, profusely illustrated book about modern architecture and modern living drawn from Le Corbusier's articles in *L'Esprit nouveau*. The second was the journal's pavilion at the Exposition des Arts Décoratifs in Paris in 1925, a full-scale model house Le Corbusier designed. A startling new building in whitewashed concrete and plate glass, the pavilion suggested the possibilities for using industrial materials in mass-produced housing. Since it was not only designed by Le Corbusier and decorated with Purist paintings but also endorsed publicly by Madame de Monzie's husband, then minister of public education and the arts, the Stein–de Monzie household had every reason to take an interest in it.[45]

The pages of *Vers une architecture* are filled with the sort of high-minded pronouncements about the links between spiritual and aesthetic experience in architecture that would have attracted the interest of these prospective clients. From the very first page Le Corbusier's text recalls the theories of two of their heroes – Henri Matisse and Mary Baker Eddy:

The Architect, by his arrangement of forms, realizes an order which is a pure creation of the spirit; by forms and shapes he affects our sense to an acute degree and provokes plastic emotions; by the relationships which he creates he wakes profound echoes in us, he gives us the measure of an order which we feel to be in accordance with that of our world, he determines the various movements of our heart and of our understanding; it is then that we experience the sense of beauty.[46]

Just as *Science and Health* advised readers that the way to happiness was by replacing "sense-testimony" with "perfect models in thought," so Le Corbusier proposed that higher consciousness arises from the perception of ideal forms:

These forms, elementary or subtle, tractable or brutal, work physiologically upon our senses (sphere, cube, cylinder, horizontal, vertical, oblique, etc.) and excite them. Being moved, we are able to get beyond the cruder sensations; certain relationships are thus born which work upon our perceptions and put us into a state of satisfaction (in consonance with the laws of the universe which govern us and to which all our acts are subjected), in which man can employ fully his gifts of memory, of analysis, of reasoning and of creation.[47]

For Christian Scientists like Sarah Stein and Gabrielle de Monzie, Le Corbusier's highly legible, elemental architecture could be viewed as the material realization of the harmonies of Divine Mind, visual aids to finding happiness and spiritual harmony. Le Corbusier also emphasized the link between creativity and happiness:

Art is poetry: the emotion of the senses, the joy of the mind as it measures and appreciates, the recognition of an axial principle which touches the depth of our being. Art is this pure creation of the spirit which shows us, at certain heights, the summit of the creation *to which man is capable of attaining. And man is capable of great happiness when* he feels that he is creating.[48]

For Le Corbusier the modern house was both "a machine for living in" and – like Matisse's "good armchair" for "every mental worker" – a retreat and a restorative: "The man of initiative," he wrote, "of action, of thought, the LEADER, demands a shelter for his meditations in a quiet and sure spot; a problem which is indispensable to the health of specialized people."[49] These lofty statements are given a thoroughly modern twist by their inclusion in a text dotted with photographs of machines – cars, airplanes, steamships – and of Greek temples and other classic works from the history of architecture. These images are compared and studied as models of good design (fig. 11).

For prospective clients like the Steins and Madame de Monzie, Le Corbusier's message was inescapably seductive. Here was an architect who understood that they were tired of the city but still cared deeply about contemporary art, that they were people who were accustomed to thinking of themselves as modern consumers, for whom progress was represented by the elegance and efficiency of mass-produced *things* – cars, household objects, furniture, clothes – that could be bought and owned. For these clients, as for a handful of other expatriates, art collectors, and businessmen, Le Corbusier's greatest

appeal lay in his ability to define a suburban way of life and to create an elegant environment in which to enjoy it. In his work the Steins and Madame de Monzie once again found something to believe in.

By the end of 1925 Le Corbusier had backed up the promises of his writings with an impressive group of buildings, including the Villa La Roche–Jeanneret, in Auteuil, the Lipchitz-Miestchaninoff studios, in Boulogne-sur-Seine, and the Pavillon de l'Esprit Nouveau, at the Exposition des Arts Décoratifs. The Stein–de Monzie household made a decision to hire the architect early in 1926; at almost the same moment Gertrude Stein's old friend William Cook, an American painter, and his French wife, Jeanne, also decided to build a house, albeit a much smaller one, and they hired Le Corbusier as well.[50]

Les Terrasses

Though the legal contract for the house would ultimately be drawn up between Le Corbusier and Madame de Monzie, the initial contact came in the form of a phone call from Sarah Stein to Le Corbusier's office on May 7, 1926, in which she described the program: four people would share the house, and thus in addition to a large and well-lighted living room and dining room, they would need two bedrooms for Madame de Monzie (one to be occupied by her daughter) and one large bedroom for the Stein couple.[51] What was needed, in effect, was two private suites of equal size rather than the conventional arrangement of "master" bedroom with smaller quarters for childen or guests, and the earliest sketches for the house (fig. 12) interpret this unusual program quite literally. The design that was ultimately worked out (fig. 13), with its parallel organization of complex, syncopated rhythms, retains the impress of the initial concept in its balanced composition.

The brilliance of the design lies in the tension between symmetry and irregularity, both in plan and elevation. In a famous comparison between the Villa Stein–de Monzie and Palladio's Villa Malcontena, Colin Rowe summed up the unique characteristics of the project: "At Garches, central focus is consistently broken up, concentration at any one point is disintegrated, and the dismembered fragments of the center become a peripheral dispersion of incident, a serial installation of interest around the extremities of the plan."[52] While Palladio consistently focuses attention on the central axis, Le Corbusier forces the visitor to confront each element independently. Distinct features such as the gate-lodge, the front entrance with canopy, the projecting balcony on the top floor, the curved wall of the dining room enclosure, or the circular stair are each encountered in turn, yet each is an integrated part of an overall composition. William Curtis thus compared the house to a Purist painting: "To explode the form of Les Terrasses into an axonometric drawing is quickly to grasp how one level differs from another and how real and illusionistic planes are compressed together with curved objects to make an equivalent to a Purist still life inhabitable."[53] Contrasts abound, most notably between

FIGURE 11

Greek temples and cars, from Le Corbusier's *Vers une architecture*, 1923

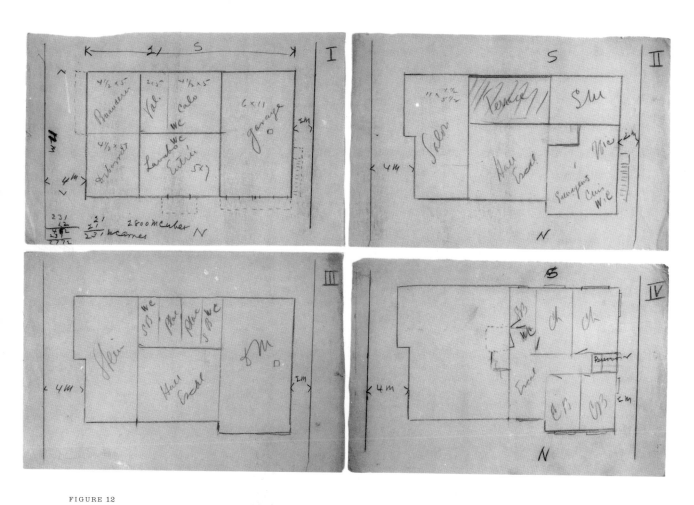

FIGURE 12

Villa Stein–de Monzie, preliminary plans. 1926

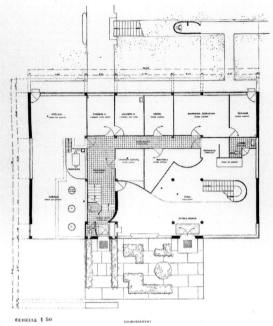

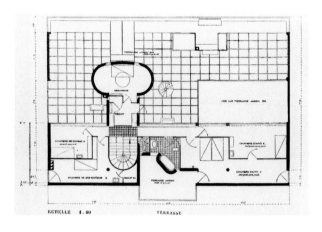

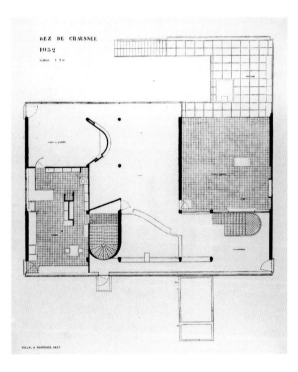

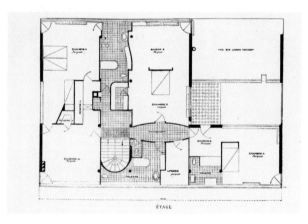

FIGURE 13

Villa Stein–de Monzie, plans.
Counterclockwise from upper left:
a. ground floor b. second floor
c. third floor d. fourth floor and
roof terrace

FIGURE 14

Panoramic view of the Villa
Stein–de Monzie and neighboring houses. ca. 1930

the closed, planar surface of the front facade and the
open, permeable forms of the garden facade (see plate
1). The serpentine concrete path and loose, varied plantings on the garden side (the work of landscape architect
Lucien Crépin) create a further contrast of color, texture,
and form.[54] Thus the visitor is forced to confront a
sequence of experiences in much the same way that
one reads an abstract painting that resists resolution as
a unified image.

The site, chosen well after the project was under
way, is on a high ridge between Vaucresson and Garches.
Le Corbusier's decision to set the house far back on the
property enabled him to create the long, formal vista he
preferred. Despite the fact that published images of the
house present it in dignified isolation, it is fairly close to
its neighbors and bordered by trees (fig. 14). Approaching by car from the road, the visitor passes the gate-lodge
and proceeds down the drive. The garage and service
entrance are encountered first; an open courtyard in
front of the house provides just enough space for a car
to make a semicircular turn and discharge passengers at
the main entrance beyond. From the beginning, then,
the parts of the house are experienced sequentially via a
series of loops or winding paths. This "promenade archi-
tecturale," as Le Corbusier called it, continues on the
interior, as one moves through the entrance hall, up a

circular staircase, and into the large living area or salon on the main floor. Here the visitor is confronted by an unusually complex arrangement of spaces and forms: on one side a large window looks out onto the terrace; in front a curved wall forms a low parapet bordering the open space of the hall below; beyond lies the wall of the dining room and a view of the garden. One explores each of these in turn, moving across, through, and eventually up again, via another staircase, to the private living area, and above that to the roof terrace. Throughout this journey one is continually made aware of the central axis – marked by the double-height hall, for example – which one must crisscross in moving about the house. In this way both the interior and the exterior become part of an eloquent, extended elaboration of the symmetry of the program with which Le Corbusier began.

The Steins and de Monzie were clearly committed to modern architecture and willing to pool their resources to finance the project generously. Les Terrasses cost over 1,500,000 francs, making it the most expensive house built by Le Corbusier's office in the 1920s.[55] Moreover, they were very conscious of the leadership role they were playing as patrons of the new style. In a letter to an old family friend in the U.S., written about 1930, Michael made this clear: "We were here all through the war and my son did fine work as a captain in the American Red Cross. Now I have a grandson and live outside Paris in an ultra modern house of which I enclose a postal card. After having been in the vanguard of the modern movement in painting in the early years of this century, we are now doing the same for modern architecture."[56]

In Michael Stein, Le Corbusier had an ideal client: an ever-patient and resourceful collaborator, a man who was interested in construction and in machines, who tinkered with cars and was willing to visit the site every day as the building was going up.[57] Michael had a lifetime of experience dealing with other people's idiosyncracies, and he coped by anticipating problems and making sure things ran smoothly; besides, he probably wanted to avoid the sort of unpleasant experience Cook had written to Gertrude about the previous summer:

I have had a real row with both the architects and the contractor…of course they are mad but that is the least of my worries as long as the house is going as it should. The architect is somewhat of a temperamental genius and he put my house one corner on my land and the other corner fifty centimetres over on my neighbors land. I thought this was a thing that was just not according to Hoyle and he told me I seemed to be a type absolutely without gratitude. Gratitude be damned says I – what I want is to have the thing fixed up. Well it will cost me ten thousand francs before the thing is finished and he is mad because I have no appreciation of the fact that he got me fifty centimetres of land that I didn't want.[58]

During his first three years at Les Terrasses, Michael pitched in to design a drainage system to absorb ground water and helped install the oil burner for the central heating, just the sorts of things that clients wait in vain for architects to attend to after a house is "finished." Thus, while he was a man of leisure and already in his mid-sixties, Michael Stein was the kind of modern client for whom the efficient-looking garage (fig. 15) and streamlined roof terrace with its lookout platform (figs. 16, 17) were designed. He and the two ladies were a bit old to fully play the parts that Le Corbusier envisioned for them (an eighty-two-meter running track originally planned for the roof had to be eliminated, and Madame de Monzie was too fearful to venture up to the lookout), but they thoroughly enjoyed the role of modern occupants in an ideal environment. Moreover, they found the

FIGURE 15

Villa Stein–de Monzie, garage.
From *L'Architecture vivante*,
1929

house unexpectedly flexible and accommodating: when
the Steins' one-year-old grandson, Danny, came to live
with them, he moved into the large second-floor bedroom, while Madame de Monzie relocated to the suite
on the top floor. This new arrangement proved to be
highly satisfactory.[59]

Letters written by the Steins throughout the period
are full of praise for the house and pleasure in their new
surroundings. They loved the garden and the terraces
and the good air; they relaxed outdoors and entertained
friends as they had done on summer holidays. Nicknamed
Les Terrasses – the name appeared almost immediately
on the Steins' new stationery – the house became a place
of pilgrimage for artists – Mondrian, El Lissitzky, Man
Ray, Matisse – critics, and collectors.[60] In early summer
1929 Michael wrote to Gertrude: "Everything is fine here.
We are resting and haven't hung a single picture. The last
workmen left today. The Cones are here. Same as ever....
I hope you will be back in time to see our roses. The air
here is simply fine. It smells like real country. Being so

FIGURE 16

Villa Stein–de Monzie,
panoramic view of roof terrace.
ca. 1930

FIGURE 17

Roof terrace and lookout
platform. From *L'Architecture
vivante*, 1929

high we get the air from the ocean that has not touched the ground. Danny spent the whole afternoon here."[61] With French and American flags fluttering on the roof, Les Terrasses became a haven for old friends on the outskirts of the city; something of the old conviviality of rue Madame was re-created there, but Michael was right to say that they had passed their "city days" for good.

For Le Corbusier, an architect who at age forty was bursting with ideas and desperate for clients who would bring them to life, the commission was a golden opportunity. He compared his experience to pregnancy: in a letter of 1926 to Madame Meyer, a reluctant client who ultimately abandoned her project (many of its best features would be recycled into Les Terrasses), he wailed, "My paternity is suffering!… A house which remains on paper is a stillbirth. Let me tell you that my suffering is truly that of an expectant father."[62] The appearance of the Steins and Madame de Monzie in his life must have seemed like a dream come true.

The house represented an enormous professional turning point for the architect. Writing in *Une Maison – Un Palais* in 1928, he described it as a "type form" for architectural design, a perfect response to the complexities of the domestic program – a "machine for living" that achieved the status of a palace.[63] The house was also a critical success, and Le Corbusier was praised for demonstrating that modern forms and materials could be successfully used in a luxurious, high-budget project.[64]

Where Le Corbusier remained at odds with his clients, however, was on the question of furnishings. Although he had been aware from the beginning that the Steins were intending to bring many of their antique pieces (some acquired years before in Florence) with them, he never quite got used to the fact that the house was filled with heavy, dark furniture (fig. 18). He may not have pressed the point with his clients, but he made his feelings clear a few years later in *Précisions*: "Big

pieces of furniture, understandable at the time of castles or in the rooms of country houses, are a disaster in the modern dwelling."[65] When he published his work, he preferred to show the rooms completely empty (fig. 19) or as settings for evocative, dreamlike tableaux (fig. 20) suggesting absence rather than the presence of real-life occupants with their own tastes and preferences.

Within months life at Les Terrasses began to assume the familiar rhythms of the prewar years, with excursions to galleries and shops in Paris and Sunday visits from family and friends. Yet time was limited. In September 1929 Michael and Sarah received word that Claribel Cone had died in Lausanne, and with the passing of their old friend and client, things began to change for them both socially and financially. Moreover, the winds of political unrest had begun to blow in Europe, bringing back still-painful memories of the war. As the effects of the worldwide economic depression began to be felt in France, and as Hitler continued his ominous rise to power in Germany, Michael grew concerned, and he set his sights on California. In 1935 he sold Les Terrasses to a Danish banker. The entire household, including Madame de Monzie, her daughter, and Danny Stein, pulled up stakes and moved to Palo Alto, leaving bewildered friends and family behind. Gertrude Stein described her astonishment at this sudden turn of events in *Everybody's Autobiography*, published two years after their departure: *Let me tell you about my brother. As I said he had lived in France as long as I had he had a son he had a grandson here, he had his wife and friends he seemed reasonably content and happy. About five years ago he said he wanted to go back to California but why I said what's the matter you've lived here so long what's the matter, oh he said you don't understand, he said I want to say in English to the man who brings the letters and does the gardening I want to say things to them and have them say it to me in American.… And he has sold his house, it was a bad time*

FIGURE 18

Villa Stein–de Monzie, salon

FIGURE 19

Villa Stein–de Monzie, salon,
looking toward stair and terrace
windows. From *L'Architecture
vivante*, 1929

to sell and nobody could sell anything but he wandered
around until he saw a man who looked as if he was looking
for a house and he was and my brother said why not buy
mine and he did and in a week they were gone.[66]

By 1938 Michael Stein was dead from cancer. His last years were spent gardening, taking long walks, and reassuring everyone that he was going to get better. Some months after his death Sarah wrote to Gertrude to say that the ever-cheerful Mike "had smiled his way out."[67] His family never recovered from the loss. Though Sarah had found an adoring audience among the students and professors at Stanford University, without Michael her enthusiasm waned. Her finances were stretched and she was forced to sell her paintings to support herself.[68] By the time she died, in 1953, Sarah Stein's life had become diminished and difficult.

Little is known about Gabrielle de Monzie's life in California. She became active in the Christian Science Church, moved to San Francisco, and died in 1961.[69] Obscured by her famous friends, and almost completely unknown, she can now be recognized as a patron of enormous importance in the history of modern architecture. Had it not been for the life, and the vision, she shared with the Steins, the house at Garches would never have been built.

FIGURE 20

Villa Stein–de Monzie, kitchen.
From *L'Architecture vivante*, 1929

1 For the Stein family and circle, see *Four Americans in Paris: The Collections of Gertrude Stein and Her Family* (New York: Museum of Modern Art, 1970); James Mellow, *Charmed Circle: Gertrude Stein and Company* (New York: Praeger, 1974); Linda Simon, *The Biography of Alice B. Toklas* (Garden City, N.Y.: Doubleday, 1977); Linda Wagner-Martin, *Favored Strangers: Gertrude Stein and Her Family* (New Brunswick, N.J.: Rutgers University Press, 1995); Shari Benstock, *Women of the Left Bank: Paris 1900–1940* (Austin: University of Texas Press, 1986); and Brenda Wineapple, *Sister Brother: Gertrude and Leo Stein* (New York: G. P. Putnam's Sons, 1996), which features the best discussion to date of Leo and Sarah. The Steins' correspondence is held in the Collection of American Literature, Beinecke Rare Book and Manuscript Library, Yale University, New Haven (hereinafter referred to as YCAL). Unless otherwise noted, letters written by the Steins cited in this chapter are in the collection of YCAL.

2 See Brenda Richardson, *Dr. Claribel and Miss Etta: The Cone Collection of the Baltimore Museum of Art* (Baltimore: The Baltimore Museum of Art, 1985).

3 Le Corbusier viewed Les Terrasses as a turning point in his career; in 1959 he wrote on a drawing of the house, "This drawing… expresses the final flowering of the modest but passionate effort of 1918–25 – the first round of new architecture to be *manifested.*" See Tim Benton, *The Villas of Le Corbusier* (New Haven: Yale University Press, 1987), 164–89, esp. 170. For the history of the Villa Stein–de Monzie, see Benton, and William Curtis, *Le Corbusier: Ideas and Forms* (London: Phaidon, 1986); Loren Soth, "Le Corbusier's Clients and Their Parisian Homes," *Art History* 6, no. 2 (1983), 188–98; "Le Corbusier and P. Jeanneret," *L'Architecture vivante*, 2ème série, 1929; and Willy Boesiger and Oscar Stonorov, eds., *Le Corbusier and Pierre Jeanneret: Oeuvre Complète 1910– 1929* (Zürich: Editions Dr. H. Girsberger, 1937), 140–49.

4 James Ward, "Le Corbusier's Villa Les Terrasses and the International Style" (Ph.D. diss. [University Microfilms], 3 vols., New York University, 1984). The household is discussed in part 1, ch. 2.

5 Benton, *The Villas of Le Corbusier*, 166. The bilaterally symmetrical plan is discussed (though only in formal terms) by Colin Rowe, "The Mathematics of the Ideal Villa," in his *The Mathematics of the Ideal Villa and Other Essays* (Cambridge, Mass.: MIT Press, 1976), 1–28. The essay was first published in 1947.

6 "Villa Stein–de Monzie à Garches," document no. 159, H1(4), Fondation Le Corbusier, Paris.

7 For Matisse's school, see Alfred H. Barr, Jr., *Matisse: His Art and His Public* (New York: The Museum of Modern Art, 1951), esp. 116–23, and Hélène Seckel, "L'Académie Matisse," in *Paris–New York, 1908–1968* (Paris: Gallimard, 1991), 316–20 (1st ed. Centre Georges Pompidou, Paris, 1977).

8 Harriet Levy, "Recollections," unpublished memoir written around 1950, typescript in the collection of Albert Bennett. I am grateful to Mr. Bennett for granting me permission to quote from this text. A second copy is in the Bancroft Library, University of California at Berkeley. For Levy's anger at Sarah Stein, see p. 13.

9 The family's tastes in art have been written about extensively; see Wineapple, *Sister Brother*, 214–21.

10 Wineapple, *Sister Brother*, 333–36; Janet Flanner, ed., *Two: Gertrude Stein and Her Brother and Other Early Portraits* (New Haven: Yale University Press, 1951).

11 For Otto Weininger, see Allan Janik and Stephen Toulmin, *Wittgenstein's Vienna* (New York: Simon and Schuster, 1973), 71–72.

12 Levy, "Recollections," 36.

13 The citation occurs in a letter from Leo Stein to Gertrude Stein (hereinafter referred to as L. Stein and G. Stein, respectively): "I dislike quite as intensely and probably more deeply than you do hygiene all forms of homosexuality so it must be understood that except when I am away from the house or have gone to bed, you and Alice except when you are in one of your rooms must be as Browning has it 'of friends the merest,'" undated (1910?).

14 The story of the Steins' life in California is told in Wineapple, *Sister Brother*, 20–48, 65–67, 102–3.

15 Sarah Stein (hereinafter referred to as S. Stein), letter to G. Stein, Oct. 30, 1899.

16 Sarah's best friend was Adele Jaffa, a homeopathic physician; see Wineapple, *Sister Brother*, 78–82.

17 S. Stein, letters to G. Stein, Nov. 1896 (?), Aug. 27, 1899, Nov. 11, 1899.

18 Michael Stein (hereinafter referred to as M. Stein), letter to G. Stein, Jan. 12, 1901.

19 For Sarah's San Francisco visit, see Simon, *Toklas*, 22–25.

20 S. Stein, letter to G. Stein, Oct. 8, 1906.

21 For Jewish conversions to Christian Science, see John J. Appel, "Christian Science and the Jews," *Jewish Social Studies* 31 (Apr. 1969), 100–121; Samuel N. Deinard, *Jews and Christian Science* (Minneapolis: Samuel N. Deinard, 1919); and Max Wertheimer, *Why I Left Christian Science* (1916), reprinted in Gary Ward, ed., *Christian Science: Controversial and Polemical Pamphlets* (New York: Garland Press, 1990), 389–446.

22 In the Christian Science version of the Lord's prayer, God is addressed as "Father-Mother God, all harmonious"; Mary Baker Eddy, *Science and Health with a Key to the Scriptures* (Boston: The First Church of Christ, Scientist, 1875), 16; reprinted in 1994.

23 For the history of Christian Science and the role of Mrs. Eddy, see Rennie B. Schoepflin, "Christian Science Healing in America," in Norman Gevitz, ed., *Other Healers: Unorthodox Medicine in America* (Baltimore: Johns Hopkins University Press, 1988), 192–214; Stuart E. Knee, *Christian Science in the Age of Mary Baker Eddy* (Westport,

Conn.: Greenwood Press, 1994); and Robert David Thomas, *With Bleeding Footsteps: Mary Baker Eddy's Path to Religious Leadership* (New York: Knopf, 1994). See also Anne Braude, "The Perils of Passivity: Women's Leadership in Spiritualism and Christian Science," in Catherine Wessinger, ed., *Women's Leadership in Marginal Religions: Explorations Outside the Mainstream* (Urbana and Chicago: University of Illinois Press, 1993), 55–67.

24 Although Christian Science had been presented rather critically in a series of articles by Willa Cather and Georgine Milmine in 1907–8 in *McClure's Magazine*, which the Steins read, it was treated far more positively by William James in *The Varieties of Religious Experience*, a book to which both Gertrude and Leo were devoted. See Willa Cather and Georgine Milmine, *The Life of Mary Baker G. Eddy and the History of Christian Science* (Lincoln: University of Nebraska Press, 1993); and William James, *The Varieties of Religious Experience: A Study in Human Nature* (Cambridge, Mass.: Harvard University Press, 1985), 83–99.

25 Levy, "Recollections," 47.

26 See ibid., 8. For Sarah Stein's relationship with Matisse, see also Annette Rosenshine, "Life Is Not a Paragraph," unpublished typescript, Bancroft Library, 97. Matisse came to Sarah's defense when Gertrude failed to mention her role as his patron in *The Autobiography of Alice B. Toklas* (1933); see Georges Braque et al., *Testimony Against Gertrude Stein, Transition Pamphlet*, no.1 (supplement to *Transition*, no. 23) (The Hague: Servire Press, 1935), 3.

27 Henri Matisse, "Notes d'un peintre," *La Grande Revue* 2 (Dec. 25, 1908), 24, 731–35, trans. Jack Flam, "Notes of a Painter," in Flam, *Matisse on Art* (Berkeley and Los Angeles: University of California Press, 1995), 30–43, esp. 42. See also Roger Benjamin, *Matisse's "Notes of a Painter": Criticism, Theory and Context, 1891–1908*

(Ann Arbor: UMI Research Press, 1987), and John Elderfield, *Henri Matisse: A Retrospective* (New York: Abrams, 1992), esp. 17–18.

28 Eddy, *Science and Health*, 247–49.

29 Flam, *Matisse on Art*, 39. Flam relates this statement to Henri Bergson's *Creative Evolution* (1907); see pp. 33–34.

30 For De Stijl and modern theory, especially Theosophy, see Reyner Banham, *Theory and Design in the First Machine Age* (London: Arch Press, 1960), 150–60.

31 For Sarah's and Gabrielle's involvement with the Christian Science Church, see Ward, "Le Corbusier's Villa," 21 n. 7, 26 n. 29.

32 For Sylvia Salinger, see Albert S. Bennett, *Just a Very Pretty Girl from the Country: Sylvia Salinger's Letters from France, 1912–1913* (Carbondale: Southern Illinois University Press, 1987). I am grateful to Mr. Bennett for sharing his knowledge of Christian Science as well as his mother's photographs and papers, and for allowing me to quote from the letters.

33 For Sarah Stein's letter about Sylvia's spiritual cure, see Bennett, *Salinger*, 39; the quotation about Harriet Levy is on p. 47; for the visit to the automobile show, see p. 143.

34 Paul Ivey, "Christian Science Architecture: Reform in America and Britain, 1910–1930," paper presented at the annual meeting of the Society of Architectural Historians, Philadelphia, 1994. Other notable patrons of architecture who were also Christian Scientists include Frank Lloyd Wright's clients Darwin Martin and Avery and Queene Ferry Coonley, who claimed that they saw "the countenances of principle" in Wright's work; see Frank Lloyd Wright, *An Autobiography* (New York: Longmans Green, 1932), 185; reprinted in Bruce Brooks Pfeiffer, ed., *Frank Lloyd Wright: Collected Writings*, vol. 2 (New York: Rizzoli, 1992), 218.

35 Daniel Stein, telephone interview with Alice Friedman, Jan. 22, 1997. I am grateful to Mr. Stein for his help with my research. James Ward's extensive search of the documents and interviews with Mr. Stein

revealed only the barest outlines of Mme de Monzie's biography. Gabrielle de Monzie was the daughter of a Dutch father and a South African mother (Ward, "Le Corbusier's Villa," 28); she married Anatole de Monzie in 1904 (29), separated from him in 1922 (33), was divorced in 1927 and reassumed her maiden name, Colaço-Osorio (58), and died in 1961 (28).

36 D. Stein, telephone interview with Friedman.

37 The properties owned by Mme de Monzie, her husband, and her extended family were researched by Ward, who provides a detailed picture of the relationship between the Steins and Mme de Monzie in this period; see Ward, "Le Corbusier's Villa," 32 and ch. 2.

38 M. Stein, letter to G. Stein, June 1918.

39 M. Stein, letter to G. Stein, June 26, 1918; "Tuesday," late fall 1918 (?); Apr. 17, 1919.

40 See Ward, "Le Corbusier's Villa," 56 n. 139.

41 A friend of the Steins, Therese Ehrman Jelenko, remembered that the Steins collected works of art for the Cones in the 1920s, storing them in their basement in Passy and then shipping them to the U.S. Jelenko, "Reminiscences," typescript of recorded interview, ca. 1965, Bancroft Library, 9.

42 See Russell Walden, "New Light on Le Corbusier's Early Years in Paris: The La Roche–Jeanneret Houses," in Walden, ed., *The Open Hand: Essays on Le Corbusier* (Cambridge, Mass.: MIT Press, 1977), 116–61.

43 Walter Pach, *Queer Thing, Painting: Forty Years in the World of Art* (New York: Harper and Brothers, 1938), 142–43. See also Hélène Seckel, "L'Armory Show," in *Paris–New York, 1908–1968*, 376–406, esp. 393. Sylvia Salinger wrote to her family (Nov. 14, 1912) about seeing the house at the Grand Palais with its full-scale mock-ups of individual rooms: "They are completely furnished, even to the books on the shelves. It is a splendid way to get ideas"; Bennett, *Just a Very Pretty Girl*, 27.

44 See Stanislaus von Moos, ed., *L'Esprit nou-veau: Le Corbusier et l'industrie, 1920–1925* (Zürich: Museum für Gestaltung, 1987).

45 See Mary McLeod, "Urbanism and Utopia: Le Corbusier from Regional Syndicalism to Vichy" (Ph.D diss., 2 vols., Princeton University, 1985), ch. 1, esp. p. 67, and Philippe Boudon, *Lived-In Architecture* (Cambridge, Mass.: MIT Press, 1972), 11. Letters from friends and family of Gertrude Stein refer to Anatole de Monzie in passing: Mildred Aldrich to G. Stein, July 20, 1926, YCAL; M. Stein to G. Stein, Tuesday 1929 (?), asks Alice to send "a typed copy of de Monzie's letter" if she has time; Rose Ellen Stein to G. Stein, June 16, 1945, writes: "I was interested that de Monzie was around enough to be coming to see you. I thought he was completely beyond the pale politically and I had a feeling that he would be liquidated or about to be."

46 Le Corbusier, *Towards a New Architecture*, trans. Frederick Etchells (London: Architectural Press, 1927), 7.

47 Ibid., 20–21.

48 Ibid., 205–7.

49 Ibid, 89, 24. See Beatriz Colomina, *Privacy and Publicity: Modern Architecture as Mass Media* (Cambridge, Mass.: MIT Press, 1994), esp. 207–8, on the marketing of the International Style to "the department store public, middle-class and mainly women."

50 See M. Stein, letter to G. Stein, 1926 (?), where "Jeanneret" is referred to as "the architect of Cook," and M. Stein, letter to G. Stein, July 20, 1926.

51 The contract is dated Nov. 10, 1926; Mme de Monzie made the down payment on Nov. 22, 1926. Stein–de Monzie, dossier 1, Fondation Le Corbusier.

52 Rowe, "The Mathematics of the Ideal Villa," 12. For a discussion of Le Corbusier's planning, see also Kurt Forster, "Antiquity and Modernity in the La Roche–Jeanneret Houses of 1923," *Oppositions* 15–16 (Winter–Spring 1979), 130–53.

53 Curtis, *Le Corbusier*, 81.

54 See Benton, *The Villas of Le Corbusier*, 174.

55 Ibid., 175.

56 M. Stein, letter to Mr. P. G. Byrne, n.d. (1930?).

57 Michael wrote to Gertrude, "The house is at a stage where I have to go out every day"; M. Stein, letter to G. Stein, n.d. (summer 1927?).

58 William Cook, letter to G. Stein, Sept. 8, 1926, YCAL. For the cost of the house, see Benton, *The Villas of Le Corbusier*, 175.

59 In a film by Pierre Chénal, *L'Architecture d'aujourd'hui*, of ca. 1930, Le Corbusier cast himself in the role of homeowner at Garches, hopping out of a car at the front door, smoking on the terrace, and bounding up the stairs to the lookout platform (a copy of the film is in the collection of The Museum of Modern Art, New York). By contrast, home movies made in the early 1930s show a portly Michael Stein, dressed completely in white as though just having returned from a day of tennis or cricket, proudly showing off his villa to family and friends (the home movies are in the collection of YCAL). For the running track, see Benton, *The Villas of Le Corbusier*, 169. For Mme de Monzie's fear of heights, see du Pasquier, letter to Le Corbusier, July 2, 1927, Stein–de Monzie, dossier 1, Fondation Le Corbusier; in the same letter he mentions "rumor has it that the house is to be called 'Mont'là-d'sus'" (Up You Go!). Additional information on the use of the house was provided by D. Stein, telephone interview with Friedman.

60 Man Ray visited and took Danny's photograph (S. Stein, letter to G. Stein, May 27, 1929); Carl van Vechten came with his wife (S. Stein, letter to G. Stein, Aug. 11, 1930); Mondrian and El Lissitzky visited (see photograph on p. 234 of Jacques Lucan, ed., *Le Corbusier, Une Encyclopédie* (Paris: Centre Georges Pompidou, 1987); and the Cones came and went (S. Stein, letter to G. Stein, May 27, 1929).

61 M. Stein, letter to G. Stein, early summer 1929.

62 Le Corbusier, letter to Mme Meyer, Feb. 24, 1926, dossier Meyer, Fondation Le Corbusier; quoted by Benton, *The Villas of Le Corbusier*, 144.

63 Le Corbusier, *Une Maison – Un Palais* (Paris: Crès, 1928; reissued Paris: Editions Connivences, 1989), 66–72, esp. 68–69.

64 Ibid.; see, for example, Siegfried Giedion, "Le Problème du luxe dans l'architecture moderne," *Cahiers d'art* 5–6 (1928), 254–56.

65 Le Corbusier, *Précisions* (1930), trans. Edith Schreiber Aujame (Cambridge: MIT Press, 1991), 109. For Le Corbusier's presentation of the interiors, see Jacques Lucan, "The Search for the Absolute," in Carlo Palazzolo and Riccardo Vio, *In the Footsteps of Le Corbusier* (New York: Rizzoli, 1991), 197–207.

66 Gertrude Stein, *Everybody's Autobiography* (New York: Random House, 1937), 14. For the later history of the house, see Ward, "Le Corbusier's Villas," 65–74.

67 S. Stein, letter to G. Stein, Oct. 13, 1938.

68 Through the foresight of Elise Stern Haas, a devoted friend, a number of paintings, including the portraits by Matisse, were purchased and then donated to the San Francisco Museum of Modern Art in memory of the Steins. See Elise Stern Haas, "The Appreciation of Quality," transcript of an interview with Harriet Nathan, Regional Oral History Office, 1979, Bancroft Library.

69 Ward, "Le Corbusier's Villas," 41 n.92, 28 n.41.

PLATE 1

Ludwig Mies van der Rohe.
Farnsworth House, Plano,
Illinois. 1945–51

The Farnsworth House (1945–51; plate 1), in Plano,
Illinois, by Ludwig Mies van der Rohe (1886–1969) is
one of a handful of modern buildings that always seem
extraordinary: it is among the most frequently illustrated
of all twentieth-century houses, yet like Le Corbusier's
Villa Savoye (1929–30) and Wright's Fallingwater (1936),
the sight of the Farnsworth House still takes one's breath
away. Countless architecture students have memorized
its canonic image, its plan, the name of its architect, and
the date and place of construction, but the house remains
surprising, elusive, ungraspable. Once seen, it lingers
in the mind's eye, but somehow it never becomes completely familiar.

Perched in the middle of a grassy meadow on the
bank of the Fox River, some fifty miles west of Chicago, the
Farnsworth House appears to be the perfect embodiment
of Mies's dictum "Less is more." Even from a distance
one is struck by the elegance and simplicity of its form.
Eight slender columns of white-painted steel support a
transparent glass box; two horizontal planes – crisp,
parallel bands of steel hovering above the ground – represent the floor and the roof. Though barely making
physical contact with its site, the house seems securely
anchored in the green sea that surrounds it; there is a
toughness and immutability to the structure, which contrast with the thinness and apparent insubstantiality of
the forms. With its low terrace and ladderlike suspended
staircases, the house appears to be a life raft or a tent
platform, a place of refuge from the turbulence of nature.
This image (and experience) of insularity is reinforced
by the fact that the interior of the house is almost totally
sealed off from the outside world: the only openings in
the glass "skin" are a door on one short side of the rectan-
gle, which serves as the entrance, and two small windows
set low on the opposite wall.

Edith Farnsworth. ca. 1940

People Who Live in Glass Houses:

Edith Farnsworth, Ludwig Mies van der Rohe, and Philip Johnson

A thin but seemingly impermeable membrane of glass thus forms the boundary between inside and outside on all four sides of the box; grass, trees, and river are visible through the "walls," yet they seem distant and abstracted, like elements in a landscape painting. This is not simply because the views from the house are framed by the rectilinear structure, but because objects and landscape beyond the glass appear recessed and diminished, as though the surface of the wall were a picture plane and the objects behind it were imaginary, not real. When one looks at things inside the house, however, this equation is reversed: there is an immediacy that is inescapable – one's awareness of the material world is heightened. In part this is due to the fact that the interior is simply one large room (the entire platform measures 77 x 28 feet), subdivided by a freestanding wooden core, which encloses two bathrooms, a fireplace, and a galley kitchen. This block at the center and a lower bank of cupboards at the far end of the house screen and subdivide the space to some degree, but the living areas remain essentially open and unbounded. Within this interior environment, sights and sounds are magnified, people and objects move closer and seem more tangible and tactile.

Mies's architecture thus calls attention not only to itself but also to the physical and aesthetic experience of the occupant. It is important to note that the experience is not always positive. As Mies's grandson, the architect Dirk Lohan, explained:

[The house] owes its stature as one of the highlights of modern architecture to its spiritual rather than its functional values. The concept, a country retreat from the big city, has been elevated to such a spiritual abstraction that it demands complete acceptance of its inner logic from the occupant. So unconventional is the house that every move and every activity in it assume an aesthetic quality which challenges behavior patterns formed in different surroundings.[1]

The "occupant" in this case was Edith Farnsworth (1903–1977), an unmarried doctor who lived and worked in Chicago. In her mid-forties and financially secure, Farnsworth had begun to think about the advantages of owning a small weekend house in the country some months, or even years, before she met the German architect Ludwig Mies van der Rohe, in 1945. Through Mies, who had emigrated to the United States in the late 1930s and was already well known among American architects and critics for the unrelenting discipline and formality of his work, Farnsworth later came to view her project as an important statement about modern architecture, but at the outset her concerns were those of a typical client: what she was looking for was "a really fine [design] solution for an inexpensive weekend retreat for a single person of my tastes and pre-occupations," as she later recalled in her memoirs.[2] She assumed that whatever else happened in the process of working with an architect, her new house would be a place in which she could relax and find some relief from the strain of her life as a doctor. There is no evidence to suggest that she sought to have her behavior challenged by the "inner logic" of Mies's unyielding architectural vision; on the contrary, she seems to have had a clear idea about how she wanted to live and she expected the architect to respect her views.

Farnsworth's assumptions about her role and rights in the architect-client relationship proved to be unfounded; she soon discovered that what Mies wanted, and what he thought he had found in her, was a patron who would put her budget and her needs aside in favor of his own goals and dreams as an architect. By 1945 Mies and his followers (including Philip Johnson, an architect himself and head of the Department of Architecture at The Museum of Modern Art in New York) were acutely aware of the fact that what he needed most was a wealthy patron and a job. The lack of opportunities for building in wartime Germany, combined with the strict minimalism of his formal language, had ensured that Mies had few clients and even fewer realized buildings over the last fifteen years. He had built a handful of well-known works in Europe, including the German Pavilion at the Barcelona World's Fair in 1929 and the Tugendhat House in Brno, Czechoslovakia, in 1930, but the majority of his designs remained on paper. This was especially true of his houses: although he had come up with some radically new ideas for living spaces and produced some extraordinary drawings, nothing much had come of them in either Germany or the U.S.[3] Mies's reputation was impressive and his work was admired in elite and academic circles, but he needed exposure – he needed to build. Dr. Edith Farnsworth seemed to be the answer to his prayers.

The first part of this chapter looks at the history of the Farnsworth House and at the process through which it came to be designed and constructed. As one of the most important monuments of twentieth-century architecture built for a woman client, the Farnsworth House is a significant example of the type discussed in this book. Yet the fact that Farnsworth was a woman and that her house is so widely admired is only the beginning of the story. Throughout the long process of design development we can identify and analyze multiple ways in which attitudes about gender and sexuality influenced the project; we can also look at how these and other factors contributed to the house's uncertain reception by the American public in the early 1950s. Nevertheless, it is very important at the outset to be clear about what this approach to the house does, and does *not*, tell us. Neither Farnsworth's conflict with the architect nor the unprecedented design of the Farnsworth House was simply the result of her being a woman. Many works of architecture, built for a variety of clients and purposes, have similar histories: there are often persistent and unresolved questions about power, professional status, money, and, ultimately, about who is in control of the project. Architects and clients frequently struggle, both publicly and privately, to enlist support for their points of view, using all the personal and professional artillery available to them. Moreover, gender values – assumptions about how men and women should behave in their daily lives – often play a role in architectural design, particularly in domestic architecture, since these values shape both the explicit and the implicit requirements of a building's program. There is no guarantee that architect and client will agree on these matters, especially in cases where unconventional ways of living are being planned for. Architecture is a process of negotiation.

What is unusual in this case, however, as in many of the other examples discussed in this book, is that questions of gender and sexuality were explicitly focused on by the participants, and that they came to assume an unusually prominent and complex role in the design process as it was discussed and described at the time. Edith Farnsworth may have been a successful doctor, but the fact that she was also a single woman made her more dependent on the architect both personally and professionally.[4] Ambiguities about their roles, not simply as architect and client but also as man and woman, blurred the boundaries of their relationship, which was especially problematized by the attitudes and prejudices of 1950s America. This opened the way for deep-rooted conflicts between them, which were played out in questions about authority, money, and control of the project.

Although this situation clearly tainted the undertaking for both of them, it is possible that these factors, especially Mies's assumptions about his own power and his willingness to disregard the client's wishes, actually set the stage for the greatness of the design by freeing Mies to pursue his vision of the weekend house as a work of "pure" architecture, a building almost completely devoid of a program. Whatever way we look at it – whether we are dismayed by Mies's desire to exploit the situation or by Farnsworth's tardy realization that she was not the all-powerful client she expected to be – it is clear that gender and sexuality played an unusually prominent role in shaping this extraordinary house.

The second half of the chapter focuses on Philip Johnson's Glass House/Guest House complex (1949), in New Canaan, Connecticut, a weekend retreat in the country, north of New York City. Johnson (b. 1906) played a significant part in creating a reputation for Mies van der Rohe in the United States: not only had Johnson prominently featured Mies's buildings in the influential International Style exhibition of 1932 at The Museum of Modern Art, but he had also been Mies's first American client, having commissioned the architect to remodel his own New York apartment in 1930.[5] As an influential curator and critic, Johnson had a hand in shaping American ideas about contemporary design, publicizing and promoting work by European architects who conformed to a hard-edged, elegant, modern style. His own Glass House in New Canaan emulated Mies's Farnsworth House and served as a commentary on it. Although the Glass House was finished a year before Mies's project was completed, it was universally viewed as having been derived from it; a model of the Farnsworth House was shown at The Museum of Modern Art in 1947 as part of an exhibition of Mies's work that Johnson curated, and his Glass House incorporated many of its most innovative features. Johnson reinforced this patrilineal connection by describing his debt to Mies in a widely read article published in the *Architectural Review* in 1950.

Nevertheless, close examination of the two projects reveals the profound differences between them. Despite Johnson's debt to Mies, his Glass House is in many ways less rigid than the Farnsworth House, more picturesque in its siting, more decorative in its details, and more open to the landscape around it. Moreover, paired with the windowless brick Guest House (which stands opposite the Glass House but is often overlooked in discussions of the project), the Glass House calls attention to the complexity of the domestic program, especially to issues of sexuality and privacy, raising questions about how a glass-walled, modern building can be a usable home and not simply an architectural object in an ideal landscape. The dialogue between the Farnsworth House and the Glass House is especially resonant because of the way in which Johnson framed his architectural argument, quoting Mies directly and incorporating elements of vernacular architecture and popular culture in subtle yet significant ways.

As an architect and as a patron and connoisseur, Johnson knew as much about the meaning of style in architecture as any critic or designer in America. Because he is also gay, and because he seems to have drawn on "camp" gay culture in his use of ironic quotations and popular motifs in this design, the Glass House/Guest House complex raises further questions about how modern architecture in its various forms accommodated and challenged values in 1950s America. Moreover, as a weekend retreat designed and built not for a single woman but for a gay man, the project reminds us of the fundamental points this book intends to make: that many of the most original ideas in the domestic architecture of this century were forged in a crucible of contested values about gender and sexuality, and that what heated up the mixture, so to speak, making the transformation from old to new modes of thinking possible, was the realization that conventional building types and patterns of domestic planning were inadequate responses to the needs, both programmatic and ideological, of atypical clients. Since the conventions of domestic planning are as closely linked with heterosexual norms as they are with prevailing gender values, it is hardly surprising that we find some of the same incentives and opportunities for originality in a project for a gay man whose aim was in some ways autobiographical as we do in projects for female heads of households who were seeking to represent their alternative modes of living. Thus the comparison between the Farnsworth House and Philip Johnson's Glass House/Guest House complex not only sheds light on Mies's architecture, it also highlights the fundamental connection between originality in design and radical challenges to prevailing categories of normalcy and difference.

FIGURE 1

Ludwig Mies van der Rohe at
the Farnsworth House. ca. 1950

The Farnsworth House

According to her unpublished memoirs, which she wrote while living in Italy in the 1970s, Farnsworth first met Mies (fig. 1) in Chicago in November 1945, at a dinner party at the home of mutual friends.[6] She was forty-two years old, single, and a successful nephrologist at a large Chicago hospital; Mies, fifty-nine, was separated from his wife and three grown daughters in Germany, a former director of the famous Bauhaus, and much admired within the field of architecture, yet virtually unknown beyond the art world and the academy. Mies was head of the Department of Architecture at the Armour Institute of Technology (later renamed the Illinois Institute of Technology), a position he had held since his arrival in the U.S. in 1938, but aside from some buildings on the campus of IIT, he had built nothing in this country. He was a man of great charm and charisma, and Edith, according to her memoirs, was painfully lonely, bored, and overworked. At dinner she mentioned that she was thinking of building a weekend house outside Chicago, and she wondered whether someone in his office might design it; Mies replied that he "would love to build any kind of house" for her himself.[7] Thus each of them found the thing they believed they needed most: the architect now had an American client; the doctor, a friend who would help her create a retreat in which to escape the loneliness of weekends in the city.[8] The two immediately planned a trip to Plano to look at the site she had acquired some months before. Thinking back on that night, Farnsworth remembered her excitement: "The effect," she wrote, "was tremendous, like a storm, a flood or other act of God."[9]

The experience of being a single, professional woman in the Midwest in the late 1940s played a critical role in Farnsworth's decision to build a custom-designed weekend house, and it colors the entire history of the project. A wide range of sources, from women's magazines to popular novels and private diaries, celebrated marriage and home ownership in 1940s America, establishing them as virtually unchallenged prerequisites for success and social acceptance. From 1944 on, for example, mortgage programs administered by the Federal Housing Administration favored returning veterans in making loans, thus promoting the ideal of suburban family life.[10] Women were encouraged to embrace motherhood and homemaking in newly built single-family homes: books like Benjamin Spock's *Common Sense Book of Baby and Child Care* (1946) suggested that good mothers would be attentive to the "natural" rhythms of a child's experience, rejecting rigid rules and feeding schedules – which effectively made motherhood a full-time occupation. Suburban houses, with their playrooms, TVs, backyards, and picture windows, were intended not simply as retreats from the city and its "old-fashioned" ways (including jobs for women) but as havens for children and the young families whose activities increasingly focused on their needs.[11]

For anyone outside the network of family life as it was then narrowly defined, the opportunities for either casual or formal social relations were severely curtailed. According to one survey, conducted in 1957 and published under the title *Americans View Their Mental Health*, childless people, particularly women, were viewed with compassionate condescension "as people who have missed the full richness of adult experiences." Moreover, in the popular imagination, single men and women were regarded with suspicion and could be subject to accusations of mental instability or homosexuality. The unmarried woman was seen as a "frustrated old maid" who had "failed so seriously in her understanding of a woman's role that she hadn't even established the marriage prerequisite of having a home." As such, she forfeited her place, both physical and symbolic, within American society, despite her not infrequent role as doting aunt or beloved eccentric, the latter being the role Edith Farnsworth played in her own family.[12]

Given these prejudices, it is not surprising to read Farnsworth's recollections of the unhappy period in which she decided to build her house, a period of "tired, dull Sundays" when she would have nothing else to do but stretch out on the sofa and listen to the New York Philharmonic on the radio. A similar story is told in another unpublished autobiography, written in about 1959 by Anne Parsons, the unmarried daughter of Harvard sociologist Talcott Parsons, who complained of the loneliness of living as a single person in America: "Life for the unmarried person after twenty five or so is simply not very easy because by this fact one is thrown out of all the better-worn social grooves so that even relatively simple things as what to do on Sunday become impossibly difficult." In a letter to Betty Friedan, the author of *The Feminine Mystique*, Parsons wrote that for mainstream America the single woman was like "some sort of poison in the social system [that] has to be cast out," and pointed in particular to the "long spaces between [her] apartment and the suburban houses where [she] occasionally got invited for dinner to hear about the local school system."[13]

Recognizing the fusion of the terms "family" and "home," Farnsworth approached the design of her own house as a typological problem, as a scientist would attack the morphology of an organism or disease. Having found a site by the Fox River some fifty miles west of the city, she began leafing through books and bulletins on modern architecture that she discovered on the "shelves of bookstores and the coffee tables of [her] friends." She marveled that she:

had been so slow to take an interest in architectural forms and purposes. The interest once found, the erection of even a small house in an out-of-the-way spot began to seem an action calling for a certain sense of responsibility. As in every other situation, there must be a really fine solution

*for an inexpensive weekend retreat for a single person of my
tastes and pre-occupations and, conversely, it would
be unbearably stupid to "put up" some contractor's cottage
which could only ruin the site and remain as a token of
empirical mediocrity.*[14]

Two key themes circulate throughout Farnsworth's
narrative: uncertainty about the contradiction between
family life and singleness, and concern with cultural
values, particularly the choice between taste and "mediocrity." These issues would resurface throughout the
project, structuring Farnsworth's experience as she was
to represent it in interviews and in her writings, and
shaping critical reaction in the professional and the popular press. Because they also loomed large on the
broader American scene, fueled by the growth of suburban consumer culture and contact with European art
and architecture, the Farnsworth House would become
an emotional *cause célèbre* invested with meaning that
went far beyond matters of architectural design.
Although the principal players in this drama – Ludwig
Mies van der Rohe, Edith Farnsworth, and the weekend
house in Plano, Illinois – were in every respect atypical
of the categories they were supposed to represent, they
became the focus of an intense debate, hashed out in
newspapers and magazines, about American domesticity, sexuality, and the politics of modern architecture.

Long before she met Mies, Farnsworth had revealed
an interest in the arts and an affinity for European culture.
Born in 1903, she attended classes in English literature
and composition at the University of Chicago in the early
1920s, but she focused her attention on the violin and
traveled to Rome for further study.[15] In 1927 Farnsworth
returned to America, although she made numerous trips
to Europe until the outbreak of the war. She took her
medical degree at Northwestern University in 1939 and
built a successful practice in Chicago. Her interest in
architecture came relatively late, given her broad travel

experience, but once awakened, it developed quickly.
Returning from that first evening with Mies at the home
of her friends, Farnsworth consulted her books and found
illustrations of the Barcelona Pavilion and Tugendhat
House. Her perception of his work was astute: "I searched
the sundry texts which lay about the apartment, and saw
in them an architect whose austerity had kept him from
popularity and whose manner was determined by his
insight."[16] Although these texts (which probably included
some of the publications of The Museum of Modern
Art) said very little about the work aside from comment-
ing on the unusually luxurious materials, Farnsworth
recognized in Mies's most important European projects
both his minimalism and his single-mindedness in exploring the discipline of architectural design. Farnsworth,
like everyone else, seems to have been unclear about
what his "insight" may have been – the characteristically
laconic Mies said little about it – but she was intrigued
by what she read and heard. She was also pleased with
Mies's enthusiasm for her project.

The visit to the site in Plano (fig. 2), which Mies
agreed was beautiful, was the first of many "Sunday excursions" they would take over the course of the next two
years; sometimes the two were accompanied by "the boys"
from Mies's office or by others. Mies and Farnsworth also
began to socialize together in the city, and she frequently
stopped by the office and even cooked dinners for the
young associates in the practice. For Farnsworth the
office became "a club-room, a sanctuary and a kibbutz."[17]

Although it was widely assumed that the two were
romantically involved, there is nothing in Farnsworth's
memoirs to support that contention. Throughout her
life she developed strong attachments to the powerful
men she admired – to her teachers and supervisors at the
hospital, to Mies himself, and, late in her life, to the poet
Eugenio Montale, whose work she translated – but her

closest relationships seem to have been with women.[18] Nevertheless, it is clear that for Farnsworth, a headstrong, proud, and rather snobbish person, the friendship with Mies represented a profound emotional and intellectual connection. She immersed herself in Mies's world, struggling through the writings of philosophers who were important to him. She read the work of the Catholic theologian Romano Guardini in order, as she put it, to "lend [her]self to the concept of liturgy," a subject of concern to Mies as it affected architecture. In her enthusiasm, she recalled, she would read "anything which might enrich [her] own awareness, presumably by showing [her] how Mies had been enriched."[19]

FIGURE 2
The Fox River, view from the Farnsworth House

Thus Farnsworth became a "disciple," and when, in 1947, the model of her house (fig. 3) was exhibited at The Museum of Modern Art, she felt proud of the project and of her role in it: "It was the pivotal point of the exhibit, and I was happy as I boarded the train back to Chicago, reflecting that our project might well become the prototype of new and important elements of American architecture."[20] Although she was no doubt unaware of it, Farnsworth had by this point made a critical transition from client to patron in the minds of her architect and his supporters, unconsciously blurring the boundaries between her own self-interest in the house and her enthusiasm for the larger intellectual and artistic implications of the project. At the same time that Farnsworth was allowing an unusually long time to elapse in the design development phase and was taking part in the emotional life of the office, she was permitting financial, programmatic, and scheduling questions to slide – a dangerous condition in any architectural project but one that was particularly grievous for a client of Mies, for whom theoretical and formal considerations always came before practical ones. Moreover, Farnsworth seemed to have trusted what she saw in presentations like the model for her house – which was at best a sketch of the overall form and not only showed the glass walls as opaque, but gave no indication at all of how the interior would be configured – and never insisted on an explanation of the details. Her failure to understand fully how the plans and models might translate into built form and space would come back to haunt her.

The house as built (plates 2, 3; fig. 4), with its open plan, glass walls, and freestanding partitions, was as pure an exercise in architectural minimalism as Mies could have hoped for; he would later cite the fact that it was intended for a single person as a significant opportunity because programmatic demands intruded so little on his

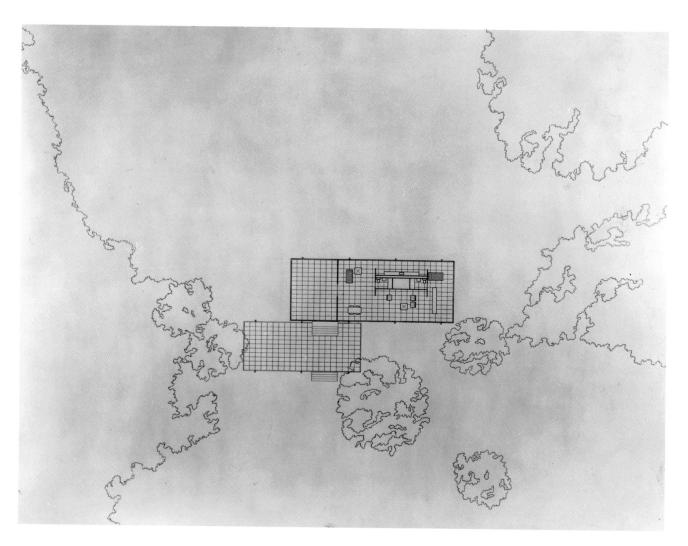

Farnsworth / Mies van der Rohe

PLATE 3

Farnsworth House, living room.
ca. 1987

PLATE 2

Farnsworth House, entrance

thinking.[21] As Fritz Neumeyer has shown, Mies's work was shaped by philosophical principles, in particular a search for architectural order and truth based on a rational approach to design. His goal was to develop a language of form that reflected universal, rather than particular, aspects of human activity and concern.[22] Principles of design and form, rather than programmatic or even typological concerns, always came first. Thus, while Farnsworth may have been, for Mies, an entertaining companion and a committed partisan, as a client she represented a means to an architectural end. Just as the Barcelona Pavilion, designed for no other function than to provide the king and queen of Spain with a place in which to sign a guestbook, receive visitors, and drink champagne, was the perfect vehicle for Mies's thinking in 1929, so the Farnsworth House was to be a pure expression of architectural ideas developed in his later career.

In his inaugural speech as director of the Department of Architecture at Armour Institute on November 20, 1938, Mies made his views on architecture clear in his typically terse, aphoristic manner:

The long path from material through purpose to creative
    work had only a single goal:
to create order out of the godforsaken confusion of our time.
But we want an order that gives to each thing its proper
    place, and we want to give each thing what is suitable
    to its nature.
We would do this so perfectly that the world of our creations
    will blossom from within.
More we do not want; more we cannot do.
Nothing can unlock the aim and meaning of our work
    better than the profound words of St. Augustine:
"Beauty is the radiance of truth."[23]

Beauty was produced by analyzing and recapitulating the structure of the natural order. At the riverbank site in Plano, the immediacy of nature would permit an unprecedented closeness with the work of architecture. Mies was quite clear about this. Farnsworth recalled

that on one occasion, as the two of them stood by the Fox River on one of their Sunday visits, she asked what sort of materials he was thinking of using for her house. He replied that he would not approach the problem in that way:

I would think that here where everything is beautiful, and privacy is no issue, it would be a pity to erect an opaque wall between the outside and the inside. So I think we should build the house of steel and glass; in that way we'll let the outside in. If we were building in the city or in the suburbs, on the other hand, I would make it opaque from outside and bring in the light through a garden-courtyard in the middle.[24]

This statement, with its emphasis on the view of natural beauty from inside the house, reveals an approach that was new to Mies and peculiar to his work in America. As in the project for the Resor House (1938), in Jackson Hole, Wyoming, which Mies represented with a photomontage showing a view of the Rocky Mountains through the living room windows, Mies's thinking for the Farnsworth House rested on a concept of uninhabited open landscape; the issue of privacy, and the possibility of being seen from outside, were not considered as problems. In European projects of the late 1920s and 1930s, by contrast, Mies explored the relationship between the glass curtain wall and the courtyard plan, most significantly in the Nolde House (1929), the house at the Berlin Building Exposition (1931), the Gericke House (1932), and the Hubbe House (1935; fig. 5).[25] Mies's approach to the Hubbe House is particularly revealing since it was to be occupied by a single woman. His concern for the client's privacy in the Hubbe House offers a striking contrast with his attitude toward the Farnsworth project: "Although living alone in the house [the client] wanted to cultivate a relaxed social life and hospitality. This also is reflected by the interior arrangement. Here also, the required privacy combined with the freedom of open room forms."[26]

The Farnsworth House represented a radical departure from this view of the domestic environment. Concerns about privacy, or about sexuality and social life, were repressed; for Mies, the house was a place for contemplation, an ordered space free of distractions. Speaking to an interviewer in 1959, he said that he felt the house had been misunderstood: "I was in the house from morning to evening. I did not know how colourful nature really was. But you have to be careful inside to use neutral colours, because you have the colours outside. These absolutely change and I would say it is beautiful."[27] In conversation with Christian Norberg-Schulz in 1958 Mies extended his argument further:

Nature, too, shall have its own life. We must beware not to disrupt it with the color of our houses and interior fittings. Yet we should attempt to bring nature, houses and human beings together into a higher unity. If you view nature through the glass walls of the Farnsworth House, it gains a more profound significance than if viewed from outside. This way more is said about nature – it becomes a part of the larger whole.[28]

FIGURE 5

Ludwig Mies van der Rohe. Hubbe House (project), Magdeburg, perspective of court seen from living room terrace. 1935. Mies van der Rohe Archive, The Museum of Modern Art, New York. Gift of the architect

By the late 1940s Mies believed in his architecture's ability not only to transcend nature but also to provide a framework for interpretation, a screen through which to look and understand. If Edith Farnsworth agreed in principle – or hoped she did, in the early days – it is clear that for her a great deal was lost in the translation from the model to the house in which she was supposed to live.

Relations between Mies and Farnsworth had begun to cool by the time construction was started in the summer of 1949: the two socialized together less, and Edith spent less time at the office. The reasons for this change remain unclear, but the situation deteriorated further as problems with the building became evident. When Farnsworth moved in, in December 1950, the roof leaked badly and the heating produced a film that collected on the inside of the windows. A local plumber, seeing that the systems were all gathered together in one inaccessible stack, suggested the house be named "My Mies-conception." The electrician advised that the wiring be completely redone. Nevertheless, according to Mies's office notes, the two were "still on good terms in February 1951."[29]

The final rupture was precipitated by disagreements over money.[30] With costs mounting to almost twice the original estimate of $40,000 (already a high figure considering that a house in a suburban development such as Levittown could be bought in 1950 for less than one quarter of that price) and under pressure from family and friends, Farnsworth began to voice some of her concerns about the unconventional design and construction methods used in her house. Mies reportedly told her "to stick to her nephritis."[31] To add insult to injury, he also seems to have decided at this point to charge a fee for his services, something that Farnsworth claimed had never been discussed; this demand was especially galling as Farnsworth had acted as his physician without fee.[32]

Having spent nearly $74,000, Farnsworth refused to pay any more bills or to take delivery of the furniture,

designed by Mies, that he had intended to place in the house. By the spring of 1951 she and Mies had stopped speaking altogether. Fearing that Mies never really wanted "a friend and a collaborator…but a dupe and a victim," Farnsworth wrote a letter dated March 1, 1951, in which she informed him that she was turning the matter over to her lawyer. In July, Mies sued for the outstanding balance of $3,673.09. He also claimed he was owed fees of $15,000 and $12,000 for architect's and supervisory services. Farnsworth filed a counterclaim in October 1951, which accused him of fraud, alleging that he had falsely represented himself as "a skilled, proficient and experienced architect" and demanding the return of $33,872.10, the amount she had paid to date above the original estimate.[33] After a trial that dragged on until June 1953, Mies was awarded $14,000; Farnsworth's lawyers appealed, and the matter was finally settled out of court on May 11, 1956, with Farnsworth paying a far smaller sum.

The most important battle, however, was not fought in the courtroom, but in the press. Once the case was brought to the attention of the public, the architect and his costly building were treated with incredulity and derision. Farnsworth too was ridiculed. To her horror, crowds of people came on weekends to look at the house "reputed to be the only one of its kind" but in reality "a one-room, one-story structure with flat roof and glass and steel outer walls."[34] She wrote that she found it "hard to bear the insolence and boorishness of those who invaded the solitude of [her] shore and [her] home…flowers brought in to heal the scars of the building were crushed by those boots beneath the noses pressed against the glass."[35]

Disdainful of the public yet furious at Mies, Farnsworth made statements in the press that fueled curiosity and provided antimodernist journalists with the ammunition they needed. In an article by Elizabeth Gordon entitled "The Threat to the Next America," published in *House Beautiful* in April 1953, the author used

Farnsworth's case as a starting point for a far-reaching denunciation of modernism:

I have talked to a highly intelligent, now disillusioned woman who spent more than $70,000 building a 1-room house that is nothing but a glass cage on stilts.... There is a well-established movement in modern architecture, decorating and furnishings which is promoting the mystical idea that "less is more"... they are promoting unlivability, stripped-down emptiness, lack of storage space and therefore lack of possessions.

Gordon pointed to "a self-chosen elite who are trying to tell us what we should like and how we should live." For her, such architectural totalitarianism and the denial of American consumerism paved the way for fascism; the threat was especially menacing because the architect in question was German:

For if we can be sold on accepting dictators in matters of taste and how our homes are to be ordered, our minds are certainly well prepared to accept dictators in other departments of life. The undermining of people's confidence is the beginning of the end....

So, you see, this well-developed movement has social implications because it affects the heart of our society – the home. Beyond the nonsense of trying to make us want to give up our technical aids and conveniences for what is supposed to be a better and more serene life, there is a social threat of regimentation and total control.

Does it work? The much touted all-glass cube of International Style architecture is perhaps the most unlivable type of home for man since he descended from the tree and entered a cave. You burn up in the summer and freeze in the winter, because nothing must interfere with the "pure" form of their rectangles – no overhanging roofs to shade you from the sun; the bare minimum of gadgets and possessions so as not to spoil the "clean" look; three or four pieces of furniture placed along arbitrary pre-ordained lines; room for only a few books and one painting at precise and

permanent points; no children, no dogs, extremely meager kitchen facilities – nothing human that might disturb the architect's composition.[36]

The following month another author, Joseph A. Barry, weighed in in the same magazine with his "Report on the American Battle Between Good and Bad Modern Houses." Again Farnsworth played the role of outraged antimodernist. Citing the many rave reviews of the house in such journals as *Architectural Forum* and *House and Garden*, Barry asked, "How about Dr. Farnsworth herself on the subject of her house?":

"Do I feel implacable calm?" she repeated. "The truth is that in this house with its four walls of glass I feel like a prowling animal, always on the alert. I am always restless. Even in the evening. I feel like a sentinel on guard day and night. I can rarely stretch out and relax....

"What else? I don't keep a garbage can under my sink. Do you know why? Because you can see the whole 'kitchen' from the road on the way in here and the can would spoil the appearance of the whole house. So I hide it in the closet farther down from the sink. Mies talks about 'free space': but his space is very fixed. I can't even put a clothes hanger in my house without considering how it affects everything from the outside. Any arrangement of furniture becomes a major problem, because the house is transparent, like an X-ray."[37]

While it is unlikely that these concerns were as grievous as Farnsworth made them sound in the thick of combat with Mies – she did, after all, remain in the house for twenty years – they nonetheless contain critical indices for the meaning of the building in its time and place. Concerns over family, gender, and the control of appearances, particularly in the domestic environment, loom large. Much of what was said against the house and modern architecture generally focuses on its departure from the traditions of the American home, and the vulnerability of its occupant to the prying eyes of others. Farnsworth complained more than once, in

her memoirs and to the press, about the problem of
being looked at by people both inside and outside her
home. In an interview published by *Newsweek* she complained that Mies had wanted to build the interior
partitions 5 feet high "for reasons of art and proportion"
but that she had objected: "I'm six feet tall," she said,
"and I wanted to be able to change my clothes without
my head looking like it was wandering over the top of
the partition without a body."[38]

The way the house foregrounded Farnsworth's single
life and her middle-aged woman's body struck at the
heart of American anxiety. As Lynn Spigel has shown, the
popularity of television in the U.S. in the 1950s stemmed
in part from American preoccupations with privacy,
consumerism, and family life. Through its ability to provide a close-up look at other people's lives and homes,
television filled a need to know and compare that was
fueled by the ever-present lure of the marketplace through
advertising. Moreover, television, like the picture window
itself, blurred the distinction between public and private
realms and problematized the very act of looking, particularly at women.[39] In this cultural climate Farnsworth's

FIGURE 7

"When Modesty Demands,"
advertisement from *House
Beautiful*, May 1953

FIGURE 6

"Pretty as a Picture," advertisement from *House Beautiful*,
May 1953

insecurities found a wide and attentive audience. Even the ads that appeared next to Barry's article in the May issue of *House Beautiful* (figs. 6, 7) harped on this theme, showing women as the guardians of home and interior privacy, displaying their clean, modern kitchens, which were as "pretty as a picture" thanks to modern ventilation systems, but drawing the Levolor venetian blinds "when modesty demands."

Gendered language pervades Farnsworth's own expression of her doubts about the workability of the house. She complained that it had two bathrooms, including one for guests, but no enclosed bedroom. In addition, guests were expected to sleep on the sofa or on a mattress on the floor. While Mies may have seen this arrangement as liberating, for Farnsworth, the real-life occupant of the house, it was embarrassing. She complained that she and her guests would "inhabit a sort of three-dimensional sketch, I in my 'sleeping space' and he in his – unless sheer discomfort and depression should drive us together."[40] In a house for a single woman, such an arrangement in fact represents a repressed (or negated) rather than a freed sexuality, just as the doubling of the bathrooms suggests a desire to modestly hide the female body and its functions. Despite pronouncements about freedom, Mies let it be known that the provision of a "guest bathroom" at the Farnsworth House was meant to keep visitors from "seeing Edith's nightgown on the back of the bathroom door."[41] Ultimately, this piece of women's clothing, this emblem of femaleness, sexuality, and the body, had to be hidden away precisely because it served as a reminder of the very things that Mies (and mainstream culture generally) wanted to deny.

The choice of furnishings also caused friction between architect and client, as it had in other modern projects (notably Le Corbusier's Villa Stein–de Monzie), and here again the conflict raised broader issues concerning domesticity and gender. Mies's theories about interior design are summarized by the poster for the Werkbund exhibition, *The Dwelling*, held in Stuttgart in 1927 (fig. 8): in response to the question "How to live?" (Wie wohnen?), a large red "x" has been drawn across an image of a Victorian interior. As a number of writers have suggested, this approach cut to the heart of consumer culture and seriously undermined the means by which bourgeois women constructed identity and memory in the late nineteenth and early twentieth centuries.[42] As a single woman, and as a member of the American upper class, Farnsworth took the threat to the heirlooms and personal mementos in her home very seriously, and she had strong feelings about what her house would say about her. She "could never consent to Mies's furnishing ideas," she wrote in her memoirs. Apparently Mies had planned to put pink suede Barcelona chairs in her house; these, she claimed, would not only be too heavy but would "make the house look like a Helena Rubenstein studio."[43] Besides, she commented, "There is already the local rumor that it's a tuberculosis sanitorium."[44] As snapshots taken in the 1950s (figs. 9, 10) show, her own ideas about furnishing the house favored heirloom antique chairs in the dining room and Fu dogs on the terrace, which to her mind suggested continuity and American tradition.

The severity of Mies's vision at the Farnsworth House is brought into sharp focus by comments made in 1931 by another of his clients, Grete Tugendhat, whose house in Brno is among Mies's most famous works. Replying to the question "Is it possible to live in the Tugendhat House?" she called the spaces of the house "austere and grand," and continued:

This austerity forbids merely passing time by "relaxing" and letting oneself go – and it is precisely this being forced to do something else that today's people, exhausted and drained by their professional work, require and sense as a liberation. For just as one sees each flower in this room in

Willi Baumeister. *Wie Wohnen?
Die Wohnung Werkbund
Ausstellung* (How to Live? The
Dwelling Werkbund Exhibition).
1927. Offset lithograph printed
in color, 44¾ x 32⅝ in. The
Museum of Modern Art, New
York. Gift of Philip Johnson

*quite an uncommon way, and every piece of art seems
more expressive (for example, a piece of sculpture standing
in front of the onyx wall), so too a person appears, both
to himself and to others, to be more clearly set off from his
surroundings.*[45]

Two points in this statement stand out. First, in the
Tugendhat House, as in other houses by Mies, rich
materials, colors, and works of sculpture play a defining
role in the interior scheme in a way that is denied in
the Farnsworth House; in Mies's idea of the Farnsworth
House, the occupant, a surrogate for Mies himself, would
focus on architecture and nature, not on objects in the
home. Second, the experience of being "set off" from
one's surroundings by an architectural stage was, at the
Farnsworth House, inescapable; this was precisely what
Farnsworth so resented. At the Tugendhat House, the
rule of order was not so rigidly enforced or the gaze of
the outsider so unrelenting. In Mies's view, it seems,
Farnsworth had very little of a "private life" to conceal: as
a single woman, the only thing that could possibly be
worth hiding was her nightgown, the sign for her body.

It is well worth asking, by way of conclusion, how
Farnsworth could possibly have been as offended and
shocked by her house as she professed to be, given her
frequent visits to Mies's studio and close association with
the project over the five or six years of design development. Having seen the model and the plans, Farnsworth
ought to have known better. She could see that the house
was going to have glass walls, so why was she so surprised when they finally appeared? The obviousness of
the question pushes us to look further for answers, for,
of course, the essence of Mies's design, and of Farnsworth's
objections to it, ultimately lie less with the exterior walls
than with the severity of the interior. The latter is something Farnsworth could have known little about from the
model, and even if she knew the drawings well, she would
hardly have recognized – as, indeed, very few critics have –

FIGURE 9

Farnsworth House, living area
and entrance. ca. 1955

FIGURE 10

Farnsworth House. ca. 1955

how the subtleties of interior planning and furnishing
profoundly alter the experience of the house. Mies's rigid
axial planning, evident in the rectilinear arrangement of
the freestanding core and minimalist furniture, is what
gives the house its discipline and creates the effect of a
domestic theater – in which Farnsworth became an isolated object of scrutiny, a moving figure in a landscape of
immovable forms. Unlike Johnson's Glass House, which
features clusters of large and small objects throughout
the interior and doorways on all four walls, the interior
of the Farnsworth House is unrelenting in its ordered
geometry – and this was something Farnsworth discovered only through living in the house over time.

In the end Farnsworth gave up the struggle, but she
fought a good fight. She spent twenty years in her glass
house, furnishing it with her family heirlooms, working
to make it a home; in spite of her complaints, she was no
doubt aware of the fact that the house was widely recognized as one of the masterpieces of modern architecture,
not only in the United States but in the world. She bat-
tled Mies in court and in the press, and she managed to
win support for her position. Yet having sold the house
(to a Mies enthusiast who filled it with furniture designed
by the architect) and moved to Italy in the early 1970s,
she looked back on the whole experience with bitterness.
She had been for too long the focus of other people's
curiosity, too long a nonconformist. Now she wanted
nothing more than to become invisible: "I would prefer
to move as the women do in the Old Quarter of Tripoli,
muffled in unbleached homespun so that only a hole is
left for them to look out of." Best of all, she said, the world
outside would "not even know where the hole was."[46]

PLATE 4
Philip Johnson. Glass House,
New Canaan, Connecticut. 1949

Philip Johnson's Glass House/Guest House as "Gay Space"

In a 1993 interview Philip Johnson (then age eighty-seven)
was asked to respond to the suggestion that there were
some people who had interpreted his Glass House, in New
Canaan, Connecticut (plate 4; fig. 11), as "a form of exhibitionism." He replied:

*Yes, needless to say a great number of them have said that.
In fact, they went so far as publishing in a magazine, "People
that live in glass houses should ball in the basement." But I
don't have a basement, so I don't ball in the basement. But
much more important than exhibitionism is the interface
of architecture and the desire for all kinds of sexual experiments. Whether you want to close yourself in is Freudian in
one way, but exposing yourself is Freudian in another way.*

*As a good Puritan Unitarian, it did not come to mind,
but there are other ways of having it come to mind. I mean
the idea of a glass house, where somebody just might be
looking – naturally, you don't want them to be looking. But
what about it? That little edge of danger in being caught....*[47]

Although this statement was made more than forty
years after the Glass House was completed, it serves as
an appropriate starting point for a comparison between
Johnson's house in New Canaan and Mies's Farnsworth
House, the building that was its acknowledged source and
inspiration. Johnson's provocative comments immediately
highlight the differences between his and Farnsworth's
experiences as occupants of their houses, raising a wide
range of questions about how each of the houses responds
to issues of gender, household structure, and the roles
of the architect and client. Surprisingly, given the enormous fame of both buildings and the volume of critical
writing that has been produced – including a 1993 anthol-
ogy of texts entitled *Philip Johnson: The Glass House*,
edited by David Whitney and Jeffrey Kipnis – very little
has been said about how each of the two houses confronts
and interprets questions of sexuality or about how each

represents and accommodates domesticity. Yet it is precisely the way in which each house responds to these
concerns that gives it its particular character as a work
of domestic architecture.

Perhaps the repression of these questions in the
critical and historical literature is not so surprising after
all. Farnsworth was a single woman; Philip Johnson is gay.
The fact was well known to his friends and, indeed, to
the broad circle of colleagues and critics he knew through
The Museum of Modern Art, the New York art scene,
and the East Coast architecture schools.[48] But, true to the
taboos of the time, Johnson's gayness was never openly
acknowledged, let alone publicly discussed in connection
with his life and work. When he came out in a number
of published magazine interviews in the early 1990s, his
frankness in disclosing his sexual orientation was considered newsworthy because he was, and is, a powerful
public figure and because an admission of this sort is so
rare among men or women of his class and status (of
whatever age) and still considered compromising.[49] The
subject simply wasn't discussed. The notion that sexual
orientation might be relevant to Johnson's work – even to
a design as intimate at that of his own home – was com-

pletely suppressed. Moreover, for most architecture critics, this suppression hardly presented a problem, given the formalist preoccupations that continue to dominate the field. Johnson's New Canaan project, like Mies's house for Edith Farnsworth, was about architectural design. That was all.

In a 1950 article in the *Architectural Review*, Johnson himself established the direction for critical appraisal of his house by offering up, in his most polished art-historical manner, a systematic listing of the sources in the history of architecture and design from which he had drawn. He presented a list of twenty-two points, each accompanied by an illustration, which ostensibly provided a guide to the design process and thus to the house's meaning as a work of architecture. The *Review*'s editor added introductory comments that express his gratitude for this process of demystification: "Since the work is proclaimed by the architect as frankly derivative, in this publication of it and the adjacent guest building, Mr. Johnson has taken the unusual and, it should be granted, praiseworthy expedient of revealing the sources of his inspiration. These are presented in consecutive order and precede the illustrations of the two houses."[50] Johnson dutifully ran through the first ten points, which included such exalted and obscure examples as Le Corbusier's Farm Village plan of 1933, Mies's site plan for the Illinois Institute of Technology, the plan and perspective of the Acropolis from Choisy's *L'Histoire de l'art grec* (to illustrate the oblique approach), the front and rear facades of Schinkel's casino near Potsdam (to illustrate siting), Ledoux's design for a spherical guard-house at Maupertuis (an example of "absolute" form), and Malevich's *Suprematist Element: Circle – 1913,* which, Johnson noted, is "obviously the inspiration for the plan of the Glass House."

A photograph of the model of the Farnsworth House from the 1947 Museum of Modern Art exhibition of Mies's work is presented as point number 8. Here Johnson included the following caption:

The idea of a glass house comes from Mies van der Rohe. Mies has mentioned to me as early as 1945 how easy it would be to build a house entirely of large sheets of glass. I was sceptical at the time, and it was not until I had seen the sketches of the Farnsworth House that I started the three-year work of designing my glass house. My debt is therefore clear, in spite of obvious differences in composition and relation to the ground.[51]

The remaining points present the plans and views of the two houses, with commentary about Johnson's design and Mies's influence on his work.

Despite the apparent usefulness of Johnson's art-historical self-analysis, confidence in and gratitude for his so-called revelations seems entirely misplaced. Far from the "praiseworthy expedient" the *Review* editor welcomed, Johnson's description of his sources brings to mind another image: that of the wily fox leading a pack of hounds farther and farther off his scent – and ultimately popping up behind them, laughing with glee at their inability to catch him. Philip Johnson as designer, client, *and* critic all rolled into one? Johnson providing a checklist of sources and monuments with which his work could be decoded? The very notion suggests an element of parody (and self-parody), which published discussions of the Glass House and its sources have entirely missed.

Johnson's quick wit, erudition, and acerbic humor are by now quite legendary; in lectures, panel discussions, and interviews, he is always ready with the *bon mot* that will disconcert friends and foes alike – to the delight of his audiences. Honed by a lifetime of social and institutional maneuvering, his skills as a critic and conversationalist stem from the same fundamental talents that underlie his success as an architect: a gift for understanding and responding to the particular anxieties and preoccupations of a given audience at a specific time, and the quickness to keep one step ahead of them. These are not merely the facile charms of the polished, high-society socialite nor even the blandishments of the successful New York architect; on the contrary, Johnson deploys his wit defensively, and his parodic charm has the effect of disarming, and dazzling, those around him. Such "camp" devices and mannerisms – elegance, distance, outrageousness, trenchant humor, cunning, charm, parody, and above all a certain imperviousness to hurt – though largely unfamiliar to mainstream observers, are the stock in trade of the gay male culture in which he has moved throughout his life. Like other gay men, no matter what class they belonged to, Johnson had to learn to "pass" by wearing a mask in public, and he mastered the art of playing a role, assuming whatever protective coloration was appropriate for the context in which he found himself. He also had to confront the homophobia of straight friends and colleagues, as well as his own self-doubt in an era before gay liberation. One suspects that his camp humor and deftly wielded one-liners were useful weapons in the battle.[52] With consummate skill Johnson brought this bittersweet sensibility to the world of architecture and architectural criticism. Nowhere is this more evident than in his discussion of the Glass House/Guest House complex, where the sophisticated formalist genealogy presented in the *Architectural Review* serves as a mask that conceals as much about the architect's identity as the transparent walls of the house reveal. This is not to say that one or the other was Johnson's "true" self; on the contrary, what the New Canaan project makes clear are the multiplicity of personae Johnson and his gay contemporaries could assume and the overarching sense of humor that colored the entire process.

Johnson's use of irony and self-parody have not gone unnoticed, but this practice has been interpreted (in the few instances where anyone has taken the trouble to analyze it) as an indication of some deeper psychological conflict rather than as a strategy for dealing with homophobia. For example, in his 1978 introduction to *Philip Johnson: Writings*, Peter Eisenman focused on "the metaphor of glass" to analyze Johnson's elusive manner: *Johnson is at his most opaque when he is speaking of himself – the historian speaking of the architect, the critic reviewing his own book, the architect presenting his house. It is Johnson as a surrogate for Johnson.*

One finds the often repeated cadence, particularly in his presentations to university audiences, of Johnson taking off on Johnson, of Johnson being flippant at his own expense.... His words, seemingly casually chosen, are diabolical mirrors. Not only do they mask his intentions, they also strip and fracture his audience. They beam yet another multiple inversion. Words and audience: first, belief; second, irony and disbelief. So far this is obvious. It is the third mirror that is crucial. It penetrates beneath his own facade. It is his own attempt to make himself believe what he is saying – to suspend his own disbelief. For in this final turn, words attempt to cover the fragility of Johnson's own uncertainty about himself and his own art. Whether he can deceive us or not, he can never wholly deceive himself. He alone lives locked within the reality of his works – they reveal to him what his words attempt to hide.[53]

This metaphor serves as a foundation for Eisenman's analysis of the Glass House and of the architect himself. "Johnson is at his most transparent – the lucid ideologue," wrote Eisenman, "when speaking of his own house." Oddly enough, he then went on to praise Johnson's *Architectural Review* piece as "modest, straightforward and telling," calling it "the first instance in which Johnson talks seriously, without his usually self-deprecating irony." What follows comes as a surprise. In a passage that has become a much-quoted milestone in the critical response to the house, Eisenman suggested a personal rather than an architectural reading of the imagery of the Glass House. He began by quoting the caption for Johnson's illustration number 17, which showed the "Glass Unit at Night": "The cylinder, made of the same brick as the platform from which it springs, forming the main *motif* of the house was not derived from Mies, but rather from a burnt wooden village I saw once where nothing was left but foundations and chimneys of brick."[54] For Eisenman, this is a reference to Johnson's deep, psychological conflict over his well-known involvement with fascism during the Second World War: "How are we to interpret such a metaphor? Who builds a house as a metaphoric ruin? Why the burnt-out village as a symbol of one's own house? But further, that Johnson should reveal the source of his imagery seems the most telling of all: the Glass House is Johnson's own monument to the horrors of war. It is at once a ruin and also an ideal model of a more perfect society."[55] Thus Eisenman concluded that the house was an expression of Johnson's "personal atonement and rebirth as an individual."

The burnt-out village, the house as ruin, drained of gay content and severed from the company of its companion Guest House, Johnson's artistic metaphor at the Glass House seems to point to wartime tragedies. Johnson, with the memory of his pro-Nazi activities kept always in the foreground by critics and historians, seems content to accept this view, at least in public.[56] Yet if we restore Johnson's gay identity to the historical picture, and once again open up a space for gay culture within the heterosexist world of architecture, a completely different set of meanings emerges.

New Canaan in the late 1940s wasn't wartime Poland but suburban America, and the most obvious war there was a bitterly fought struggle over who was, and who was not, a "normal" American, a member of a family, living life in the "right" way. Just as Edith Farnsworth confronted these issues, so did Philip Johnson. Americans

were increasingly suspicious about the lives of single men and women, and it is clear from popular books and magazine articles about social behavior and family life that the pressure to conform to accepted norms was enormous.[57] Additionally, because of widely publicized negative attention by the federal government and by psychologists, attitudes toward homosexuality had become more fixed and narrow-minded. Efforts to ferret out "sexual perverts" in the U.S. government and in the armed forces (Johnson himself had briefly served as a private in the army, but his superiors seem to have been far more nervous about his right-wing politics than about his homosexuality) put gay men and lesbians at a new disadvantage by creating a climate of anxiety about sexuality, conformity, and loyalty – even among those not directly involved with the military.[58] According to George Chauncey, antigay sentiment – which had been gaining force since the early years of the century, particularly among middle-class men – was closely tied to a "growing concern that the gender arrangements of their culture were in crisis."[59] Changes in the structure of work and family life, the increasing visibility and power of women, and ambiguity about the definition of masculinity in an increasingly "feminized" society all contributed to a marked and growing antipathy toward gay people, which peaked in the 1950s; markers of nonconformity – such as effeminate behavior for men, masculine behavior for women, or anything about the ways in which people lived that looked unconventional – were subject to scrutiny.[60] Questions about surveillance and privacy, and heightened attention to codes of meaning in social behavior and in the material world of American postwar consumer culture helped produce a new awareness of the importance of being, and appearing, "normal."

Gay men and lesbians coped with this repressive situation in a multiplicity of ways. They developed a rich "underground" culture of their own, with a separate system of language, dress, and behavior, which main-stream American society knew little about. For gay men in particular, camp behavior, attitudes, and objects – with a heavy emphasis on irony, exaggeration, artifice, and of course humor – provided a way to live a separate and safe existence within heterosexual culture and afforded much-needed distance and protection from hostility.[61] Moreover, camp was not only theatrical in itself but cast doubt on the whole weighty, self-sustaining system of gender roles, social norms, and conventional appearances. As Jack Babuscio put it in an essay entitled "Camp and Gay Sensibility":

To appreciate camp in things or persons is to perceive the notion of life-as-theater, being versus role playing, reality and appearance. If "role" is defined as the appropriate behavior associated with a given position in society then gays do not conform to socially expected ways of behaving as men and women. Camp, by focusing on the outward appearances of role, implies that roles and, in particular, sex roles, are superficial – a matter of style. Indeed, life itself is role and theater, appearance and personification.[62]

Johnson's Glass House must be understood within the context of this sophisticated manipulation of culture and language. The house appeared to be a fishbowl in which his life was put on display for all to see, but it actually raised more questions than it answered, focusing attention on the very theatricality of its own form and of the life that was lived within its transparent glass walls. Rather than actually enabling outsiders to satisfy their curiosity about what went on inside (as the Farnsworth House did), the Glass House screened, distorted, and overtly denied visual access through the landscaping of the hilly site and by a series of architectural devices, especially the long, tree-lined driveway that leads to the house from the main road and entrance gate (fig. 12). This handling contributed to the irony of transparency

and to a more acute representation of the double-sided nature of domestic life, particularly for gay men who were compelled to hide their private lives from outsiders.

Paired with the solid block of the Guest House (fig. 13), which faces it, the Glass House becomes more meaningful. Linked by a paved pathway, which forms a diagonal axis between the two rectangles, the open and closed spaces of the two houses become an essay on the overt and hidden sides of domestic life. The Guest House appears to be a windowless bunker, a defensible space of intimacy as well as a "closet" containing the unseen apparel of a gay man's life. Like the nondescript gay bars of the period, it turns its back on its surroundings, "passing" behind its blank walls in a way that is diametrically opposed to the celebratory transparency of the Glass House.

For Johnson, who unlike Farnsworth had a sophisticated grasp of architectural language, there was no question that each element in the design had a carefully constructed meaning. Thus, the cylindrical brick chimney at the core of the Glass House (fig. 14) makes an obvious and clearly ironic reference to the architecture of the traditional American family home and to the sentimentalized view of domesticity that had gained widespread currency since the late nineteenth century. Rather than invoke the image of wartime Poland, this freestanding chimney seems to refer to the tragedies of the domestic battlefield inhabited by the American family of the late 1940s, and to Johnson's outsider's view of that way of life. The fact that the house was a comfortable weekend retreat where Johnson entertained gay friends from New York at elegant cocktail parties and dinners only served to reinforce this sense of remove.[63] Moreover, with his deep understanding of the work of Frank Lloyd Wright – in a 1949 article entitled "The Frontiersman," Johnson called him "the greatest living architect" – Johnson produced a highly pictorial, American commentary on family and tradition, hearth and shelter that is about as

FIGURE 12

Philip Johnson. Philip Johnson estate, New Canaan, Connecticut, site plan showing the Glass House/Guest House and later buildings

FIGURE 13

Philip Johnson. Guest House, with the Glass House at left, New Canaan, Connecticut. 1949. Photograph by Ezra Stoller © ESTO

Farnsworth/Mies van der Rohe

153

far from Mies's world (and Wright's) as one can imagine.[64] While some people accused Johnson of "exhibitionism" because they felt that what they were seeing through the glass walls of the house was private life, it is quite clear that their inquiring looks were met instead with a theatrical parody of the very concepts of privacy and normalcy.

Further, by pairing the Glass House with the virtually windowless Guest House (described by Arthur Drexler in an early review of the house – in an unconsciously apt phrase – as the "neighboring block of closet-like rooms"[65]), Johnson acknowledged not only his own need for privacy but also the impossibility of the Glass House's serving as a family home. The brick Guest House represented an unequivocal drawing of the curtain and an emphatic rejection of all those prying eyes that had suddenly become so ubiquitous in American society.

FIGURE 14
Glass House, plan

House-Body/Home-Body

From here it is a long way back to the Farnsworth House. Even the most cursory glance at the plans of the two glass-walled houses immediately reveals how different they really are. The Farnsworth House, a glass box on stilts, is suspended above the ground, cut off from its surroundings and yet completely permeable to the gaze of outsiders. The service core has the effect of constricting and focusing the life of the occupant. The fireplace, kitchen, and bathrooms become signs for the most basic functions within the home, but there are no "signposts" for social spaces, beyond the furniture groupings, to guide movement from one moment or activity to the next. The house thus reads more like a diagram of life-sustaining bodily activities than as a social or relational environment. Mies's inspiration for this view of domestic life may have come from his reading of a series of lectures entitled *What Is Life?*, written by the physicist Erwin Schrödinger; in her memoirs Farnsworth noted that the book was important to Mies because of his "preoccupation with death."[66]

According to Schrödinger life in organisms is maintained by continually "extracting 'order' [or 'negative entropy'] from the environment" and thus delaying the slow process of "decay" into "maximum entropy," that is, death. The concluding summary of Schrödinger's lecture "Order, Disorder and Entropy," though complex and challenging, is worth quoting here:

Thus the device by which an organism maintains itself stationary at a fairly high level of orderliness (=fairly low level of entropy) really consists in continually sucking orderliness from its environment. This conclusion is less paradoxical than it appears at first sight. Rather could it be blamed for triviality. Indeed, in the case of higher animals we know the kind of orderliness they feed upon well enough, viz. the extremely well-ordered state of matter in more or less complicated organic compounds, which serve them as foodstuffs. After utilizing it they return it in a very much degraded form – not entirely degraded, however, for plants can still make use of it.[67]

Taking Schrödinger's view to its logical conclusion, the service core at the Farnsworth House becomes a diagram of the house as a machine for extracting order from the environment: the kitchen and the back-to-back bathrooms stand in a logical, utilitarian relationship to one another; the fact that the slender, black soil stack is the only atectonic connection between the glass box and the ground lends credibility to this view. Moreover, while the fireplace, which is itself used for extracting energy (in the form of heat) from "organic compounds," is bundled into the core, it too is purely functional and treated diagrammatically; its projection beyond the glass box as a chimney, and therefore its value as a symbolic or pictorial expression of the domestic, is completely suppressed.

Johnson's approach, on the other hand, is metaphoric, discursive, and picturesque. Changing views of the architectural "events" that form the domestic landscape – the cylindrical chimney/bathroom, the bedroom storage partition, the kitchen bar, the luxurious, white living room rug with its grouping of chairs, chaise longue, and table – encourage movement through the space. The surfaces are covered with carefully chosen objects of the sort that Mies would never have tolerated, such as flowers, an ashtray, and a small table sculpture by Johnson's friend Mary Callery; these items also function as episodes in an unfolding story. The low parapet, a sort of wainscot or chair rail of steel that encircles the house, not only establishes a human scale but serves as a reminder of the traditional New England vernacular. Doors on each of the four sides of the house help define interior "rooms" by providing access to outdoor spaces and changing vistas. As Kenneth Frampton noted in a 1978 article, "The Glass House Revisited," where Mies is "always tectonic, Johnson is invariably scenographic."[68] Compared to Mies's unrelenting discipline, the Glass House is almost frivolous. In effect, the architecture

begins to form a narrative on the subject of domesticity as interpreted by Johnson: elegant, precise, social, hospitable.

Johnson's Glass House was meant to be part of a complex of buildings that offered a choice of environments to Johnson and his many visitors. Unlike the Farnsworth House, in which the experience of seeing and concerns about domestic privacy were never resolved, Johnson's Glass House/Guest House accommodates both. Frampton described this double function:

The conceptual conflict between the belvedere and the court house was to be finally resolved by treating the whole bluff as a court house on a mini-acropolis, in which the trees surrounding the house serve as the perceptual limits of the domain. These limits are unambiguously established at night by floodlit trees, while during the day the domain is determined by the extent of the manicured lawn, the tapis vert *upon which the* open *and* closed *boxes are nothing but revealed chambers within a much larger conceptual but "invisible" domain of domesticity.*[69]

Each of the "chambers" in Johnson's domain served a different aspect of his life: the Glass House represented the public side of that life, the Guest House the hidden, private side.[70] Just as the processional route through the entire complex is carefully choreographed, so too are the interiors of both the Glass House and Guest House. The Guest House was originally quite simple, with two identical bedrooms flanking a sitting room; with its 1953 remodeling as a luxurious and seductive pleasure palace (figs. 15, 16), an exotic room within a room defined by tall, spindly arches and pink Fortuny fabric wall-coverings, it became a virtual celebration of queenly camp, about as close as any modern architect could come to Las Vegas–style, floor-show drag. Johnson himself pointed to John Soane as a source of his use of stepped arches and indirect lighting, but it seems evident that what is being suggested here has more to do with a camp reading of popular culture than with historical precedent.[71] That this decorative, arcuated mode within Johnson's oeuvre is sometimes referred to as "ballerina classicism" only serves to confirm the point. Unlike Mies, Johnson recognized that, for Americans at least, Architecture with a capital "A" would never triumph over individualism, nor would it have absolute authority to dictate the rhythms and choices of daily life.

Johnson was clear about the fact that his New Canaan complex was a highly personal essay about domesticity and architecture and not a realistic solution to the problem of the modern American family home. Speaking of his Wiley House, also in New Canaan (1953), a glass box set atop a low, stone base, Johnson commented that it was: *one more attempt to reconcile the (perhaps) irreconcilable. Modern architectural purity and the requirements of living American families. Why can't people learn to live in the windowless spheres of Ledoux or the pure glass prisms of Mies van der Rohe? No, they need a place for Junior to practice the piano while Mother plays bridge with her neighbors.... The Wiley House "solution" of putting private functions below...gives the architect great freedom. The client can design downstairs as he pleases.... The architect can design the pavilion above.*[72]

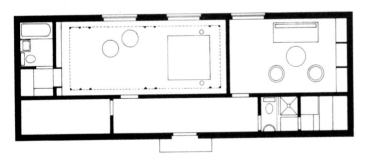

FIGURE 15
Guest House, plan, after the 1953 remodeling

While Johnson's Glass House was, in a sense, both a negation of and a memorial to the middle-class family home in which "Mother" and "Junior" go about their daily rounds, the Guest House was a celebration of the messy "private functions" of the domestic realm. By exaggerating the feminine, the sensual, the secret, and the decorative sides of architecture in the Guest House, Johnson not only created a foil to the International Style Glass House but also offered a further parody of the rigid sex roles so beloved by middle-class America. The Guest House, as remodeled in 1953, smacked of exactly the sort of vulgar, ultrafeminine salon decor that Farnsworth referred to when she made her comment about how Mies's pink Barcelona chairs reminded her of a Helena Rubenstein studio. Johnson and his gay friends recognized the Guest House as a camp stage set, remodeled, according to Johnson, because he "wanted to play."[73] While the architect in him may have designed the glass pavilion, it was the client (indeed, the gay client) who recognized and accommodated the program in the brick bunker.

Ultimately this is what distinguishes Johnson's New Canaan complex from Mies's Farnsworth House: the profound understanding of the fact that while the architect of a house can remain fully clothed at all times, the client must ultimately strip naked if the house is to become a home. Thanks to Johnson's gay sensibility, he also recognized that how, where, and when we dress and undress is as critical to architecture as the form of the buildings we inhabit. This knowledge may not make the house a better work of architecture as Mies or other professionals understood it, but it certainly made for a more successful project from the client's point of view. The Glass House/Guest House complex thus serves not only as a self-portrait of the architect and as a statement about the successes and failures of architecture, but also as a home for the client who had to live there – and happily continues to do so to this day.

FIGURE 16

Guest House, bedroom. 1953.

Photograph by Ezra Stoller ©

ESTO

1 Dirk Lohan, *Mies van der Rohe: Farnsworth House, Plano, Illinois, 1945–50* (Tokyo: Global Architecture, 1976), 4.

2 Edith Farnsworth, "Memoirs," unpublished ms. in three notebooks, Farnsworth Collection, Newberry Library, Chicago, ch. 11, unpag.

3 For an overview of Mies's career, see Franz Schulze, *Mies van der Rohe: A Critical Biography* (Chicago: University of Chicago Press, 1985), esp. chs. 4–6.

4 Farnsworth recalled, for example, that Mies "never showed [her] the trivial courtesies – or the greater ones." He never called a taxi for an "unescorted female visitor" but left her to "scurry through the dark streets however she saw fit." Farnsworth, "Memoirs," ch. 11.

5 Terence Riley, *The International Style: Exhibition 15 and the Museum of Modern Art* (New York: Rizzoli, 1992), 21–23.

6 Farnsworth, "Memoirs," ch. 3.

7 Ibid., ch. 11.

8 The suggestion in Schulze, *Mies*, 252, that Farnsworth chose Mies from a list of architects supplied by The Museum of Modern Art is based on the transcript of a June 1, 1973, interview with Myron Goldsmith, the project architect for the Farnsworth House, but it is contradicted by Farnsworth's own recollections.

9 Farnsworth, "Memoirs," ch. 11.

10 Gwendolyn Wright, *Building the Dream: A Social History of Housing in America* (Cambridge, Mass.: MIT Press, 1981), ch. 13.

11 Clifford E. Clark, Jr., *The American Family Home, 1800–1960* (Chapel Hill: University of North Carolina Press, 1986), ch. 7.

12 Gerald Gurin et al., *Americans View Their Mental Health* (New York: Basic Books, 1960), esp. 117. The survey also found that single women were happier but worried more than single men, and that they "experienced an approaching nervous breakdown less often than other women"; 233–35.

See also Wini Breines, *Young, White and Miserable: Growing up Female in the Fifties* (Boston: Beacon Press, 1992); Elaine Tyler May, *Homeward Bound: American Families in the Cold War Era* (New York: Basic Books, 1988); and Rochelle Gatlin, *American Women Since 1945* (Jackson: University Press of Mississippi, 1987). Farnsworth's nephew, Fairbank Carpenter, remembers her "regaling the family with tales" at holiday dinners: "She was a spellbinding story teller and totally wrapped up in her own experiences. No one minded her selfishness as she was so entertaining." Fairbank Carpenter, letter to Alice Friedman, Oct. 22, 1991.

13 See Wini Breines, "Alone in the 1950s: Anne Parsons and the Feminine Mystique," *Theory and Society* 15 (1986), 805–43.

14 Farnsworth, "Memoirs," ch. 11.

15 Ibid., ch. 3.

16 Ibid.

17 Edward A. Duckett and Joseph Y. Fujikawa, *Impressions of Mies: An Interview on Mies van der Rohe* (Chicago: [no publisher], 1988), 26. See also Farnsworth, "Memoirs," ch. 12.

18 See Eugenio Montale, *Provisional Conclusions*, trans. Edith Farnsworth (Chicago: H. Regnery Co., 1970). Farnsworth's early friendships with women are described in "Memoirs," ch. 4.

19 Farnsworth, "Memoirs," ch. 11.

20 Ibid.

21 "Interview with Ludwig Mies van der Rohe," *The Listener*, Oct. 15, 1959, 620–22 (transcript of BBC interview, Ludwig Mies van der Rohe file, Library of Congress, Washington, D.C.).

22 Fritz Neumeyer, *The Artless Word: Mies van der Rohe on the Building Art*, trans. Mark Jarzombek (Cambridge, Mass.: MIT Press, 1991), esp. part 5.

23 Ibid., 317.

24 Farnsworth, "Memoirs," ch. 11.

25 See Wolf Tegethoff, *Mies van der Rohe: The Villas and Country Houses*, trans. Russell M. Stockman (Cambridge, Mass.: MIT Press, 1985), 99–104, 110–19, 121–22 (projects 12, 14, 15, 17).

26 Ludwig Mies van der Rohe, "Haus. H., Magdeburg," *Die Schildgenossen* 14, no. 6 (1935), 514–15; reprinted in English in Neumeyer, *Artless Word*, 314.

27 "Interview with Ludwig Mies van der Rohe," *The Listener*, 621.

28 Christian Norberg-Schulz, "A Talk with Mies van der Rohe," *Baukunst und Werkform* 11, no. 11 (1958), 615–18; reprinted in Neumeyer, *Artless Word*, 338–39 (the quotation is on p. 339).

29 Farnsworth folders 11, 28, Mies van der Rohe Archive, The Museum of Modern Art, New York (hereinafter referred to as Mies Archive). See also Farnsworth, "Memoirs," ch. 13.

30 The story is told in detail in Schulze, *Mies*, 252–59.

31 Farnsworth, "Memoirs," ch. 13. For costs of Levitt houses, see Kenneth T. Jackson, *Crabgrass Frontier: The Suburbanization of the United States* (New York: Oxford University Press, 1985), 234–38.

32 "Defendant's Brief," Dec. 1952, Farnsworth folder 31, Mies Archive.

33 For Mies's office notes on the house, assembled in preparation for the trial, see Farnsworth folder 31, Mies Archive. Myron Goldsmith recalled that Mies only decided to charge a fee at the suggestion of his business manager. The case was heard in the Kendall County Circuit Court in Yorkville, Ill.; the information about the suits comes from a court summary of the proceedings. The matter is discussed in Farnsworth, "Memoirs," ch. 13.

34 "Charges Famed Architect with Fraud, Deceit," *Chicago Daily Tribune*, Oct. 30, 1951, Farnsworth clipping file, Mies Archive.

35 Farnsworth, "Memoirs," ch. 13.

36 Elizabeth Gordon, "The Threat to the Next America," *House Beautiful* 95 (Apr. 1953), 126–30, 250–51; the quotations are on p. 250.

37 Joseph A. Barry, "Report on the American Battle Between Good and Bad Modern

Houses," *House Beautiful* 95 (May 1953), 172–73, 266–72; the quotation is on p. 270.

38 "Glass House Stones," *Newsweek*, June 8, 1953, 90.

39 Lynn Spigel, *Make Room for TV: Television and the Family Ideal in Postwar America* (Chicago: University of Chicago Press, 1992), esp. chs. 3, 4.

40 Farnsworth, "Memoirs," ch. 12.

41 As reported by Myron Goldsmith in conversation with Alice Friedman, Apr. 1988.

42 See Paulette Singley, "Living in a Glass Prism: The Female Figure in Mies van der Rohe's Domestic Architecture," *Critical Matrix* 6, no. 2 (1992), 47–76. See also Miriam Gusevich, "Decoration and Decorum: Adolf Loos's Critique of Kitsch," *New German Critique* 43 (Winter 1988), 97–123, and Remy G. Saisselin, *The Bourgeois and the Bibelot* (New Brunswick, N.J.: Rutgers University Press, 1988).

43 Farnsworth, "Memoirs," ch. 13.

44 Ibid.

45 Grete Tugendhat, "Die Bewohner des Hauses Tugendhats aussern sich," *Die Form*, no. 7 (Nov. 1931), 437–38; reprinted in English in Tegethoff, *Mies*, 97–98. See also Richard Padovan, "Machines à méditer," in Rolf Achilles et al., *Mies van der Rohe: Architect as Educator* (Chicago: University of Chicago Press, 1986), 17–26.

46 Farnsworth, "Memoirs," ch. 14.

47 Hilary Lewis and John O'Connor, *Philip Johnson: The Architect in His Own Words* (New York: Rizzoli, 1994), 49.

48 For Johnson's biography, see Franz Schulze, *Philip Johnson: Life and Work* (New York: Knopf, 1994).

49 See Kurt Andersen, "Philip the Great," *Vanity Fair* (June 1993), 130–38, 151–57; earlier articles contain indirect references to Johnson's homosexuality in their titles, such as John Brodie, "Master Philip and the Boys," *Spy* (May 1991), 50–58, and Denise Scott Brown, "High Boy: The Making of

an Eclectic," *The Saturday Review*, Mar. 17, 1979, 54–58.

50 *Architectural Review* 108 (Sept. 1950), 152–59; reprinted in *Philip Johnson: Writings*, foreword by Vincent Scully, introduction by Peter Eisenman, commentary by Robert A. M. Stern (New York: Oxford University Press, 1979), 212–25, and in David Whitney and Jeffrey Kipnis, eds., *Philip Johnson: The Glass House* (New York: Pantheon, 1993), 9–16; the quotation is on p. 9.

51 Whitney and Kipnis, *Philip Johnson: The Glass House*, 11.

52 For Johnson's early struggles with homophobia, see Schulze, *Johnson*, 35–36.

53 Scully et al., *Philip Johnson: Writings*, 20.

54 Ibid., 22–23.

55 Ibid., 23.

56 See, for example, Johnson's statement in a 1993 interview: "I regret having said that. Because the burned-out village was in the Second World War, and I was on the wrong side. So we don't talk about that anymore. My enemies do, of course. That's a part of my life I'd rather forget." Lewis and O'Connor, *Philip Johnson: The Architect in His Own Words*, 31.

57 See above, n. 12.

58 See John D'Emilio, *Sexual Politics, Sexual Communities: The Making of a Homosexual Minority in the United States, 1940–1970* (Chicago: University of Chicago Press, 1983), 40–49; for Johnson's military service, see Schulze, *Johnson*, 160–68.

59 George Chauncey, *Gay New York: Gender, Urban Culture and the Making of the Gay Male World, 1890–1940* (New York: Basic Books, 1994), 111.

60 Ibid., esp. 111–27.

61 For a full discussion of camp, see David Bergman, ed., *Camp Grounds: Style and Homosexuality* (Amherst: University of Massachusetts Press, 1993). See also Chauncey, *Gay New York*, esp. 286–91.

62 Jack Babuscio, "Camp and Gay Sensibility," in Bergman, *Camp Grounds*, 19–38. See also Judith Butler, *Gender Trouble: Feminism and

the Subversion of Identity* (New York: Routledge, 1990).

63 Schulze, *Johnson*, 217.

64 Philip Johnson, "The Frontiersman," *Architectural Review* 106 (Aug. 1949), 105–10; reprinted in Scully et al., *Philip Johnson: Writings*, 188.

65 Arthur Drexler, "Architecture Opaque and Transparent," *Interiors and Industrial Design* 109 (Oct. 1949), 90–101; reprinted in Whitney and Kipnis, *Philip Johnson: The Glass House*, 3–7 (the quotation is on p. 6).

66 Farnsworth, "Memoirs," ch.11.

67 Erwin Schrödinger, *What Is Life? The Physical Aspect of the Living Cell* (New York: Macmillan, 1946), 75.

68 Kenneth Frampton, "The Glass House Revisited," *Catalogue 9* (Sept.–Oct. 1978), 38–59; reprinted in Whitney and Kipnis, *Philip Johnson: The Glass House*, 92–105; the quotation appears on p. 94.

69 Frampton, "The Glass House Revisited," quoted in Whitney and Kipnis, *Philip Johnson: The Glass House*, 99.

70 As time went on, Johnson added other places to the complex: he designed the Pavilion on the lake (1962), intended as a "playhouse," complete with the thin "Syrian" arches employed in the Guest House but constructed at a reduced scale; the Painting Gallery (1965); the Sculpture Gallery (1970); the Library/Study, the "Gehry Ghost House," and the Lincoln Kirstein Tower (all completed in 1985); and he acquired two older houses at the edges of the property. See Schulze, *Johnson*, 254–55, 287–93, 386, 391.

71 Ibid., 237–38.

72 Ibid., 214.

73 Lewis and O'Connor, *Philip Johnson: The Architect in His Own Words*, 36.

The story of the Constance Perkins House in Pasadena, California (plate 1), one of Richard Neutra's "acknowledged gems," began with a verbal sparring match between architect and client that was typical of both of them. In 1952 Perkins, a professor of art at Occidental College, organized a conference there on the art and architecture of the Southwest, and she invited the most distinguished people she knew to serve as panelists. These included Grace McCann Morley, director of the San Francisco Museum of Art (with whom Perkins had worked while a graduate student in art history at Mills College some fifteen years earlier, teaching drawing to junior high school students on Saturday mornings), John Entenza, editor of the influential magazine *Arts & Architecture*, and Richard Neutra, one of the most famous architects in Los Angeles.[1]

Years later Perkins remembered that although Neutra had a supercilious manner and a well-known habit of trying to make himself appear to be "much in demand" by arranging to be called away in the middle of such events for "an important phone call," she nevertheless invited him to speak because she respected his work and, since first meeting him in 1948, had frequently taken her students to see his home and studio in nearby Silver Lake. Moreover, Neutra had enjoyed enormous success as a designer of houses in Southern California, and his work was so well known nationally that he had been featured on the cover of *Time* magazine in 1949. Though his early reputation rested on large, International Style houses like the Lovell Health House of 1929 (fig. 1) and on urban design projects such as his Rush City Reformed of the 1920s, since the 1930s Neutra had established an

Constance Perkins. ca. 1953

Southern California Modern:

The Constance Perkins House, by Richard Neutra

active practice designing middle-class, suburban homes in the Los Angeles area. At the conference Neutra argued that the future of contemporary architecture in America lay with people like his own middle-class clients: "It is not with the wealthy that the future of contemporary architecture lies. It is with the people in the middle. They are the ones who can afford to be uninhibited and imaginative and to whom living with beauty is more important than ostentation."[2]

According to Perkins the audience – which included many "middle-class" people who felt that they could never afford the services of an architect, and others who were disappointed by modern architecture's failure to live up to its promise as a low-cost housing alternative –

FIGURE 1
Richard Neutra and the Lovell Health House, Los Angeles. ca. 1950

had begun to challenge Neutra quite vociferously, when she herself stood up and asked whether his definition of the middle class "included a professor who takes her lunch to work every day in a brown paper bag because this is the only way that she can make ends meet?" "Of course everyone laughed," she recalled, "and it was relaxed, and he said yes, and he was not at all surprised, I think, when I called to see him a year later."[3]

Perkins and Neutra, both of whom were described by colleagues and contemporaries as affected, superior, and contentious, clearly recognized kindred spirits in one another.[4] The event at Occidental College sealed a strong bond of friendship and mutual respect between them, which lasted until Neutra's death, in 1970. As client and architect, they enjoyed an unusual relationship marked by Perkins's involvement in every aspect of the design of her house and by Neutra's willingness to accept and incorporate her suggestions. For Neutra, who was born in Vienna in 1892 and never lost his confidence in the authority of "experts" (including himself), Perkins's position as a professor of art conferred on her a certain respectability and lent status to her ideas about design. For Perkins, who, at age thirty-nine, had finally separated herself from her family in Denver and become an artist and teacher in her own right, Neutra's formal manner and air of intellectual superiority were marks of artistic temperament and talent, the privileges of the true aesthete. According to Perkins, for years after the house was built, Neutra would stop by to visit her if "he was feeling low"; she was unfailingly loyal to him and to his work.

Perkins was an independent, single woman who had strong opinions about art and deeply felt ideas about how she wanted to live. Having spent most of her life listening to other people's opinions, she realized, as she approached her fortieth birthday, that she could at last embrace and celebrate the very things that made her

different: her choice of career over marriage, her preference for having "her own space" rather than sharing her
life with others, her desire to give herself over completely
to her art, to her books and to the Southern California
landscape. During the war she had served with the
Red Cross in Australia and New Guinea, and the heady
experience of freedom from family and of the dense,
tropical landscape made an impression that stuck with
her throughout her life. When her house was in the
early stages of design, she wrote to Neutra about her love
for "the verdant jungle growth" of the South Pacific; as
she imagined her new house, she wrote, "I dream again
of living amidst lush green plants and exotic flowers."[5]

Perkins wanted to be constantly in touch with the
things that mattered to her, and in the house that Neutra
and she created together, the twin presences of landscape and art are palpable. For her the studio was the
core of the house, and she challenged Neutra to think of
her home in an unconventional way, as a domestic environment in which individual creativity and work, rather
than family and leisure activities, were central to the
concept. In 1959 Perkins wrote: "It happens that I sleep
in my studio – the bedroom is for guests. Perhaps my
studio is the most used part of my home. The drafting
table area serves me in all my projects and studies. I can
work, read, sleep – and still keep an eye on the mountains and the skies."[6]

She had grown up in a "little bungalow" in Denver in
which she had felt "confined and unhappy," and she was
determined to create her own environment, a retreat
and a workplace: "Why live in an environment that you
don't love?" she asked, and Neutra was delighted by the
idea. She felt that he was sympathetic with her desires,
her interests, and her "sense of design," and she knew and
respected his approach: "I think too many people have
a tendency to pull in an architect for his name or reputa-

tion or because the Joneses had him, instead of going to
him and finding out if there's something compatible in
the way you both approach this very intricate problem
of living."[7] As an artist and teacher, Perkins understood
and participated in the process of design, and in this too
she was unusual among Neutra's clients. She also loved
looking at and thinking about art: she owned a small
collection of favorite pieces – reproductions of paintings
by Matisse and Picasso, a Daumier lithograph, three
Japanese woodblock prints by Toyokuni, and a handful
of works by friends and former teachers including Roi
Partridge, from Mills College, and Harold Gebhardt, a
sculptor and colleague at Occidental. She wanted to be
able to display these art works in her home: as she wrote
to Neutra, "I cannot do without my paintings but I do
not need to have them all up at once."[8] She had a thorough
knowledge of art history and kept up with current trends
in the art world through books, periodicals, and exhibitions; in later years she would work as a curator for the
Pasadena Art Museum and the Smithsonian Institution.

Her knowledge of architecture had been extended
and enriched by travel in Europe, Canada, and Mexico;
in the summers of 1951 and 1952 she received grants
from the Rockefeller Foundation to study and photograph the architecture of the American Southwest. On
both occasions, after returning home, she organized lectures and conferences at Occidental College on the arts
and architecture of the Southwest and Mexico, including
the one at which Neutra had spoken. Like many of her
contemporaries in the art world and university community, Perkins was committed to exploring the ways in
which modern art and architecture could be adapted to
the local landscape and distinctly non-European cultural
traditions of Southern California. In many ways, then,
Neutra must have felt that she was a worthy collaborator,
if not exactly a peer.

PLATE 2
Perkins House, reflecting
pool. Photographed ca. 1975
by Constance Perkins

They seem to have genuinely liked each other. Moreover, Perkins's project – a small studio and home for a single person on a very tight budget – was exactly the sort of challenge that Neutra embraced, not only for polemical reasons but also because it provided him with an opportunity to work for an enlightened client who shared his commitment to modern design and the distinctive architecture and landscape of Southern California. The house, perched on a hillside lot in a Pasadena subdivision, hardly appears, at first glance, to be worthy of special notice. Its closed, planar facade, though softened by landscaping over the years, suggests a quiet and unglamorous accommodation to its site and context, and the approach to the front door, up a short flight of wooden stairs, does not prepare the visitor for the extraordinary experience it offers. The interior, with its open plan and enormous plate-glass windows, is light filled, spacious, and still, a secret retreat. At the far end of the living room a small reflecting pool meanders beneath a wall of glass, blurring the distinction between inside and outside (plate 2); with the dense growth of the garden as a screen, one has the sense of being completely removed from civilization, in a quiet oasis of solitude and work. Dramatic views of distant snow-covered mountains from the front windows and deck heighten the experience of the landscape and site. This is one of Neutra's most romantic interiors, where architecture and nature come together in an unusually expressive and beautiful partnership.

Richard Neutra: From Vienna to Los Angeles

In Richard Neutra, Constance Perkins found two things that were critical for her project: he was a well-regarded architect whose work combined European sophistication with sensitivity to the landscape of Southern California, and he had a solid track record, which would convince the bank to lend her the money she needed to build. Neutra was a master at public relations: handsome and ambitious, he had a knack for being in the right place at the right time and for letting others know about it. Throughout his career he made sure that his work attracted the attention of influential people and that it received a great deal of visibility through exhibitions, competitions, books, and magazines. From an early age he had known how to "network" in the world of architecture, and he labored to ingratiate himself with clients and others who could help promote his career.

Within a year of his arrival in the United States in 1923, for example, Neutra had befriended the ailing and destitute Louis Sullivan and managed to meet Frank Lloyd Wright at Sullivan's funeral, securing an invitation to visit Wright's school and studio at Taliesin.[9] This contact led to the offer of a job in the architect's office. But the most famous example of Neutra's uncanny ability to promote himself concerns the Lovell Health House, one of the first independent commissions he received after moving to Los Angeles in 1924. In California, Neutra and his wife, Dione, had been invited to stay with his old friend Rudolph Schindler, a Viennese architect who had been working for Wright on a number of projects, including Aline Barnsdall's Hollyhock House and theater complex on Olive Hill (see chapter 1 of this book). Schindler also had his own practice, and had attracted the attention of a wealthy couple, Leah and Philip Lovell, for whom he had designed three vacation houses in the 1920s, including a much-admired house at Newport Beach, completed in 1926.

The story of how the Lovells came to hire Neutra, rather than Schindler, for their next project, the enormous, high-profile Lovell Health House, has been retold many times, but in the present context it is not so much the fact that Neutra received the commission instead of his friend that is noteworthy, but what he subsequently made of the experience. Philip Lovell was a doctor and a columnist for the *Los Angeles Times* who not only wrote about the house and its healthy environment (including plentiful light, a pool, and an exercise yard) in the newspaper but also opened it to the public as a show house soon after it was finished, in 1929.[10] As the architect of this startling new home, Neutra was, of course, the focus of considerable attention. Later, as a result of his efforts, a selection of his architectural projects, among them the Lovell House, was included in the influential exhibition on the International Style held at The Museum of Modern Art, New York, in 1932. In the widely read catalogue that accompanied the show, Philip Johnson and Henry-Russell Hitchcock described the Lovell House as "without question, stylistically the most advanced house built in America since the War."[11] Neutra was on his way.

Comments such as Johnson and Hitchcock's attracted the attention of art enthusiasts, students, and prospective clients like Perkins, who turned to books and catalogues written by curators and critics as they struggled to learn more about modern art and architecture, particularly in Europe. For a broad cross-section of Americans, living in cities and towns far from New York, the widely distributed publications of The Museum of Modern Art were an invaluable source of information about the work of contemporary artists, and they provided a common-sense introduction to broad subjects such as Cubist painting or modern architecture, which many found baffling.

Perkins herself remembered how important The Museum of Modern Art's tenth anniversary volume *Art in Our Time* (1939) had been for her; she had not only read the book but traveled from Denver to New York to see the exhibition when it was presented at the World's Fair.[12] Unlike the art and architecture magazines, which were written for specialists, the museum's publications on the arts, which included Alfred Barr's *Cubism and Abstract Art* (1936) and *What Is Modern Painting?* (1943), John McAndrew's *What Is Modern Architecture?* (1942), and Elizabeth Mock's *If You Want to Build a House* (1946), were intended for the general reader, and they found their way onto coffee tables and bedside stands in homes across the country. With the museum's traveling exhibition program, which brought a selection of small exhibitions to numerous U.S. cities, these books exerted a powerful influence on the tastes and values of a generation of Americans.

Neutra recognized how effective this publicity could be in reaching a broad audience. Over the years many of his small homes were featured in popular, wide-circulation publications and traveling exhibitions. For example, the tiny Miller House and Studio, in Palm Springs, California, with its dramatic desert setting and elegant reflecting pool (figs. 2, 3), was included in a traveling show of noteworthy contemporary houses sponsored by The Museum of Modern Art in 1938, the year after it was completed. Another small house, the Beard House, in Altadena, California (1934) – which that year won the Gold Medal Award in the "Better Homes in America" competition sponsored by *Architectural Forum* magazine – was also given the museum's seal of approval when Mock cited it in *If You Want to Build a House* as an outstanding example of the use of prefabricated materials.[13] In the same volume Mock described Neutra's Nesbitt House, in Brentwood, California (1942), as "a house which takes gracious advantage of the Californian possibility of year-round outdoor living," with a garden "designed by the architect."[14]

FIGURE 2

Richard Neutra. Miller House,
Palm Springs, California. 1937

FIGURE 3

Miller House, with reflecting
pool at night

This sort of critical attention provided the architect with broad exposure among prospective middle-class clients. While glamorous mansions like the Lovell House, the Von Sternberg House, in Northridge, California (1935), and the sprawling John Nicholas Brown House, on Fisher's Island, New York (1938), were greatly admired, it was Neutra's more modest designs that secured his reputation. By the time he met Perkins, Neutra had established himself as a highly respected architect who understood the needs of middle-class home owners and their families. Thus, while she considered other Los Angeles-based architects, such as Craig Ellwood and Raphael Soriano, she chose Neutra for her project because he had built up the most solid reputation as a reliable professional who would produce the sort of house she wanted.

Arts & Architecture: Southern California Modern

Like many other people in Los Angeles who were interested in the arts, Neutra and Perkins were influenced by publisher and editor John Entenza's widely read magazine, *Arts & Architecture*, and by its distinctively Californian point of view. The magazine (known until January 1944 as *California Arts & Architecture*) had been published since the 1910s and traditionally focused on art in Southern California, but after Entenza acquired it in 1938, it became more experimental, more international in scope, more focused on the work of avant-garde artists and writers, and broader in its coverage. Emphasizing the importance of the "aesthetic environment" in shaping modern experience, the magazine included articles on painting, sculpture, and architecture as well as on music, film, theater, ceramics, and furniture design.[15] By the late 1940s and 1950s its bold graphics and large, eye-catching photographs had brought the work of artists and designers such as Charles and Ray Eames, Harry Bertoia, Alexander Calder, Jackson Pollock, Robert Motherwell,

and many lesser known figures to an audience of young Americans who were interested in the arts and considered themselves outside the mainstream of postwar American culture. Self-defined "liberals" in matters of art and politics, the readers of *Arts & Architecture* took pride in being socially and artistically aware: they read novels, went to "art" films, kept up with the latest theories about sex and psychology, and fretted about the increasing crassness and materialism of the culture they saw around them. They were uneasy about living so far from the centers of "high culture" on the East Coast or even in San Francisco, but they were also Californians, entranced by the vivid and varied landscape and the heady sense of freedom that went with living on the frontier. What's more, as often as not they too were enjoying the fruits of American prosperity – the cars and refrigerators, the green suburban lawns and frozen foods – and they were at pains to distinguish themselves from their neighbors in matters of taste.

The pages of *Arts & Architecture* are colored by the enthusiasms and insecurities that shaped the American art world during the 1940s and 1950s. Uncertainty about the impact of new technology and mass production, ambivalence about European dominance in modern art and architecture, and anxiety about the value of American art and artists contributed to a mixture of bravado, boosterism, and defensiveness in the articles published. For example, in August 1943 Entenza expressed his worries about the future of American culture in his editorial column, "Notes in Passing":

The air has been heavy with talk about the world, the house, the life of tomorrow. Everyone and his silly brother has been writing it and singing it and threatening to build it. For months the public has been asked to consider houses that will never fall down and automobiles that will always stand up and ice boxes that will never wear out.

It has been high and heartening talk and the people who have been making it have done a job of tub-thumping. "Just wait," they say. "Just wait until after the war when we stop making guns we will make the dadgumdest hairpin in the world." "Mr and Mrs America," they say, "you just wait and see."…

The only thing that can possibly delay the future we are fighting for is our own actual fear of it. There's no sense in pretending that it doesn't mean change. In some cases it means very drastic change.… It is going to force upon us considerations and reconsiderations of the complicated systems, political, social, and economic, by which we have lived up to now. We are at this late date just becoming aware of the nature of the great decisions we will be forced to make. We are only now beginning to realize that when the war ends we will be faced with something that is new, something that is strange, and something that is not going to take "no" for an answer.[16]

Like many of his readers Entenza was more interested in trying out new ideas than in spending time speculating about the future. He followed up this editorial with an article announcing the winners of the magazine's recent architectural competition, "Designs for Postwar Living," which focused on the future of the single-family home. The announcement provided an opportunity for members of the jury – architects Sumner Spaulding, Charles Eames, Richard Neutra, John Rex, and Gregory Ain – to contribute short articles describing their views on the subject. Sponsored by a handful of prominently named manufacturers of building supplies and paints, the competition established a pattern of patronage at *Arts & Architecture* that matched theory with practice and emphasized new technologies. This approach would become the magazine's hallmark, especially with the establishment in 1945 of its most famous initiative, the Case Study House Program.

In the 1940s *Arts & Architecture* offered a quirky balance of idealism and practicality, of interest in both fine art and commercial design, and a commitment to exploring the unconscious while keeping an eye on the bottom line. This odd mixture was uniquely American; the magazine's eclecticism reflects the reforming spirit that infused its pages with optimism and energy and helped define a distinctive, regional style – Southern California Modern. Linked to European Modernism of the 1910s and 1920s by an unshakable confidence in the power of industrial technology and good design to cure society's ills, the contributors to *Arts & Architecture* nonetheless sought to develop a new, non-European language of form that would engage the concerns and tastes of their own time and place in postwar America. In their search for inspiration they explored folk art, craft traditions, and the art of "primitive" cultures around the world, and they sought out new imagery and alternative approaches to modern planning in places ranging from Latin America to wartime Russia. Casting their nets wide, they gathered the resources for an approach that would soften the hard edges of the International Style with natural imagery, emphasizing individual creativity, informality, and the spontaneous expression of inspiration in "free form," biomorphic shapes, varied textures, and deep, rich colors. Although by the early 1950s the magazine would come to focus more narrowly on architecture, industrial products, and on its own Case Study House Program, it was widely recognized as a major source of information about current trends in art and design, and a distinctive critical voice that helped shape the tastes and outlook of a generation.

The range of topics covered in the 1940s provides a good cross-section of the tastes and interests of readers like Perkins. In 1944, a particularly rich and varied year for the magazine, there were numerous articles on architecture and planning in the United States, including "Prefabricated Housing" by Herbert Matter, Charles Eames, and R. Buckminster Fuller (July), "Housing Project as Progressive Community" by Hilde Reiss Friedman (August), and a profile of Richard Neutra's Channel Heights housing project (August). There were also articles on design in Latin America, such as "House in Brazil" (September) and "Town Project: A Commercial Fishing Village in Chile" (October). Film criticism, such as "Minorities and the Screen" by Dalton Trumbo (February) and "A Festival for Fascism" by Robert Joseph (August), which looked at propaganda and the film industry in Spain, Germany, and Hollywood, also occupied a prominent place in the journal. Articles on music included "Arnold Schoenberg" (February), "Charles Ives" (September), and "Primitive Music, Folk Art and Improvisation" (November), all by Peter Yates. These titles suggest the breadth of subjects and the liberal slant of the magazine as well as the effort to reexamine modern art and architecture through the lens of contemporary cultural criticism. Western, and specifically Californian, concerns occupied center stage, and the emphasis was on independence of spirit and a fresh new approach to contemporary problems.

The experimental and speculative side of *Arts & Architecture* is suggested by the regular appearance of articles about artists and art theory, often written in an awkward tone of studied informality meant to suggest a common-sense pragmatism and a fresh, antielite point of view. In September 1943, for example, the magazine published a statement and photomontage by artist Ray Eames. The text was laid out as a graphic design on the page without punctuation:

it is impossible to talk about painting without bringing up the whole weary subject of aesthetics philosophy and metaphysics
the fact is that without any talk we are influenced by the world in which we live and by the synthesis of the experiences of the world by all creators the engineer the mathematician sculptor physicist chemist architect doctor musician writer dancer teacher baker actor editor the man on the job the woman in the home and painters....
my interest in painting is the rediscovery of form through movement and balance and depth and light using this medium to recreate in a satisfying order my experiences of this world with a desire to increase our pleasure expand our perceptions enrich our lives.[17]

The montage of photos and drawings that appeared with the text – incorporating images as disparate as a detail of Picasso's *Guernica*, a drawing of a soldier's helmet, and photographs of a toy car, oil wells, high-rise buildings, machine parts, and a chair of contemporary design – suggests the chaotic jumble of stimuli that float through the artist's brain. These are things with which she must come to terms as a woman and an artist in the modern world. No longer was it acceptable to make art in isolation: science, engineering, and psychology now must all play a role in her work, helping her to "rediscover" the language of abstract form. And there were further challenges the contemporary artist had to face as well: her job was not only to "recreate" experiences in "a satisfying order" but also "to increase our pleasure expand our perception enrich our lives." This self-imposed burden, and the peculiarly American preoccupations with self, psychology, and social justice that lent it weight, reflects the concerns that came to dominate American avant-garde culture at midcentury.

The Case Study House Program

The practical, experimental, and artistically progressive slant of *Arts & Architecture* naturally led to a focus on the problem of the moderately priced single-family home, a house with an open plan and large expanses of glass in which returning veterans and their families could live active lives while enjoying their leisure time and an intimacy with the unique Southern California landscape. Comfortable homes and efficient, well-designed products were the rewards that modern technology, new materials, and the postwar American economy made possible, and the challenge was taken up by the magazine with a characteristic blend of optimism, self-congratulation, and reforming zeal.

In January 1945 the magazine announced the establishment of its Case Study House Program:
Because most opinion, both profound and light headed, in terms of post war housing is nothing but speculation in the form of talk and reams of paper, it occurs to us that it might be a good idea to get down to cases and at least make a beginning in the gathering of that mass of material that must eventually result in what we know as "house – post war."…

It is with that in mind that we now announce the project we have called THE "CASE STUDY" HOUSE PROGRAM.… *We are…proposing to begin immediately the study, planning, actual design and construction of eight houses, each to fulfil the specifications of a specific living problem in the Southern California area.…*

We of course assume that the shape and form of post war living is of primary importance to a great many Americans, and that is our reason for attempting to find at least enough of an answer to give some direction to current thinking on the matter.

Whether that answer is to be the "miracle" house remains to be seen, but it is our guess that after all the witches have stirred up the broth, the house that will come out of the vapors will be conceived within the spirit of our time, using as far as it practicable many war-born techniques and materials best suited to the expression of man's life in the modern world.[18]

The Case Study House Program was supported by the magazine and by the manufacturers whose products were used; designs for the houses (which in practice were largely paid for by the private clients who commissioned them) would be published in *Arts & Architecture* and, if constructed, would be open to the public to serve as models of good, low-cost design. The seven architects who agreed to participate were J. R. Davidson, Spaulding, Neutra, Eero Saarinen, William Wurster, Ralph Rapson, and Charles Eames (whose Case Study House #8 of 1949, a home and studio for himself and his wife, Ray, would become far better known than the program that produced it).[19]

Neutra, who was responsible for four Case Study houses over the life of the project, was an ideal participant.[20] He had considerable experience as a designer of low-cost housing, thanks in part to his training in Europe, where since World War I the type had engaged both the public and professional imagination. Moreover, throughout the late 1930s he had taken part in small-house design competitions sponsored by magazines and manufacturers, including the Los Angeles Building Center (1936), *Better Homes and Gardens* (1938), and *Ladies Home Journal* (1939).[21] Neutra became known as an architect who understood the economics of modern construction and the American way of life.

His Case Study projects exhibit the qualities that would become the trademarks of his style in the 1940s. For example, Case Study House #20, the Bailey House of 1947 (fig. 4), which was the only one of Neutra's designs for the program to be built, emphasized its site and materials: relaxed in form, flexible in plan, open to the

FIGURE 4

Richard Neutra. Bailey
House, Case Study House #20,
Santa Monica, California. 1947

outdoors, it juxtaposed industrial finishes and expanses of glass with natural materials such as brick and redwood. It was elegant and modern without being austere, and it was welcoming and homelike in a way that American families could recognize. These were precisely the characteristics that would have attracted the attention of a reader like Constance Perkins as she thumbed through the pages of *Arts & Architecture*.

In February 1951 the magazine reprinted a tribute to Neutra by Siegfried Giedion, one of Europe's most influential architecture critics, which put the finishing touches on Neutra's already glowing reputation. The text was accompanied by impressive black and white photographs of the Tremaine House, in Santa Barbara (1947). Giedion spared nothing in his praise: "F. L. Wright grew out of the prairie earth. He can almost transform himself into a piece of material; a stone, wood, or a plant. R. J. Neutra is a city dweller. He approaches nature, man and materials with the analytical eye of a scientist. Through his love for these and a sensitivity which is ever alive to them, he is near them in a particular way."[22] As if enchanted by the beauty of the house and the California landscape, the normally hardheaded Giedion waxed poetic on the subject of its relationship to its site:

What has been done by the architect? Almost nothing. He simply left the site undisturbed, so that the ground nearly reaches the window-sill. And yet, a view into a microcosme [sic] of nature has been created – unknown to me anywhere else. This power to leave nature undisturbed and simultaneously to draw her into a specific emotional situation, reveals the artist, no less than the power to transfuse a ferro-concrete skeleton with psychic value.[23]

With reviews like this, it is a wonder that any reader of *Arts & Architecture* ever chose another architect to design a house.

Collaboration

Perkins first telephoned Neutra's office in July 1952, and the two began working together soon thereafter. A few months shy of her fortieth birthday and recently tenured at Occidental, Perkins viewed the design and construction of her home as her first truly independent act as an adult. For the past five years she had been supporting her elderly father, who had moved from Denver to Altadena to live with her, but he had recently died, leaving Perkins free to do as she pleased. She was convinced that she had to "start a new chapter in her life," and the decision to hire Richard Neutra to design her house was the first step in that new beginning. A serious and deliberate person, she approached every detail of the process with care and gave even the smallest decision along the way her time and attention. Her budget was small – around $10,000 (she ended up spending about $17,000) – but the house represented her future and she poured her life savings into it.

Neutra devoted himself to the project and to his client. Through the fall and winter of 1952–53 the two searched for a site; on March 31, 1953, Perkins summarized their progress to date in one of her meticulous lists, which provided the architect with all the information that she had been able to gather about the six sites they had seen in Eagle Rock, near Occidental College. They would eventually settle on a wedge-shaped, hillside lot in Pasadena, overlooking the arroyo and the San Gabriel Mountains beyond.

Neutra's attentiveness to the question of the site reflected the high priority he always gave to the relationship between a house and its setting, but in Perkins's case, he became far more involved than was his usual practice. In part this may have been due to his old-world notions about her vulnerability as a single woman, but it is also

clear that he had decided early on to make the house and his unusual client a test case for his theories about design. These emphasized the role of individual experience and perception in the psychological response to environment; Neutra, who had been a close friend of Freud's son in Vienna and had himself undergone psychoanalysis in the late 1930s, received additional encouragement for his approach from the fashionable interest in psychology among artists, writers, and intellectuals in Southern California.[24] In 1951, for example, he published a book entitled *Richard Neutra on Building: Mystery and Realities of the Site*, in which the architect described his views on the unconscious impact of the environment:

Our awareness of most things vital to us is incomplete and this certainly holds true with what we know or think about the site on which we are to spend a good part of our life. Yet – conscious or unaware – our mental and nervous repose and stimulation very much depend on it. A great deal of relaxation or irritation derives from it or from the degree of competence with which the architect may have fitted structure to setting….

What a site produces on our total being is, in fact, a combined total impact – a magic spell, hard to gauge, to analyze or to exhaust its effectiveness. It suns or overshadows our growth and decay, our failures and successes, our dire withering away or our happy survival.[25]

Neutra, whom Giedion had praised as an architect "with the analytical eye of a scientist," had for years been working on a collection of essays in which he grappled with questions about the relationship between psychology and design. Ever the amateur, yet ever confident, Neutra eventually published these writings in 1954 under the title *Survival Through Design*. He saw himself as a new kind of architect who, like his artist contemporaries, had benefitted from the discoveries of modern science and could speak its language:

If we have learned to consider environment as the sum total of all stimuli to which a neural system is exposed, it becomes clear how the future development of brain physiology will aid and underscore with factual knowledge the design of a constructed environment. The designer, the architect, has appeared to us as a manipulator of stimuli and…their workings on the human organism. His technique is really with the organic matter of brain and nerves, however familiar he should be with the trades of the steel fabricator, the mason, the plumber, devoted to external inorganic tasks. Their outer arrangements, though, may further or harm inner physiological developments.[26]

Although he never quite got around to describing specific research in psychology or to making concrete proposals in the book (which, at Neutra's suggestion, Perkins reviewed, briefly and noncommittally, in the *Journal of Aesthetics and Art Criticism* later that year), Neutra's interest in these questions was translated into a highly original working method in practice: once he had been hired, he requested that each client write an autobiography and supply him with a list of "likes and dislikes" on every subject from textures and light levels to colors and smells. The clients' responses to this assignment varied, but of course Connie Perkins threw herself into the project with gusto.

Perkins sent her autobiography to Neutra in August 1953. Like her house, it is a little gem: carefully crafted, precise, lyrical in places. In it she works hard to describe the experiences and emotions that brought her to the present moment and to her decision to build. Her life had not been easy. Born in Denver in 1913, the child of a busy doctor and an overprotective, invalid mother, Perkins was a loner and a nonconformist, popular enough at school but constantly pulled by family responsibilities, unhappy yet outwardly stoical. She took piano lessons, elocution lessons, and dancing lessons, the latter arranged for by her parents because she "showed increasing tendencies of becoming a tomboy."[27] She felt that her only brother had been pampered, while she had to do as she was told. In high school she was good at sports (she remained a lifelong baseball fan) and at art, which she hoped to pursue in college, but, as before, her parents' plans for her future won out over her own. She yielded to their wishes only to discover that she could not live with her decision nor with the deep disappointment that came with it. She blamed herself for her inevitable failure to carry out their plans, but remained bitter:

There was no question as to where I should go to college. I had a four-year state scholarship. But Colorado University did not offer an art major with a B.A. degree and my mother did not consider a B.F.A. a real college degree. Besides, I was feeling a little inadequate at ever being able to make a living with my art; I knew that I was no prodigy. Secretly I decided to study medicine. It seemed like a natural decision until I told father. It was the only time in my life he ever laughed at any of my ideas. I entered as a literature major, pledged the sorority that I was expected to pledge, made the grades I was expected to make and went to the college functions I was supposed to go to but I was miserable. None of the decisions that I had made had been my own really and none were important enough to me to help me fight my old timidity. I was homesick. I dropped out winter quarter, went back for spring quarter but dropped out again in the fall. It was my first psychological defeat and disgraceful to me.

Eventually Perkins got her way, registering at Denver University the next fall as an art major. Then, in her senior year, her parents told her that she either had to support herself or leave school. Their decisions would lead to one of her greatest disappointments and a missed opportunity that would haunt her for the rest of her life:

As my senior year in college was coming to a close I applied to Radcliffe College for a scholarship for graduate work but did not tell my family. In the same mail that brought a favorable reply there came an appointment to one of the elementary schools in Denver. Mother opened the latter and was so overjoyed, seeing an end to some of the economic pressures that the depression years had brought, that I never had the heart to tell her of my real dreams.

She was assigned to a job teaching elementary school in Denver; she hated it and quit midway through the year. Again Perkins persevered: she took a job at the Denver Art Museum and then worked with a friend as an interior decorator. By August 1936 she was on her way to Mills College, in San Francisco, where she completed an M.A. in art history the following year.

Unfortunately, the only teaching job she could find in art history was back at Denver University. Living in the same city as her parents was difficult and confining, but Perkins had made a remarkable discovery: travel. It not only took her away from Denver but also yielded a lifetime of new experiences. In 1938 she organized a student study trip to Europe; when everyone who had signed up canceled as a result of Hitler's invasion of Austria, she borrowed $500 and took off alone. She followed the conventional tourist routes through Europe, but her letters and a photograph album show that she was keen to learn as much as she could about modern architecture, particularly in Holland, Germany, and Italy (this interest produced some rather startling snapshots of "Nazi administration buildings" in Munich and of "Mussolini's Forum" outside Rome).[28] A trip to New York City in 1939 and "a leisurely jaunt" through Canada were followed by a vacation in Mexico City. Each time she returned to teaching, she passed her newest discoveries on to her students.

With the outbreak of World War II, Perkins contrived a way to escape for good by volunteering for an overseas position with the Red Cross. This would prove to be the most remarkable experience of her life. Assigned first to Australia and then to New Guinea, she learned to "hitch-hike" around on planes and survived the rigors of life in remote jungle outposts. She was meant to be teaching crafts and setting up recreation centers for soldiers, but she had little supervision and simply pitched in where she was needed, sometimes working as a supply driver and nurses' assistant when wounded soldiers arrived in droves at the navy base where she was posted. The experience in the tropics changed her:

When I first landed in New Guinea, I never thought I would learn to ignore the heat, the endless rains, the muddy swamps, the dusty coral roads, the "bully-beef," the dehydrated foods, the little hard coconut bugs that you didn't bother to fish out of your drinking cup. But the verdant jungle growth I loved from the first. I dream again of living amidst lush green plants and exotic flowers. And I am happier warm than cold. The only fear I struggled against was of the hurricanes that sent giant trees crashing on the tents and wiping out lives; I still cringe when a high wind blows. Life was not easy but it was not lonely.... Those days were most important because I learned a new code of values and was able to develop a sustaining philosophy of life.

Forced to return home in 1945, when her father suffered a stroke, Perkins prepared to ship out again as soon as she could. On the eve of her departure, however, she herself became ill; when her health improved, she was reassigned to the domestic service of the Red Cross and took up a post at Shoemaker Naval Hospital in Oakland. "There was a great psychological chasm between those who had served over-seas and those who had not," she wrote; she had "to learn not to reminisce... [and] to become civilized again." She "yearned for the jungle" and for the independence she had known there.

When the war ended Perkins once again confronted the problem of finding a new job, and following her mother's death, she assumed responsibility for the care of her elderly father. The only work she could find was in Southern California, as executive secretary of the San Fernando and Van Nuys branches of the Y.W.C.A. With her father in tow she moved to "an unfinished and unfurnished garage" in Altadena, which cost her only $75 a month in rent. Feeling frustrated and restless, she started to look for a teaching position; by the fall of 1947 she had landed a job in the art department at Occidental College, which enabled her to move herself and her father to a bigger house in Altadena. She loved her work, did well, and received tenure. Then, in 1951, her father died.

She wrote to Neutra that "the five years that father and I shared our home and my work were as close to complete happiness as I believe it is possible to attain." The loss had convinced her that she had "to start a new chapter" in her life. She considered returning to graduate school for the Ph.D., but decided instead to build herself a house, a house for one person. She was convinced that, whatever else she might to do with her life from that point on, she would do it alone. She ended the autobiography with a remarkable list of observations:

My greatest enjoyment comes from the perception of sounds, forms, colors and rhythms. I do not believe that I could again live happily without good music and my art world. My preferences lie in the Contemporary field but do not exclude the traditional.

It is necessary for me to feel that I serve a purpose in my life of a broader nature than routine materialistic living provides.

I enjoy the close friendship that exists between faculty members, and between the faculty and student groups at Occidental College, and, unless academic freedoms were broken, would not now seriously consider employment elsewhere.

I have not lost my romantic love for travel and the unknown. I would like to take an exchange teaching position when my sabbatical comes up…but lest I would not know when to come back, I want a home that is a part of my own living and feeling that I will feel homesick for.

I am peculiarly independent, tenacious and willful, and at the same time, the opposite of all of these.

I would like to be an idealist.

Neutra no doubt read Perkins's autobiography with great interest. Confronted with a client who clearly had such a strong will and such determination to get what she wanted, he must have realized that he had met his match. Moreover, like a number of other single women clients who had preceded her in his practice (women like the psychologist and collector Galka Scheyer, or Grace Lewis Miller, a teacher of the Mensendieck System of Functional Exercise), Perkins wanted a very small house in which she could live and work, but also a place where she could entertain. These criteria required Neutra to reexamine the familiar single-family home, which had become his stock in trade, and to rework the conventional patterns of the type, dispensing, for example, with such familiar room designations as the master bedroom and pushing the limits of the open plan to achieve maximum flexibility.

Perkins's skills as an artist and critic were central to the design process. Her list entitled "Likes and Dislikes," sent to Neutra with the autobiography in August 1953, reads like a program for the house since many of its distinctive elements are described; looking back on her notes some years later, she was surprised to find how closely her preferences matched the design she got and how careful her architect had been to respect her wishes.[29]

On such matters as the open plan and the use of natural materials or large expanses of glass, Perkins's preferences were not unusual among Neutra's clients; like many people, Perkins had hired him because she liked what she had seen in his work: open spaces, large windows, and sensuous, unpainted redwood or stained pine walls and doors. But even when Perkins described fairly commonplace preferences, her distinctive voice and precise manner can be clearly heard:

For interior materials, I like natural woods if kept light and care is taken not to use too active a grain. Painted or papered plaster areas are agreeable. I like tile. Formica or similar material I like too for kitchen and bath. On the whole I do not care for other plastics. I love textiles and strong color used carefully. No tints! Textural contrasts and simple forms are wonderful.[30]

Her favorite colors, she added, were yellows, mustards, browns, greens, and golds. Perkins was at her best when describing the most abstract elements of design: "Speaking of forms, I enjoy a nicely used free form, sometimes a rigid curve is successful. I am allergic to the arbitrary rectangles and angularities that Wright uses. I like boldness but not artificial dramatization. I am not a purist but I could be." The list of "other desires," with which she ended the introductory section, is also characteristic in its specificity: "Storage areas at points where items are used, not centralized, shelves within reach, sliding rather than hung doors when possible, weather stripping and insulation, no hardware if possible, no venetian blinds, no barbecue, no door chimes."

The programs for the "living area" and "studio-den" are laid out with equal precision, and helped Neutra understand exactly how she intended to use the house. She wanted the living area to be flexible, to "accommodate a group of perhaps twenty for a seminar, and still be conducive to small conversational groups." She did not want the kitchen closed in, "even by temporary screen units," as she preferred to "talk with guests and cook at the same time." Perkins intended to display paintings and prints on the walls, and noted that she needed enough wall space or "flexible screen space" to make this possible in either the living room or studio. She also indicated her interest in showing slides "or possibly movies" on the

walls. A desk for bills and correspondence, ample bookshelves, and a built-in radio and record player were also planned for this room. A small reflecting pool "that will meander in and out of my living area" is specifically included in the wish list, and with it, "as much indoor-outdoor planting as possible." Perkins added that she "would like the definition of indoors and outdoors almost obliterated with a pool and continuous planting areas establishing the dominant background feeling."

The studio (fig. 5) was of particular importance for Perkins as she intended to both work and sleep there:

This I would also like to have open with the outdoors for I will not work when I am closed in. Granted I will need privacy at night. I have a single bed mattress, springs and frame to use. It might roll under a built-in shelf to be a couch for day use. At night I would want light for reading in bed. The other major item here would be a general work table on which I would also silk-screen – minimum 3' x 6' – with the space underneath used for storage of paintings and art supplies.

Perkins also took great care in specifying her storage needs in the living area and kitchen (fig. 6), complete with the measurements of her present storage area for cooking utensils, and she requested "a closed but ventilated space for towel rack, soaps and the like, including wastebasket." Likewise, she described her preferences for the bath and service areas in detail. The guest room was something of an afterthought for Perkins, who planned to build it only if and when she could afford it.

Very little was left to chance (Neutra even measured her height and reach), yet Perkins knew well that even with all of her needs spelled out, in the end the problem of designing her house would be Neutra's, not hers. With uncharacteristic awkwardness, she offered a word of caution to her architect as he embarked on the design of her home: "I want you to feel complete freedom within my financial limitations in your designing."

FIGURE 5

Perkins House, studio. ca. 1977

The Perkins House

Neutra completed the preliminary drawings for the house in October 1953, and Perkins responded positively. Moving on to more detailed plans the following month, Neutra, assisted by his son Dion, began grappling with serious design issues. One of these was the shape and overall conception of the reflecting pool, about which Perkins had serious doubts after seeing Neutra's preliminary suggestions. In a letter dated November 9 she wrote to Dion Neutra with tact and restraint about his design: *I think it is a tremendous idea, but not for me nor for my particular home. I feel that from the material point of view it will be out of place since I cannot use stainless steel, polished chrome, terrazzo and the like in the rest of the house. Also, for me, it would require the abstract shape of the pool to take on a surrealist nature and, although I like such forms, here I want something relaxing and more intimate.*

FIGURE 6

Perkins House, kitchen.

ca. 1977

Perkins/Neutra

FIGURE 7

Perkins House, interior with reflecting
pool. ca. 1955

FIGURE 8

Perkins House, exterior with deck and
reflecting pool. ca. 1955

*Therefore I want the top of the pool close to being flush
with the floor, and the water level below the floor level. I
want the material to be in harmony rather than contrast,
and the dramatic element to be one achieved possibly
through lighting.*[31]

Wisely, Neutra and his son suggested that Perkins do some
drawings of the shapes she had in mind. Years later she
recalled sitting down on the floor with one of her art
students, surrounded by books on Calder and Miró, trying out ideas until they found the right shape. She sent
Neutra a handful of designs, one of which was eventually chosen. The pool (figs. 7, 8), which became more
natural looking as the landscaping grew up around it, is
one of the most memorable elements in the house.
Assisted by the spider-leg extension of an interior beam,
its shape projects the interior outward in exactly the way
that Perkins had described in her notes. Working with
green foliage, white stones, and a tiny pool of water,
Perkins transformed a corner of her suburban home
into an island of natural beauty, recapturing something
of the jungle landscape – and the sense of adventure –
she so keenly missed.

The process of give and take continued through the
winter of 1953–54; one of Perkins's lists of suggestions
and questions numbered forty-three items, and Neutra
responded patiently (perhaps even gratefully) to each of
them. Realizing that her budget was too low (and that
the bank was reluctant to lend her the money for a house
with no bedroom), Perkins despaired – but then was
lucky to receive a personal loan for $3,000 from the wife
of the chair of her department.[32] The plan (fig. 9) was
changed to include a guest room, with its own separate
entrance, in place of a master bedroom. A model of compact yet open planning, the house skillfully accommodated
Perkins's unusual program and the idiosyncracies of
the site (plate 3). A flight of stairs leads from the driveway and carport to the front door; an opaque screen at
the top of the stairs shields the view of the small deck
and garden beyond (fig. 10). Inside, the front door opens
directly onto the main living space: living room, kitchen,
and studio are all clearly visible, and the large, plate-glass
wall and reflecting pool at one end of the room open

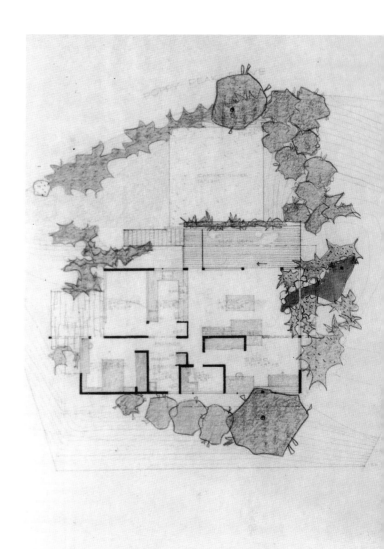

FIGURE 9

Perkins House, plan, presentation
drawing. 1954. The studio is at
the lower right, the guest room
at the lower left, the kitchen
at the upper left, and the living
room at the upper right

Perkins/Neutra

181

RESIDENCE FOR:
MISS CONSTANCE PERKINS
RICHARD J. NEUTRA
F.A.I.A.   ARCHITECT

PLATE 3
    Perkins House, perspective,
    presentation drawing. 1954

the side of the house to a vista of dense plantings, completely obscuring the neighbors' garage some twenty feet away and extending the view out into an apparently limitless tropical landscape.

Perkins moved into her new home late in December 1955, in time to celebrate Christmas there. She marked the occasion by decorating her artificial Christmas tree with the leftover brown, yellow, and orange paints she had used on the interior (plate 4). At last she had a home of her own; the final cost was $17,166, including the architect's fee, a figure of which she was justly proud. It proved that even a person on a tight budget could afford to build an architect-designed home without spending much more than others did on ordinary tract houses.[33] Perkins saw herself as a model client and her house as an unqualified success.

In photographs taken not long after its completion (figs. 11, 12) , the Perkins House appears stark and unprotected in its barren landscape, but later shots reveal how significantly this changed as the trees and plantings grew up around it. As the landscaping grew in, particularly around the perimeter of the site, the house began to seem more and more private, more completely isolated from nearby neighbors. Moreover, as Perkins acquired more artwork, furniture, and rugs, the interior appeared less harsh and more lived-in.[34]

Critical response to the house was positive, but Perkins remained its most devoted fan, unstinting in her praise.[35] She was also immensely grateful to Neutra for the care he had taken with her project. She wrote to him in April 1955, "The realization of my dreams is most exciting, a realization for which I owe you a great deal that cannot be put into words."[36] On May 31, 1956, she wrote again, "It is impossible to say how much I love my home; how relaxing and satisfying it is to go home to."[37] Perkins's most detailed and thoughtful tribute to the house came some years later, in August 1959, when she was approached by Katherine Creighton, a New York critic, who was writing a book about modern architecture. Asked by Creighton to summarize the process of design, she took some credit for her own contribution: "It is probable that I was more concerned with design

FIGURE 10
Perkins House, garden and deck. ca. 1977

details, proportions and the like than is the average client. It is the refinement of these details that is still the most enjoyable part of my home. It is the plastic use of three-dimensional space that is achieved by an artist."[38] She included a summary of the list of "likes and dislikes," but praised Neutra for thinking of things she had forgotten. Then, following an outline provided by Creighton, she undertook a critical assessment of her house as a work of modern architecture. Under the heading "large expanses of glass," for example, she commented on the question of privacy, an issue that had become something of a *cause célèbre* following the uproar over Mies van der Rohe's Farnsworth House in the early 1950s: "There is no question of privacy because of the use of the site.… The use of the exterior strip light reverses the opaque quality of the glass at night and allows one to see out, not in." This openness to the outdoors allowed her complete freedom to experience the landscape: "Needless to say, my view never becomes tiresome. This depends partly on the orientation of the house and the planning of the glass

PLATE 4

Christmas at the Perkins House.

1955

areas so that the moods of both the interior and exterior environments are constantly changing as the light changes. I personally like it best early in the morning, at sunset, and particularly at night. On a stormy day it is dramatic." She singled out Neutra's handling of the site, his flexible use of space, and his use of colors on both the interior and exterior. Leaving the best for last, Perkins thoughtfully summed up her views:

To me, a truly great architect is not one who merely skillfully manipulates a construction to meet the individual functional needs of a client, important as these are. He is one who, doing this, also creates an "art object." My home is not just my "machine for living"; it is my environment. Living includes thinking and feeling as well as mechanical existence. Living is a way of life. To be full it needs an environment that pricks every sense with which the human being is endowed, an environment that is specifically ordered to give direction to ordered thought.

Perkins's long and happy life in the house is proof of its success. Throughout the 1960s and 1970s she continued teaching and pursued a career as a popular art critic for *ArtWeek*, *ArtForum*, and the *Los Angeles Times*. In 1967, though still without a Ph.D., she was presented with a Faculty Achievement Award by Occidental College. In a sense the process of working with Neutra had been her graduate education; no one could have asked for a better student or a more devoted patron. For Perkins the house would always be exciting and fresh, a work of art, which she took great delight in sharing with students, friends, and admirers of Neutra's work. Indeed, when she died, in March 1991, she left the house to the Huntington Library and Art Gallery, where in her last years she had worked as a volunteer. Through her home she hoped that a new generation would come to know the intense pleasures – and the deep sense of order – that modern houses could impart to those who were lucky enough to live in them.

FIGURE 11

Perkins House. ca. 1955

FIGURE 12

Perkins House, living room and
studio. ca. 1955

1 The quotation is taken from Thomas S. Hines, *Richard Neutra and the Search for Modern Architecture* (New York and Oxford: Oxford University Press, 1982), 257. Hines's work is the best source of information about Richard Neutra's career: for the Perkins House, see pp. 257, 262–63; for Neutra's Van der Leeuw Research House, see pp. 110–15. The Perkins House was published in *House and Home* in Nov. 1957, in *Domus* in Nov. 1958, in *Arts & Architecture* in Jan. 1960, and in *Architektur und Wohnform* in Jan. 1961. I interviewed Constance Perkins twice in Jan. 1989 and again in Jan. 1990, in Pasadena, Calif., and she gave me access to the papers relating to her house; at her death, in 1991, Perkins's papers were left to the Archives of American Art, Smithsonian Institution. Neutra's office files are in the Neutra Archive, Department of Special Collections, University of California at Los Angeles. I am grateful to Susan Danly, former curator of American Art at the Huntington Library and Art Gallery, for introducing me to Constance Perkins in 1987.

2 Hines, *Richard Neutra*, 257; from Margaret Stovall, "Home of the Week," *Pasadena Independent Star News*, Dec. 5, 1960. Perkins paraphrased the story in an interview with Alice Friedman in Jan. 1989.

3 Perkins, interview with Alice Friedman, Jan. 1989.

4 According to Robert Winter, a longtime friend and colleague of Perkins's at Occidental College, Perkins heaped scorn on college administrators whom she felt had no "vision" about the arts; for them, her "Bryn Mawr" accent and her haughty manner were particularly grating. Robert Winter, interview with Alice Friedman, Pasadena, Calif., Jan. 1995.

5 The quotation is taken from Perkins's "Autobiography," an unpaginated manuscript written at Neutra's request in Aug. 1953. Copies of this document, and of a list entitled "Likes and Dislikes" (dated Aug. 12, 1953, unpaginated), submitted to the architect at the same time, are in the Perkins Papers and in the Neutra Archive.

6 Constance Perkins, letter to Katherine M. F. Creighton, Aug. 14, 1959, Perkins Papers (uncatalogued).

7 Perkins, interview with Friedman, Jan. 1989.

8 Perkins, "Likes and Dislikes."

9 See Hines, *Richard Neutra*, 5, 51–56, and Esther McCoy, *Vienna to Los Angeles: Two Journeys* (Santa Monica: Arts and Architecture Press, 1979).

10 Hines, *Richard Neutra*, 75–91, 303–8.

11 See Hines, *Richard Neutra*, 102–4, and Henry-Russell Hitchcock and Philip Johnson, *Modern Architecture* (New York: The Museum of Modern Art, 1932), 157–60. A book by the authors entitled *The International Style: Architecture Since 1922* (New York: W. W. Norton, 1932) was also published at the time of the exhibition; see Terence Riley, *The International Style: Exhibition 15 and The Museum of Modern Art* (New York: Rizzoli/Columbia Books of Architecture, 1992).

12 Perkins, interview with Friedman, Jan. 1989.

13 For the Miller and Beard houses, see Hines, *Richard Neutra*, 120–23; for the Beard and Nesbitt houses, see Elizabeth Mock, *If You Want to Build a House* (New York: The Museum of Modern Art, 1946), 50, 82–83.

14 Mock, *If You Want to Build a House*, 83.

15 See Elizabeth A. T. Smith, "*Arts and Architecture* and the Los Angeles Vanguard," in Smith, ed., *Blueprints for Modern Living: History and Legacy of the Case Study Houses* (Cambridge, Mass.: MIT Press, 1989), 144–65, and other essays in this volume. See also Barbara Goldstein, ed., *Arts and Architecture: The Entenza Years* (Cambridge, Mass.: MIT Press, 1990).

16 John Entenza, "Notes in Passing," *California Arts & Architecture* 60 (Aug. 1943), 21.

17 Ray Eames, *California Arts & Architecture* 60 (Sept. 1943), 16. See also "Jackson Pollock," *Arts & Architecture* 61 (Feb. 1944), 14, and Sidney Janis, "Abstract and Surrealist Art in America," *Arts & Architecture* 61 (Nov. 1944), 16.

18 [John Entenza], "The Case Study House Program," *Arts & Architecture* 62 (Jan. 1945), 37, 39.

19 Lesser-known architects, including Raphael Soriano, Craig Ellwood, and Pierre Koenig, were asked to join once the program was established. The designs of these younger architects were more fully engaged with the possibilities of modern industrial materials than the earlier projects had been, resulting in a more elegant, high-tech look to their houses. See Amelia Jones and Elizabeth A. T. Smith, "The Thirty-six Case Study Projects," in Smith, *Blueprints for Modern Living*, 41–81.

20 Neutra designed Case Study Houses 6 (1945), 13 (1946), 20, and 21 (both 1947). See Smith, *Blueprints for Modern Living*, 48–49, 60–61. The program lasted until the mid-1960s.

21 See Hines, *Richard Neutra*, 126–28, and his "Case Study Trouvé: Sources and Precedents, Southern California, 1920–1942," in Smith, *Blueprints for Modern Living*, 82–105.

22 Siegfried Giedion, "R. J. Neutra: European and American," in Willy Boesiger, ed., *Richard Neutra: Buildings and Projects* (Zürich: Editions Girsberger, 1951), 100.

23 Ibid.

24 For the influence of Freud and psychoanalysis on Neutra, see Hines, *Richard Neutra*, 12–13, 188.

25 Richard Neutra, *Richard Neutra on Building: Mystery and Realities of the Site* (Scarsdale, N.Y.: Morgan and Morgan, 1951), 16.

26 Richard Neutra, *Survival Through Design* (New York: Oxford University Press, 1954), 230.

27 Perkins, "Autobiography." Unless otherwise noted, this and the following quotations on pp. 174–76 are taken from Perkins, "Autobiography."

28 Perkins's photograph album is included with the Perkins Papers.

29 Perkins, letter to Creighton.

30 This and the following quotations on p. 177 are taken from Perkins, "Likes and Dislikes."

31 Constance Perkins, letter to Dion Neutra, Nov. 9, 1953, Neutra Archive.

32 Perkins recalled with great fondness the kindness shown her by Irene Young; her papers include a detailed accounting, plus every check she wrote to Young as she repaid the money at 6 percent interest. It took her seven years, from Dec. 1955 to Jan. 1963.

33 Constance Perkins, letter to Mrs. Dione Neutra, Sept. 28, 1956, Neutra Archive. Although Perkins (at Neutra's suggestion) had approached Entenza early on, the house was not included in the Case Study House Program.

34 In 1956 Perkins added one of Neutra's specially designed "camel" tables (with hinged legs that would allow it to convert from a coffee table to a dining table). The rugs were designed and executed by Robert Wallace, a former student, in 1971; Perkins Papers.

35 The Perkins House was declared a landmark by the Pasadena Cultural Heritage Commission in 1977.

36 Constance Perkins, letter to Richard Neutra, Apr. 16, 1955, Neutra Archive.

37 Constance Perkins, letter to Richard Neutra, May 31, 1956, Neutra Archive.

38 Perkins, letter to Creighton. All of the quotations on p. 184 are taken from this document.

PLATE 1

Robert Venturi. Vanna Venturi
House, Chestnut Hill,
Pennsylvania, view from the
street. 1961–64

Given the tastes and interests of her architectural "parents,"
it should have surprised no one that the Vanna Venturi
House in Chestnut Hill, Pennsylvania (1961–64; plate 1;
fig. 1), the first-born child of the Postmodern movement,
turned out to be a girl – not a stalwart son destined to go
forth into the world boldly proclaiming a new architectural vision, but a rather pretty, mercurial daughter who,
wreathed in diffidence and irony, made a case for change
through the subtle art of persuasion. With its thin, flat
walls – which, on the front facade, part at the center of a
broad gable to form a deep slot through which a layered
vista of voids and veils is barely visible – its festoon of
mismatched windows and decorative string courses, and
seemingly haphazard borrowing of imagery and objects
from other times and places, the house is unapologeti-
cally playful and decorative. It seemed rather unassuming,
and it entered the world of architecture quietly; nevertheless, "Mother's House," as it has come to be known,
soon showed critics and historians just how fundamentally disruptive it would be to the architectural status quo.[1]

Indeed, for its architect, Robert Venturi, the house
was not an isolated experiment but part of an ongoing
campaign of research, writing, and design. Throughout
the three-year period in which he was intensively designing (and redesigning) the little house for his mother,
he also focused his attention on writing a work of architectural theory, *Complexity and Contradiction in
Architecture* (1966), which digs deep into history to celebrate the "messy vitality" of architecture, confronting
contemporary modernism with a series of little-known
buildings that responded to "the inherent complexities and
contradictions of living."[2] Using hundreds of illustrated
examples, Venturi proposed an alternative approach to
design theory, one guided not by modern architecture's

It's a Wise Child:

The Vanna Venturi House, by Robert Venturi

FIGURE 1

Vanna Venturi sitting at the
entrance to her house

search for originality and consistency in form and theory, but by a passion for history, a love of variety, and
a deep commitment to architecture as an art of accommodation. Challenging Ludwig Mies van der Rohe's
famous saying "Less is more," Venturi wrote, "Where
simplicity cannot work, simpleness results. Blatant sim-
plification means bland architecture. Less is a bore."[3]

These values made Venturi something of an outsider
in the early 1960s, but it was his growing commitment
to vernacular and commercial architecture that ultimately separated him from many of his contemporaries.
In 1960 he embarked on a collaboration – architectural,
intellectual, emotional – with architect and planner
Denise Scott Brown (the two were married in 1967), and
it was she who, influenced by Pop art and by the London-

based Independent Group, and inspired by the theories of social planners such as Herbert Gans at the University of Pennsylvania, encouraged Venturi to turn his attention to the vernacular architecture of his own time, to advertising, to street life, and to the commercial strip as a valid architectural vocabulary for the mid-twentieth century.[4] For Venturi and Scott Brown, and for a generation of younger architects, these interests represented a fundamental change in architectural thinking, a "shift of perspective from the Champs-Elysées to Main Street," as Vincent Scully put it in his introduction to *Complexity and Contradiction*, and a rejection of the heroic statements of modernism in favor of an antiheroic approach emphasizing program, accommodation, and inclusion.[5]

As a residence for his mother, a widow of nearly seventy with strong feminist and socialist beliefs and distinctive tastes in fashion and furniture, the Vanna Venturi House had to conform to the shape of a well-defined way of life and create a comfortable setting for a small collection of antiques and other furniture acquired over a period of nearly half a century. Moreover, as a residence for an older person who was still quite healthy in the early 1960s but nonetheless needed a bit of extra looking-after (and perhaps might later need a live-in nurse/companion, as Venturi's father had at the end of his life), Venturi mother's house had to respond to an unconventional program, providing spaces for daily life on one floor, and facilitating the movements of and need for domestic privacy of a caretaker.[6] As Denise Scott Brown explained:

Although the Vanna Venturi house is usually described in stylistic and formal terms, functional requirements were not ignored in its planning, they were merely not discussed in our writing. The house works in the narrowly functional sense, but it satisfies, as well, a broader range of functions. For example, it was intended for a widow and perhaps her companion, and was designed specifically around her

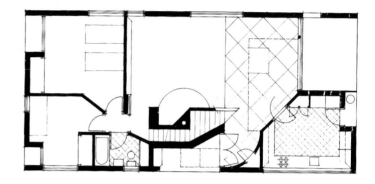

FIGURE 2

Robert Venturi. Vanna Venturi
House, Chestnut Hill,
Pennsylvania, plan, ground
floor

antique and reproduction furniture. It was located to give her accessibility to transportation and urban services yet to provide privacy as well.[7]

The main rooms – master bedroom, guest/caretaker's room, living/dining area, and kitchen – are all on the ground floor (fig. 2), clustered around a central stair and fireplace. Embracing the whole was the watchful, loving presence of the adult architect/son who, though he traveled frequently and worked downtown, still lived at home. Thus, Venturi designed a small studio/bedroom for himself at the top of the house with a half bath on the landing and a small balcony for additional space and privacy (figs. 3–5). Large windows flooded the room with light and, on the front of the house, offered a view of the street and of the approach to the front door. Venturi lived here until his marriage to Scott Brown and even for some months after.[8]

What made the house such an extraordinary sight in 1964 was its use of overscaled conventional elements – the split gable, the chimney, the arch and lintel, the wide, dark doorway at the center of the facade, the sash window and the ribbon window – which appear to have been tacked up randomly on billboardlike walls.[9] The meaning of the boldest forms, such as the sheltering gable, was immediately recognizable as one looked across the flat site from the street (see plate 1), and as one drew closer, details like the elegant wood moldings and window mullions seemed reassuringly familiar. Thus, while the house was nothing like its suburban Chestnut Hill neighbors, it, like them, drew on a vast lexicon of American and European architectural imagery to create a feeling of domestic security and continuity; the effect of the facade was, at first, rather comforting. In a fundamental way the house seemed to make sense. The broad gable, chimney, and sash window recalled such historical examples as McKim, Mead, and White's Shingle Style Low House, in

Bristol, Rhode Island, of 1887, or Frank Lloyd Wright's own home in Oak Park of 1889, and the arched lunette window at the back of the house (fig. 6) suggested, in a distant, associational way, connections with both Roman and Palladian sources.[10] More important than specific historical references, however, was the fact that the overall shape and many of the individual elements recalled a generic and familiar architectural language drawn from the storehouse of collective memory. Venturi has suggested that this is why his mother's house looks like a child's drawing: "Some have said my mother's house looks like a child's drawing of a house – representing the fundamental elements of shelter – gable roof, chimney, door, and windows. I like to think this is so, that it achieves another essence, that of the genre that is house and is elemental."[11]

Nevertheless, there was something peculiar and unsettling about the look of the oversimplified gable and the flat wall surface with all those architectural spare parts stuck onto it. Such an image of the suburban home – an image simultaneously comforting in its simplicity and jarring in its disjunctive complexity – could easily be read as an ironic commentary not simply on the traditions and language of architecture, but also on the American dream of life in a suburban, single-family home. By the early 1960s, thanks to books like Sloan Wilson's *The Man in the Gray Flannel Suit* (1955) or John Kenneth Galbraith's *Affluent Society* (1958) – or, indeed, to movies like Nicholas Ray's *Rebel Without a Cause* (1955), in which James Dean played a troubled teenager adrift in a sea of empty materialism – the seeds of doubt about postwar American prosperity, family life, and consumption had already been sown, particularly among the intellectuals and art world observers who formed a substantial part of the audience for architect-designed buildings.[12] Thus, while Venturi himself may not have wanted to focus on such a reading, there is no doubt

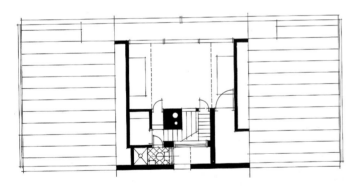

FIGURE 4
Vanna Venturi House, studio
and "nowhere stair"

FIGURE 5
Studio, showing the lunette
window and balcony beyond

Venturi/Venturi

that these themes constituted a significant part of the meaning of his works in their time, particularly for specialists who were inclined to treat any reference to popular culture as cynical, patronizing, or arcane.

On the interior (plate 2; figs. 7, 8) the design was equally unusual, though more subtle. Here one found panel doors, wood moldings, a marble floor, a mantelpiece, and antique and reproduction furniture brought together with more contemporary elements such as the large plate-glass window and freestanding column in the dining area. This mixing of styles and materials constituted a serious challenge to modern architecture in America: since the appearance of Wright's Prairie houses in the 1890s, the unity and integration of architecture and interior furnishings had been assiduously pursued, and it was a basic tenet in the teachings of Mies, Walter Gropius, and Louis Kahn. Here again Venturi's irreverence toward modernist dogma was immediately recognizable.

FIGURE 6
Vanna Venturi House,
rear elevation

FIGURE 7
Vanna Venturi House, dining
area

FIGURE 8
Vanna Venturi House, view of
the stair, fireplace, and window

PLATE 2
Living/dining area, entry,
and stair

Venturi's mother's house was meant to be experienced both associationally – as a series of architectural signs – and spatially, as a series of physical and aesthetic sensations; often these two types of experience overlapped.[13] The house is filled with devices intended to enhance the user's awareness of his or her centrality in a playful, animated dialogue with the architect and with the building itself. As in the Mannerist architecture of sixteenth-century Europe (which Venturi studied with particular enthusiasm during the 1950s), this dialogue is most effectively achieved by manipulating the conventions of architectural form and the expectations of the observer.

As we look down the macadam "driveway" toward the house, for example, it gradually becomes clear that there is no garage door at the end of it (Vanna Venturi did not drive); the closest thing to an opening of the size and shape that we expect in such a suburban setting is the broad entrance in the center of the facade, which was clearly meant for human beings and not for cars. Such contradictions abound. Entering the house through the main doorway, we expect to move forward on axis but instead are forced to turn sharply to the right and proceed along a diagonal path; in the porch and foyer the wall changes three times – first it is parallel with the facade, then diagonal, and finally drops away entirely to reveal the stair. Once inside, we are confronted by an assortment of awkwardly juxtaposed architectural elements: the chimney and the stair seem to compete for space with the oddly shaped window ledge in the front wall; this struggle is ultimately "won" by the chimney, which, halfway up the flight, constricts the stair to a narrow passage, hardly wide enough for a person to pass through. Viewed from the back of the house (fig. 9), the broad "chimney" that we first encountered on the street facade is revealed to be simply the front wall of the large room on the upper story; from here, the actual chimney looks puny

and inconsequential. A large lunette window, also visible only from the back, establishes another unexpected intermediary plane of enclosure at the upper level; the slot of space between this wall and the back of the house becomes a narrow balcony with a low parapet. These are only the most obvious examples of the many architectural ironies, false starts, and rhetorical flourishes that we encounter, and they suggest that "fun house," rather than the farm house of rosy memory, is the more apt metaphor here.

At the Vanna Venturi House, the logic and coherence of plan and elevation, ideas so fundamental to modernist aesthetics, are intentionally disrupted. Responding to the complexities of the program (Venturi called this "allowing form and function to go their separate ways"), and by a need to communicate with the user through architectural form, the house was transformed from a static object into a series of aesthetic and intellectual operations that are "performed" by the building visually, spatially, and symbolically.[14] As in other early projects – the Guild House elderly housing complex, in Philadelphia (1963), for example, or the North Pennsylvania Visiting Nurses Association, in North Ambler, Pennsylvania (1961) – Venturi acted as an agent and advocate for the client/occupant rather than as a distant form-giver.

Because Venturi wanted his architecture to be legible and accessible to his audience, he drew on familiar vernacular and commercial sources, assembling a pastiche of signs and motifs; this characteristic of his work is fundamental to its contribution to Postmodernism.[15] But it was the reinscription of the user/participant/observer at the very heart of the architectural project that marked Venturi's most radical break with modernism. Now the client became not simply a passive recipient but a participant in a process of communication and experience; this notion substantially undermined the belief in the architect as an independent, original creator with mastery

FIGURE 9

Vanna Venturi House, rear
elevation

over form, an idea central to the identity of the artistic
avant-garde.[16] It was this fundamental change in the definition of the architect's role that, perhaps more than any
other aspect of his work, made Venturi an outsider: as
Scully once noted, Venturi was hated by the architectural
profession (and by many critics) because by successfully
challenging the concept of originality, he "took its most
satisfying, its most childish myth, away."[17]

    The Vanna Venturi House, like other cases described
in this book, is an example of a project in which ideas
that were circulating in architectural culture and significant for a particular architect were expanded and
explored in an unconventional home for an atypical client.
Although the house, like many architects' first houses
done for relatives, provided her son with an opportunity
to build his ideas (rather than simply to write about
them), it was nonetheless very specifically a residence for
Vanna Venturi herself: her age, her unconventional way

of looking at the world, and her relationship to her son were not only symbolically represented but gently accommodated in the spaces and points of view that the design of the house made possible. Moreover, the house became a meditation on the passage of time, an architectural essay on the significance of fragmentary images and chance memories within the complex reality of the present. Here originality was secondary: the architectural source in history and memory were celebrated instead. That this important reassessment of the value of the past for modern architecture was undertaken in a house for the architect's mother was not a coincidence; on the contrary, the project provided Venturi with the opportunity to draw a portrait not so much of an individual but of a loving relationship between generations, which represented, in essence, the importance of history.

The Vanna Venturi House: Complexity and Contradiction

In many ways the Vanna Venturi House was intended as a demonstration of the approach to architecture described in *Complexity and Contradiction in Architecture*, and thus it makes sense to consider the main points of its design in the context of Venturi's theory.

On first reading, the most surprising thing about *Complexity and Contradiction* is its rational, conversational tone: speaking in the first person, Venturi made his ideas seem eminently reasonable and accessible. With characteristic modesty, he began the book with a chapter entitled "Nonstraightforward Architecture: A Gentle Manifesto," describing the observations and preferences that guided his work. These he discussed in terms of his personal responses, perceptions, and experiences rather than as pseudo-scientific discoveries that might serve as proof of the validity of immutable rules; the approach was perfectly suited to a generation of readers increasingly anxious about the failure of systems and weary of the language of absolutes.[18] Indeed, Venturi explicitly rejected the "moral language" of modernism:

Architects can no longer afford to be intimidated by the puritanically moral language of modern architecture. I like elements which are hybrid rather than "pure," compromising rather than "clean," distorted rather than "straightforward," ambiguous rather than "articulated," perverse as well as impersonal, boring as well as "interesting," conventional rather than "designed," accommodating rather than excluding, redundant rather than simple, vestigial as well as innovating, inconsistent and equivocal rather than direct and clear. I am for messy vitality over obvious unity. I include the non sequitur and proclaim the duality.... I am for richness of meaning rather than clarity of meaning; for the implicit function as well as the explicit function. I prefer "both-and" and "either-or," black and white, and sometimes gray, to black or white. A valid architecture evokes many levels of meaning and combinations of focus: its space and its elements become readable and workable in several ways at once.[19]

While this discussion focused the reader's attention on the intricate formal language of architectural design, Venturi was also concerned with the ways in which program would be accommodated – order had to give way in the face of functional requirements:

A valid order accommodates the circumstantial contradictions of a complex reality. It accommodates as well as imposes. It thereby admits control and spontaneity, "correctness and ease" – improvisation within the whole. It tolerates qualifications and compromise. There are no fixed laws in architecture, but not everything will work in a building or city. The architect must decide, and these subtle evaluations are among his principle functions. He must determine what must be made to work and what is possible to compromise with, what will give in, and where and how. He does not ignore or exclude inconsistencies of program or structure within the order.[20]

This was a rare admission on the part of an architect: Venturi not only acknowledged the limitations of architectural order but intentionally set out to identify and underline them through design. He continued with a series of statements that provide a key to his approach, stressing the need to deal with things as they are rather than as we would wish them to be. This takes him beyond architecture to social planning:

Mies refers to a need to "create order out of the desperate confusion of our time." Kahn has said "by order I do not mean orderliness." Should we not resist bemoaning confusion? Should we not look for meaning in the complexities and contradictions of our times and acknowledge the limitations of systems? These, I think, are the two justifications for breaking order: the recognition of variety and confusion inside and outside, in program and environment, indeed, at all levels of experience; and the ultimate limitation of all orders composed by man. When circumstances defy order, order should bend or break: anomalies and uncertainties give validity to architecture.[21]

Ultimately, this cluster of concepts gives rise to one of Venturi's fundamental ideas about architecture and urban planning: that the wall, in particular the facade, acts as a boundary between public and private. As such, it should be treated as a screen that both represents the public face of the institution (or home) and indicates something of the nature of interior space:

Designing from the outside in, as well as the inside out, creates necessary tensions, which help make architecture. Since the inside is different from the outside, the wall – the point of change – becomes an architectural event. Architecture occurs at the meeting of interior and exterior forces and use of space. These interior and environmental forces are both general and particular, generic and circumstantial. Architecture as the wall between the inside and the outside becomes the spatial record of this resolution and its drama. And by recognizing the difference between the inside and the outside, architecture opens the door once again to an urbanistic point of view.[22]

In Venturi's architecture, the individual building, with its signifying boundary wall, is seen as part of a flexible community of architectural forms, just as the individual room in a house or building becomes part of an overall network of spaces that interact and intersect. These relationships are dynamic rather than static and transcendent, and thus become fully legible only in the presence of an observer or user. Because the starting point in design is the client, or rather the ever-changing experience of the human user who lives in historical time, architecture cannot remain rigidly systematic; to reflect and respond to complex and contradictory experiences, it must contain these qualities within itself.

At the Vanna Venturi House these principles were given three-dimensional form:

This building recognizes complexities and contradictions: it is both complex and simple, open and closed, big and little; some of its elements are good on one level and bad on another; its order accommodates the generic elements of the house in general, and the circumstantial elements of a house in particular. It achieves the difficult unity of a medium number of diverse parts rather than the easy unity of few or many motival parts.[23]

For Venturi, the primacy of the program in shaping the plan, with its irregular (yet clearly rectangular) outer edge and distorted interior spaces, was among his most important innovations:

The inside spaces, as represented in plan and section, are complex and distorted in their shapes and interrelationships. They correspond to the complexities inherent in the domestic program as well as to some whimsies not inappropriate to an individual house.... The contradiction between inside and outside, however, is not total: inside, the plan as a whole reflects the symmetrical consistency of the outside;

outside, the perforations in the elevations reflect the circumstantial distortions within.[24]

Questions of function and economy clearly took precedence here, followed by spatial composition and the shaping of perceptual experience. In *Complexity and Contradiction*, Venturi discussed elements like the stair and chimney in terms of their function and spatial position without reference to symbolism; his description recalls the tensions created between crowded arches and pilasters in Michelangelo's architecture of the 1520s:

A more violent kind of accommodation occurs within the central core itself. Two vertical elements – the fireplace-chimney and the stair – compete, as it were, for central position. And each of these elements, one essentially solid, the other essentially void, compromises in its shape and position – that is, inflects toward the other to make a unity of the duality of the central core they constitute. On one side the fireplace distorts in shape and moves over a little, as does its chimney; on the other side the stair suddenly constricts its width and distorts its path because of the chimney.[25]

According to Venturi the stair is meant to be seen as both awkward and efficient: its shape is altered by its position next to the chimney, but because it is wider at the bottom than at the top, it offers both a place to sit and a place to put things before taking them upstairs. This combination of aesthetic and functional thinking is summed up in Venturi's description of the "nowhere stair" (fig. 10), which leads from the studio to the top of the house:

The little "nowhere stair" from the second floor similarly accommodates awkwardly to its residual core space: on one level, it goes nowhere and is whimsical; at another level, it is like a ladder against a wall from which to wash the high window and paint the clerestory. The change in scale of the stair on this floor further contrasts with that change of scale in the other direction at the bottom.[26]

FIGURE 10

"Nowhere stair"

201

Ultimately, this balance between form and function, as well as the overlapping of architectural elements, spaces, and systems of signification, provides the key to the Vanna Venturi House. In a characteristically layered description, Venturi made his final point about the complexities of the plan by referring not to the plan itself but to the structure:

The exceptional point in the plan refers to the expedient column support, which contrasts with the otherwise wall bearing structure of the whole. These complex combinations do not achieve the easy harmony of a few motival parts based on exclusion – based, that is, on "less is more." Instead they achieve the difficult unity of a medium number of parts based on inclusion and on the acknowledgement of the diversity of experience.[27]

The single column (see fig. 7) is, in part, an ironic element: it recalls the systematic grid of *pilotis* in Le Corbusier's projects of the 1920s, but by eliminating the grid – and at the same time reintroducing the load-bearing wall – Venturi lets the single element both stand in for the absent system and signify its disruption. He thus focuses attention on the complexities of representation in architectural design; his mother's house is, as he says, both "generic" and "circumstantial," both broadly significant and specifically meaningful. Using some forms that communicated widely recognized meanings (such as the gable, the stair, or the fireplace) and others that constituted references to a fairly arcane language of architectural history, as well as elements with specific associations known only to his mother and to himself (for example, in the furniture, or in ways in which the doors reminded him of the house he grew up in), Venturi was able to create an image of domesticity that was multilayered and rich in content. It is this complexity at all levels of experience, and his willingness to acknowledge the contradictions that underlie it, that makes Venturi's mother's house an extraordinary work of architecture.

Vanna Venturi: The Client's Role

Vanna Venturi was born in 1893 and grew up in Philadelphia. Her family was from Apuglia, Italy; because she had to go to work at an early age she did not finish high school.[28] Largely self-educated, she had a lifelong interest in books, and she took a particular interest in history, current events, and biography.[29] She was a socialist, a vegetarian, and a feminist, and she married relatively late, in 1924; her husband, Robert Venturi, Sr., was twelve years older than she, and their son, born the following year, was an only child. The family lived comfortably in Philadelphia, where Robert Venturi, Sr., ran a successful fruit and produce business.

It was Venturi's father who introduced him to architecture. His friendships with the Philadelphia architects Phineas Paiste and Edmund Brumbaugh (the latter designed a small store for him in 1922) suggest that he encouraged his son to pursue a professional interest in the subject.[30] Yet Vanna Venturi also played a significant role in the development of her son's intellectual and artistic interests. With her love of fashion (she made many of her own clothes), her interest in antique furniture, and her commitment to social justice, it was she who introduced him to politics, to ethical values, and to art and design. He admired the clarity of her beliefs and her "elegant" tastes. Looking back on his childhood, Venturi described how, like him, Vanna was an outsider:

As a child of immigrants, my mother also did not fit the mold. . . . As a young woman [she] became interested in literature and socialism and liberal causes. She loved the Fabians and Bernard Shaw and the Webbs. Norman Thomas, the socialist, was her choice for President the five times that he ran for that office. . . . Being a pacifist, my mother was attracted to the Quakers because of their stand against war, and so she became a member of the Society of Friends. . . . I never went to a public school: pledging allegiance to the flag – "coercive patriotism," my mother called it – was anathema to her. So she couldn't send me to a school where that kind of ritual was performed in the morning: this was an expression of her pacifism."[31]

Motivated by Vanna Venturi's interests, the family made summer excursions to the socialist community at Arden, Delaware, and to Rose Valley, an early arts and crafts community in Pennsylvania.[32] At the Pritzker Prize award ceremony in 1991, Venturi noted that his mother's "sound but unorthodox positions, socialist and pacifist, worked to prepare [him] to feel almost all right as an outsider."[33] All right or not, as the only child of an older couple with unconventional interests, Venturi learned to compromise, and he learned to care for his parents as they grew older.

At his death, in 1959, Venturi's father had left a modest inheritance, more than enough to live on, and with some of this money his widow purchased a lot at 8330 Millman Street, in the suburb of Chestnut Hill, on which to build a house for herself. Her decision to provide her son with the opportunity to design a house was, according to Venturi, fairly easy – as he put it: "I think it was very simple: she had a son, she loved architecture and he did, and she trusted him. I guess that's it."[34]

In discussing the process of designing his mother's house, Venturi emphasized the deep sympathy, attachment, and understanding that they shared. Having lived together for over thirty-five years, mother and son knew a great deal about one another; moreover, having completed one building already, Venturi felt that he was "reasonably knowledgeable and understanding."[35] He remembered only two incidents during the course of their collaboration as problematic. One occurred when the house was nearly three-quarters completed and he drove her to the site to inspect the building in progress. Looking at the ordinary nineteenth-century house next door, she remarked wistfully, "Oh, isn't *that* a nice house."[36] Apparently the incident passed without further comment; if Vanna Venturi had genuine concerns, she

was surely unusual – as a client and as a parent – in keeping them to herself, but the fact that her son worried about this relatively mild expression of anxiety gives a good indication of the sympathetic relationship between them.

The second problem arose in connection with Venturi's plan to put a marble floor in the entrance and at the dining end of the large room; Vanna Venturi rejected this scheme as ostentatious. Despite Robert's explanation that such floors were found in eighteenth-century farmhouses and served a practical purpose, Vanna wanted none of it, but in the end her son prevailed. Venturi remembered that "when the house was half finished, I said, 'Oh, I really need this marble; I really need to make the distinction between this end of the room and the other end.' I went to her and I said, 'Look Mother, I really want this,' and she said, 'O.K.'"[37] Adjustments had to be made by the contractor (and in the end the marble cracked), but the architect got his way and the client seemed satisfied. In this anecdote, as in the first one, Vanna's tolerance and trust seem extraordinary, suggesting that Venturi's recollection of the process as a positive one is correct. Even the final price – around $43,000 – which in 1963 was a great deal of money for a house, was agreeable to both of them.[38]

Vanna Venturi's trust in her son was rewarded in her house, and she lived there happily until 1973. Indeed, the house became almost a living human presence, an indispensable part of a three-way conversation between the client, her environment, and the many visitors who came to see it. As Scott Brown recalled:

The house provided Vanna with company and solace when she was an old woman, living there with an architecture student on the second floor for protection. Carloads, sometimes busloads, of visitors, mainly architecture students, would come by, and we would find her with a seminar seated around the dining table giving lectures on the architecture of the house and the babyhood of its architect.

The house filled some long hours for her. As her son put it, "Architecture is the opiate of the mothers."[39]

The house was designed to be lived in comfortably by more than one person, and at various times Vanna shared it with her caretakers: with her son until his marriage; with her son and daughter-in-law for a period after their marriage; with an architecture student; and finally, at the very end, with a live-in nurse. She entered a nursing home in 1973 and died in 1975; in 1973 the house was sold to Thomas and Agatha Hughes, a professor of history and technology at the University of Pennsylvania, and a potter, respectively, who have lived there ever since.[40]

Vanna Venturi was the central figure in her son's conception of the house: it was lovingly designed to reflect her interests and to meet her needs. But the house projected an image of its client in a broader sense as well. In the often-reprinted, canonical black and white photograph of the house (see fig. 1), she is shown at the center of its overscaled entrance, sitting quietly on a chair in the sun with a pot of flowers beside her and reading a book. Scully compared this modest image to Leonardo da Vinci's well-known illustration of the Vitruvian ideal man inscribed within a circle and a square, citing it as evidence of Venturi's rejection of architectural machismo: *All previous embodiments of human centrality in this diagram had been of the heroic male figure, an athletic, aggressive being who fits into but basically dominates the essential shapes of the world. But here it is Vanna Venturi, seated in her kitchen chair with a pot of geraniums beside her. She is tiny, but the space detonates around her. Directly above her head the gable splits to release her energy beyond the circle and the square to the empyrean. There the rich balance of apposites, or complementarities, which was to shape all of Venturi's later work, achieved its first and still its most compelling image. Contrasted with the traditional male figure, Vanna Venturi is at once antiheroic and feminist in meaning. She is stronger than he; at rest, she breaks the mold. It was this combination of subversive attitudes that caused so many architects to hate Robert Venturi so earnestly. He was striking at their heroic image of themselves as godlike creators, an idea fundamentally ridiculous in itself and dangerous to architecture but one which was deeply rooted in romanticism and which late modernism had done everything to encourage. The fact that Vanna Venturi was Robert Venturi's mother fueled the fires. Everybody knew all about mothers in 1960. It was risky for a male to admit that he had ever had one. The truth is that the macho pretensions of architects have always rested upon rather shaky foundations in the modern period. Such could easily be read in the early sixties in their destructive urbanism and brutalist constructions alike. Modernism had trapped them in an unreal and untenable mythology from which they needed release very badly. Venturi went to the heart of the matter with his gentle feminist image, a harbinger of healthier things to come.*[41]

Though exaggerated and poetic, Scully's reading captures a fundamental aspect of the meaning of the house as a loving gesture between a son and his mother. Assuming the traditional parental role of oversight in the home, Robert Venturi used architecture to create an environment in which he could literally watch out for his mother, ensuring her comfort, security, and pleasure in her old age.

Postmodernism, Social Activism, and Everyday Experience

Although the Vanna Venturi House is often described as a Postmodern building, it is important to recognize that as a project conceived and designed in the early 1960s, it is significantly different in character and meaning from the many works of architecture, painting, and literature that appeared subsequently, especially those dating from the height of the movement, in the late 1970s and 1980s. Compared to buildings by Michael Graves, Charles Moore,

PLATE 3

Richard Hamilton. *What Is It*
That Makes Today's Homes So
Different, So Appealing? 1956.
Collage on paper, 12 x 18 in.
Kunsthalle Tübingen, Collection
G. F. Zundel

Venturi/Venturi

or Frank Gehry, the Vanna Venturi House seems tame in its use of conventional imagery, applied ornament, and layered space – that is, until we recall that it preceded the Postmodern buildings of these architects by fifteen to twenty years.[42] While the later works of Graves, Gehry, Peter Eisenman, and even Venturi himself were conceived within the context of Structuralist and Deconstructivist notions of history, representation, and subjectivity as presented in the writings of Michel Foucault, Roland Barthes, Jacques Derrida, and their followers (books published in France in the late 1960s and early 1970s, but which appeared in English translation only later), Venturi's earliest buildings drew on other sources for inspiration. These sources, based in the intellectual, artistic, and academic countercultures of Europe and America in the 1950s, opened up the space and offered the raw materials for an interrogation of contemporary values and of the systems (economic, social, literary, artistic) that regulated them. In the history of Postmodernism, the Vanna Venturi house should be viewed as a foundational – yet somewhat ambivalent – first step, and an early manifestation of the erosion of confidence in postwar culture that would result in a torrent of change in the 1970s.

Through Scott Brown – who as early as 1960 was in the process of formulating a theory of populist and socially responsible architecture – Venturi's interests and sphere of reference were significantly broadened. Having studied at the progressive Architectural Association in London during the late 1950s, Scott Brown was influenced by the work of the Independent Group in England and by the populist architectural projects and theories of Peter and Alison Smithson.[43] Her concerns and those of the Independent Group artists overlapped in two significant ways: first, in their fascination with commercial imagery and American consumer culture, and second, in their commitment to a "straight-forward" and antielitist architecture, designed and built, as Scott Brown put it,

"for community life as it is and not for some sentimentalized version of how it should be."[44] The Smithsons' architectural projects and housing designs of the 1950s focused on urban experience, street life, and the creation of working-class neighborhoods; as artists, they turned away from modernist abstraction to confront mass production and the culture of everyday life. As Scott Brown noted, their appeal for her lay "in combining the Dadaist found-object aesthetic with an interest in community development."[45]

A collage like Richard Hamilton's *What Is It That Makes Today's Homes So Different, So Appealing?* (plate 3), which he produced for the 1956 Independent Group exhibition, suggests the broad range of artistic ideas, social commentary, and experimental techniques that were being proposed at the time.[46] Using images taken from popular American magazines, Hamilton not only emphasized the randomness and transience of the work of art but, through his choice of sources and subjects, offered an ironic critique of American consumerism, media culture, sexism, and obsession with youth and novelty.[47] Using irony and visual puns he constructed an effective commentary on the shaping of contemporary identity through the detritus of commerical culture. Moreover, he focused attention on the domestic realm and on women's roles as consumers, housewives, and sexual objects. This juxtaposition of disparate images raised numerous questions about class, race, sexuality, authenticity, and the nature of experience in time and space (we realize only very slowly that the surface of the moon hovers over the room) that would later become fundamental to the Postmodernist project.

The combination of artistic experiment, populism, and social commentary represented by the Independent Group's projects was immensely appealing for Venturi and Scott Brown; transposed to an American context, it fueled their own investigations of contemporary archi-

206

tecture. Through the grass-roots political activities of the early 1960s – disarmament rallies, sit-ins by black students pressing for integrated lunch counters in the South, opposition to "urban renewal," and so on – they, like many of their colleagues, became increasingly aware of the need to question the certainty with which Americans had congratulated themselves for over a decade. In part, this meant listening to the viewpoints and experience of people unlike themselves, people who were excluded from discussions of urban policy, planning, and design. Widely read books like Michael Harrington's *The Other America* (1962) and Jane Jacobs's *Death and Life of Great American Cities* (1961) revealed the deep divisions in American society and opened the eyes of educated, white, middle-class readers (most of whom lived in the suburbs) to ways of living – among poor people, people of color, immigrants – different from their own.[48] For women and men on the American Left, these books and experiences would prepare the way, in a broad sense, for the fundamental concepts of Postmodern theory: the recognition that language and art were both malleable systems of representation that defined cultural values, and the realization that control over these systems was an instrument of power.[49] It is clear from their work in this period that Venturi and Scott Brown were developing a strong sense of the ways in which they, as architects, might make use of these ideas.

Here again it was Scott Brown who led the way: through her exposure to the urban planning department at the University of Pennsylvania, which advocated a fusion of social activism and urban policy-making, she formulated an approach to architecture that confronted the realities of American life. As she noted, "the continued existence of poor people in America was a real discovery for students and faculty in the late 1950s."[50] In her own work, and in her collaborations with Venturi, Scott Brown made an effort to come to terms with these challenges.

Venturi and Scott Brown (though she was not an official partner in the studio until 1968) implemented their antielitist and antiheroic approach to architecture through what might be called an "architecture of care" in the early 1960s. This architecture, though not explicitly feminist, is characterized by a number of qualities that would become integral to American feminism in the 1970s: first, the validation of individual experience through a focus on the needs of users (including the elderly and children) and on the program; second, the recognition of the importance of routine household chores and of planning for these activities; third, the commemoration, through the language of monumental architectural form, of the mundane, the ordinary, and the apparently inconsequential; fourth, the recognition of the importance of individual and cultural memory, even if this is articulated in colloquial language and commonplace imagery.[51]

We can recognize a number of these qualities not only at the Vanna Venturi House but also in Guild House, the ninety-one-unit elderly housing complex designed for the Society of Friends in Philadelphia in 1960–63.[52] A great deal has been written about the building, yet it is worth noting in this context how much of the description of it in *Complexity and Contradiction* is devoted not only to its "ordinary and ugly" materials and imagery but also to its program and the needs of its occupants.[53]

In the later 1960s and early 1970s Venturi and Scott Brown would extend their research to the commercial strip of Las Vegas (*Learning from Las Vegas*, 1972) and to the American suburbs (*Signs of Life: Symbols of the American City*, 1976), investigations that deepened the Postmodernist tendencies in their work. But in *Complexity and Contradiction*, Venturi offered an explanation that placed his book, and with it the Vanna Venturi House, firmly in an earlier historical moment, one that occupies the middle ground between the realist cultural and social

Venturi/Venturi

commentary of the 1950s and the full-scale social and political activism of the later 1960s and 1970s:

The main justification for honky-tonk elements in architectural order is their very existence. They are what we have. Architects can bemoan or try to ignore them or even try to abolish them, but they will not go away. Or they will not go away for a long time, because architects do not have the power to replace them (nor do they know what to replace them with), and because these commonplace elements accommodate existing needs for variety and communication. The old clichés involving both banality and mess will still be the context of our new architecture, and our new architecture significantly will be the context for them.... I am taking the limited view, I admit, but the limited view, which architects have tended to belittle, is as important as the visionary view, which they have tended to glorify but have not brought about. The short-term plan, which expediently combines the old and the new, must accompany the long-term plan. Architecture is evolutionary as well as revolutionary.[54]

By focusing on the expedient rather than on unitary theory, Venturi's work demonstrates the deep connection between populism, feminism, and liberal activism in the earliest years of Postmodernism. These foundational principles are worth recalling here, especially in light of the commercial and consumerist turn that the Postmodern movement would take in the 1980s.

History and Memory

Venturi's commitment to popular imagery was ultimately rooted in his sense of history and in his keen awareness of the vast differences in architectural language that existed at various places and times. History thus provides the final key to Venturi's work and enables us to form a more complete picture of his goals and aspirations.

In 1954, a few years after completing his studies in architecture and architectural history, Venturi won the Rome Prize in Architecture; he lived at the American Academy there between 1954 and 1956.[55] This experience marked a turning point in his education. Travel in Europe and the pleasures of first-hand experience provided him with the opportunity to know and understand a broad range of architectures, from Renaissance Classicism to Elizabethan Mannerism and English Baroque, and the richness and variety of these forms is lovingly – even euphorically – re-created in the profusion of tiny illustrations that dot the pages of *Complexity and Contradiction*. The complex surfaces of Michelangelo's late works and the intricate spatial layering of Palladio's villas made an enormous impression, suggesting ideas that would resurface in Venturi's own work. Moreover, ever conscious of his role as a practicing architect, Venturi also kept a close eye on the present, using his time in Italy to study postwar European architecture. Like the historical forms and compositions observed on his travels, such contemporary devices as the enormous split gable of Luigi Moretti's apartment house on the Via Parioli in Rome (ca. 1952, illustrated in *Complexity and Contradiction*) were incorporated into Venturi's encyclopedic mental portfolio and reused, in varying degrees of literalness and abstraction, throughout his career.

Returning to Philadelphia in 1956 Venturi took a job in the office of the widely respected modern architect Louis Kahn, and he began teaching at the University of Pennsylvania. Through his relationship to Kahn, Venturi came to define his own manner as an independent architect, and in particular to formulate a distinctive new vision of architecture as a system of representation, both contemporary and historical. Kahn, like a number of architects working in the 1950s, was deeply engaged in an effort to reinvest modern architecture with a sense of the past; in many of the buildings he designed during this period, historical forms – monumental arches, vaults, and lintels – are abstracted into a unified system of geometrical elements, recalling both the rigor and the authority of Roman architectural precedents.[56] In Kahn's work these forms are integral to the structure of the building, suggesting a fundamental order in architecture that links the past with the present.

Venturi learned a great deal from Kahn about the power of simple, direct imagery, and he shared Kahn's love and respect for history, but the two architects had very different ideas about the role of history in architecture. Their differences are made plain enough through a comparison of Kahn's Margaret Esherick House (fig. 11) of 1959–61 and Venturi's house for his mother, which is located just down the street from it.[57] In Kahn's building the evident principles of geometry, symmetry, and proportion not only recall the architecture of the classical past and Kahn's own roots in the Beaux-Arts tradition, but also serve to bind the parts of the building to the whole and the interior to the exterior. The "disruptions" in this unifying order – for example, the asymmetrical massing of the two parts of the house and of the window and door openings – create tension in the composition, but this only serves to reinforce, rather than to undermine, the overall sense of rationality and integration. Moreover, true to Kahn's modernist allegiances, there is no hint of surface ornament and no sense of the wall as a planar boundary between interior and exterior. On the contrary, the wall is massive and three-dimensional, evoking, however distantly, the solid, authoritative architecture of antiquity and suggesting that it is a natural expression of the volumes inside.

In the Vanna Venturi House the separate elements appear as fragments and not as parts of a whole; they "pull away from the whole, denying its internal consistency and thus distinguishing themselves in purely representational terms," as Neil Levine has aptly put it.[58] Each part

209

– the split window, the chimney, the ribbon window, the enlarged "sash window," the Palladian window, the arched molding, the concrete lintel – reads as a fragmentary component in an allegory in which its original meaning is altered by the new context.[59] Craig Owens described the way this process works in Postmodern literature and art:

Allegorical imagery is appropriated imagery; the allegorist does not invent images but confiscates them. He lays claim to the culturally significant, poses as its interpreter. And in his hands the image becomes something other. (allos = other + agoureui = to speak). He does not restore an original meaning that may have been lost or obscured: allegory is not hermeneutics. Rather he adds another meaning to the image.[60]

Owens makes three further points about allegory that are particularly relevant here: first, that allegory is "consistently attracted to the fragmentary, the imperfect, the incomplete – an affinity that finds its most comprehensive expression in the ruin"; second, that it is "the common practice" of allegory "to pile up fragments ceaselessly" in a strategy of accumulation that appears to be an end in itself; and third, that in the allegorical impulse there is a desire to preserve "the traces of something that was dead, or about to die," and thus a feeling of melancholy and impending loss – in the latter instance, the allegorical fragment is transformed into a sort of *memento mori.*[61]

In describing his own use of what he called "conventional elements" in architecture, Venturi revealed his understanding of the ways in which meaning, and particularly historical meaning, is communicated through such displaced or recontextualized images:

Conventional elements in architecture represent one stage in an evolutionary development, and they contain in their changed use an expression of some of their past meaning as well as their new meaning. What can be called the vesti-gial element parallels the double-functioning element. It is distinct from a superfluous element because it contains a double meaning. This is the result of a more or less ambiguous combination of the old meaning, called up by associations, with a new meaning created by the modified or new function, structural or programmatic, and the new context. The vestigial element discourages clarity of meaning; it promotes richness of meaning instead.[62]

What is striking about the Vanna Venturi House, and about much of Venturi's other work, is how much emphasis is placed on the fragment – or rather, the series of fragments deployed in hybridized compositions: throughout the house individual elements are encountered sequentially and not as parts of a structured whole. This is a central and fundamental difference between Venturi and Kahn: for Kahn, abstracted historical, specifically classical, references were intended to recall the organic unity and rationality of buildings and of systems of design that connect the culture of the present to that of the past; in Venturi's work, by contrast, the fragmentary element is removed from its historical context and made to speak in a new relationship to the other elements around it; this is entirely an operation of the present, and of an architecture aware of its own culture and of the limitations of cultural retrieval. Thus, ironically, it is Venturi the historicist, the architect who reintroduced historical imagery into contemporary architecture, who most emphatically draws the line that marks the past as foreign and unreachable.

While the exterior of the Vanna Venturi House makes reference to various traditions in architectural history, the interior mixes the general with the specifically biographical and autobiographical. Some elements – the panel doors, the moldings, the fireplace, the marble floor in the dining area – recall details of vernacular domestic architecture, while others – the vaulted ceiling, the freestanding column – serve as signs of more monumental precedents. The antique and reproduction furniture is also made to fulfill a double function: like the fragmentary parts of the exterior, each object is read as part of a series of images, but it also functions as an element in a more coherent portrait of the client and of Venturi himself; through the planning and decor of the interior, the "ordinariness" of vernacular forms in general is tied to the specific experiences of an individual life. Since Venturi grew up with the furniture in the house, it represented for him not only his mother's way of life but also his connection to her and to their shared family past:

There are things about that house that are just sort of ordinary, that are accepted now, that were very un-ordinary for the time. It was not a historical revival house at all, but it was also not modernist in the sense that it did use familiar forms that symbolized house and shelter.... I think in a way that it was sympathetic [to his mother]; it was not right for her to move into a "modern" house... maybe partly that was because this was for my mother and I didn't want to do something show-off for me that didn't really relate to her, but fundamentally it was based on a respect for her, and a sentimental liking for this furniture and for her way of life.... I knew her well, and I was not trying to put her into something [that was not appropriate for her].... This suited my own interests as an evolving artist, but I was not putting this old woman into a jazzy modern house that she didn't connect with.[63]

The Vanna Venturi House represents a rare instance, at least since the advent of modernism, of an avant-garde architect embracing – rather than rejecting – the client's wish to furnish a house with disparate objects of personal value; the history of twentieth-century architecture is littered with examples (including a few discussed in this book) of the bitter conflicts that resulted from a rigid adherence to the principles of uniformity in interior design.

Venturi's own emotional attachment to his mother and to the objects with which she surrounded herself ensured that the Vanna Venturi House would be a project of a highly specific nature; it could not have been designed by any other architect for any other client. Yet, through its emphasis on individuality, it served as an eloquent essay on the importance of memory and domestic history not just for women – the traditional conservators of family heirlooms – but as a fundamental principle in architectural design. Venturi's understanding of the compensatory pleasure of memories – his own, his mother's, society's – triggered by the everyday experience of living with old things, stood in stark contrast to the opinions of architects and critics who condemned the popular taste for antiques and period revival interiors in contemporary homes.[64] At the Vanna Venturi House, Robert Venturi was not simply creating meanings as an architect but also as a son, coming to terms with his mother's past and his own. This process was playful and open-ended: with its fragmentary structure, and with its reliance on individual memory and association, the narrative that he created remained fluid and unfinished. In this way, Vanna Venturi was perpetually present and alive, and the architect/son could be connected to her through the contemplation and recapitulation of his work.[65]

Scully has said that Venturi "touches the core of modesty and intelligence in all of us and endows the rather frightening monster of modern America with a curious sweetness of heart."[66] In his mother's house Venturi demonstrated that he – and by extension, we – could stand in a new relationship to history, to ourselves, and to each other, allowing a multiplicity of images, points of view, and experiences to coexist. The house served as a model of intimacy and continuity in a time obsessed with rationalism and the new. With humor, tolerance, and skill, Venturi thus offered up the elements of a new architecture.

1 For surveys of Postmodern architecture, see Charles Jencks, *The Language of Postmodern Architecture* (New York: Rizzoli, 1977), and Heinrich Klotz, *History of Postmodern Architecture* (Cambridge, Mass.: MIT Press, 1988). There is a handful of useful critical works that deal with the Vanna Venturi House; these include Stanislaus van Moos, *Venturi, Rauch and Scott Brown: Buildings and Projects* (New York: Rizzoli, 1987), esp. 244–48; Ellen Perry Berkeley, "Complexities and Contradictions," *Progressive Architecture* 46, no. 5 (May 1965), 168–73; Yukio Futagawa, *Venturi and Rauch: Vanna Venturi House* (Tokyo: Global Architecture/A.D.A. Editions, 1976), 9–17; and Rosemarie Haag Bletter, "Transformations of the American Vernacular: The Work of Venturi, Rauch and Scott Brown," in *Venturi, Rauch and Scott Brown: A Generation of Architecture*, exh. cat. (Champaign-Urbana, Ill.: Krannert Art Museum, 1984), 2–19.

2 Robert Venturi, *Complexity and Contradiction in Architecture* (New York: The Museum of Modern Art, 1966), 22, 46.

3 Ibid., 25.

4 Denise Scott Brown, "Learning from Brutalism," in David Robbins, ed., *The Independent Group: Postwar Britain and the Aesthetics of Plenty* (Cambridge, Mass.: MIT Press, 1990), 203–7, esp. 205. See also her "A Worm's Eye View of Recent Architectural History," *Architectural Record* (Feb.1984), 69–81.

5 Vincent Scully, Introduction, in Venturi, *Complexity and Contradiction*, 16.

6 Robert Venturi, interview with Alice Friedman, May 10, 1996.

7 Denise Scott Brown, "On Houses and Housing," in James Steele, ed., *Venturi, Scott Brown and Associates: On Houses and Housing* (New York: St. Martin's Press, 1992), 13.

8 Venturi, interview with Friedman. See also Frederic Schwartz, ed., *Mother's House: The Evolution of Vanna Venturi's House in Chestnut Hill* (New York: Rizzoli, 1992), 21, 22, 25. An architecture student lived in the house in later years.

9 In addition to the passages from *Complexity and Contradiction* discussed below, see Robert Venturi, "Diversity, Relevance and Representation in Historicism, or *Plus ça change*… Plus a Plea for Pattern All Over Architecture with a Postscript on My Mother's House," in Robert Venturi and Denise Scott Brown, *A View from the Campidoglio: Selected Essays, 1953–1984*, ed. Peter Arnell, Ted Bickford, and Catherine Bergart (New York: Harper and Row, 1984), 108–19.

10 For the historical sources of the Vanna Venturi House, see Vincent Scully, "Robert Venturi's Gentle Architecture," in Christopher Mead, ed., *The Architecture of Robert Venturi* (Albuquerque: University of New Mexico Press, 1989), 8–33.

11 Venturi, "Diversity, Relevance and Representation in Historicism," 118.

12 See Todd Gitlin, *The Sixties: Years of Hope, Days of Rage* (New York: Bantam Books, 1987), esp. chs. 1, 2.

13 See Deborah Fausch, "Knowledge of the Body and the Presence of History – Toward a Feminist Architecture," in Debra Coleman, Elizabeth Danze, and Carol Henderson, eds., *Architecture and Feminism* (New York: Princeton Architectural Press, 1997), 38–59, in which she presents a reading of two works by Venturi, Rauch, and Scott Brown where the sense of the past is "embodied" through physical experience.

14 Venturi, "Diversity, Relevance and Representation," 111.

15 For a general introduction to Postmodernism, see David Harvey, *The Condition of Postmodernity: An Enquiry into the Origins of Cultural Change* (Oxford, England: Basil Blackwell, 1990).

16 See Rosalind Krauss, *The Originality of the Avant-Garde and Other Modernist Myths* (Cambridge, Mass.: MIT Press, 1985), and Carol Duncan, "Virility and Domination in Early Twentieth-Century Vanguard Paint- ing," in her *The Aesthetics of Power: Essays in Critical Art History* (New York: Cambridge University Press, 1993), 81–108.

17 Scully, "Robert Venturi's Gentle Architecture," 15.

18 Although it was not Venturi's intention, his words appealed most to people who, like Elizabeth Gordon of *House Beautiful*, feared and hated European modernism as a coercive, antidemocratic, and anti-American approach to design; the best-known spokesman for this antimodernist position was Tom Wolfe in his *From Bauhaus to Our House* (New York: Farrar, Straus and Giroux, 1975).

19 Venturi, *Complexity and Contradiction*, 23.

20 Ibid., 46.

21 Ibid., 46–47.

22 Ibid., 88–89.

23 Ibid., 117.

24 Ibid.

25 Ibid., 117–19. This description recalls Rudolf Wittkower's analysis of Michelangelo's Laurentian Library vestibule in "Michelangelo's Biblioteca Laurenziana," *Art Bulletin* 16 (1934), 123–218.

26 Venturi, *Complexity and Contradiction*, 119.

27 Ibid., 121.

28 Schwartz, *Mother's House*, 17.

29 Venturi, interview with Friedman.

30 Linda Brandi Cateura, *Growing Up Italian* (New York: William Morrow, 1987), 199.

31 Ibid., 196–97.

32 Venturi, interview with Friedman.

33 Transcript of Robert Venturi's speech at Pritzker Prize award ceremony, Mexico City, May 16, 1991, 2.

34 Venturi, interview with Friedman.

35 Ibid.

36 Ibid.

37 Ibid.

38 Ibid.

39 Denise Scott Brown, "On Houses and Housing," 13.

40 Schwartz, *Mother's House*, 26.

41 Vincent Scully, "Everybody Needs Everything," in Schwartz, *Mother's House*, 39–57, esp. 40–41.

42 Frank Gehry's house in Santa Monica, Calif., of 1979 is discussed at length as a work of Postmodernist architecture in Fredric Jameson's *Postmodernism, or the Cultural Logic of Late Capitalism* (Durham, N.C.: Duke University Press, 1991), 107–29, one of the most thoughtful analyses of the movement. See also Suzanne Franck, *Peter Eisenman's House VI: The Client's Response* (New York: Whitney Library of Design, 1994), in which she describes her own experience as a client.

43 I am indebted to a recent essay by Mary McLeod, "Everyday and 'Other' Spaces," in Coleman, Danze, and Henderson, *Architecture and Feminism*, 1–37, for providing the outlines of this history and suggesting possible directions for a feminist analysis of Venturi's work. See also David Robbins, "The Independent Group: Forerunners of Postmodernism?" in Robbins, *The Independent Group*, 237–47. For Venturi's discussion of the influence of Pop art, see "A Definition of Architecture as Shelter with Decoration on It, and Another Plea for a Symbolism of the Ordinary in Architecture," *A & U* (Jan. 1978), 3–14, reprinted in Venturi and Scott Brown, *A View from the Campidoglio*, 62–67.

44 Denise Scott Brown, "Learning from Brutalism," 203–7; the quotation is on p. 203.

45 Ibid., 204.

46 For Hamilton, see Robbins, *The Independent Group*, 68–69.

47 I am indebted to Patricia Berman for her reading of the Hamilton collage.

48 McLeod, "Everyday and 'Other' Spaces," 23, cites Elissa Rosenberg, "Public and Private: Rereading Jane Jacobs," *Landscape Journal* 13, no. 2 (Fall 1994), 139–44, as the source of a feminist reading of Jacobs, noting that it was written from the perspective of the everyday urban experience of a woman.

49 See Craig Owens, "The Discourse of Others: Feminists and Postmodernism," in Scott Bryson, Barbara Kruger, Lynn Tillmann, and Jane Weinstock, eds., *Beyond Recognition: Representation, Power and Culture* (Berkeley and Los Angeles: University of California Press, 1992), 166–90.

50 Scott Brown, "A Worm's Eye View of Architectural History," 75.

51 Scott Brown's commitment to feminism in the 1970s is evident in a number of her writings, notably "Room at the Top? Sexism and the Star System in Architecture," first presented at the Alliance of Women in Architecture, New York, in 1973 and published in Ellen Perry Berkeley, ed., *Architecture: A Place for Women* (Washington, D.C.: Smithsonian Institution Press, 1989), 237–46.

52 In particular, see van Moos, *Venturi, Rauch and Scott Brown*, 22–31, and Neil Levine, "Return of Historicism," in Mead, *The Architecture of Robert Venturi*, 58–62.

53 Venturi, *Complexity and Contradiction*, 116. In this context, it is notable that Venturi also designed the very modestly programmed headquarters of the North Pennsylvania Visiting Nurses Association in Ambler, Penn. (1961), with an uncharacteristically monumental entrance, and that he used this device to create an image for a largely female institution quite unaccustomed to such architectural attention.

54 Venturi, *Complexity and Contradiction*, 49.

55 For the details of Venturi's education and early career, see Schwartz, *Mother's House*, 18–21.

56 Levine, "Robert Venturi and the 'Return of Historicism,'" 45–67.

57 For the Margaret Esherick House, see David B. Brownlee and David G. De Long, *Louis I. Kahn: In the Realm of Architecture* (New York: Rizzoli, 1991), 152–55.

58 Levine, "'Return of Historicism,'" 56.

59 See Craig Owens, "The Allegorical Impulse: Toward a Theory of Postmodernism," and "The Allegorical Impulse, Part 2," in Bryson, et al., *Beyond Recognition*, 52–69, 70–87.

60 Owens, "The Allegorical Impulse," 54.

61 Ibid., 55, 56. For an overview of the subject of memory and history, see David Lowenthal, *The Past Is a Foreign Country* (New York: Cambridge University Press, 1985).

62 Venturi, *Complexity and Contradiction*, 44.

63 Venturi, interview with Friedman.

64 See, for example, Edgar Kaufmann, Jr., *What Is Modern Design?* (New York: The Museum of Modern Art, 1950), 7. The book was part of the Introductory Series to the Modern Arts, published by the museum in the 1940s and 1950s.

65 In *The Practice of Everyday Life*, Michel de Certeau suggests that there is a similar process at work in the experience of walking in unknown parts of the city: in moving from the familiar to the unfamiliar and back again, the walker re-creates the child's playful experiments with separation from the mother. See *The Practice of Everyday Life*, trans. Steven Rendall (Berkeley and Los Angeles: University of California Press, 1984), 109–10. On children and "found objects," see Walter Benjamin, "Construction Site," in *One Way Street and Other Writings*, trans. Edmund Jephcott and Kinsley Shorter (London: New Left Books, 1979), 52–53, and Graeme Gilloch, *Myth and Metropolis: Walter Benjamin and the City* (Cambridge, England: Polity Press, 1996), esp. 88–89.

66 Scully, "Robert Venturi's Gentle Architecture," 33.

PLATE 1

Morphosis. Bergren House,

Venice, California, rear elevation.

1985

Much has changed in the lives of American and European women in the wake of the women's movement of the 1970s. Thanks to the "second wave" of feminism, more women work outside the home, attaining higher levels of economic, professional, and educational achievement than their mothers or grandmothers could have imagined possible.[1] Moreover, through the sustained efforts of activists, researchers, and educators at both the grass-roots and professional levels, women have gained greater control over their health and sexuality: issues such as birth control, abortion, mental health, lesbian rights, and the needs of older women are more openly discussed, and access to services – as well as information and community supports – relating to all these topics has increased dramatically.[2] Patterns of marriage and divorce have also changed since the 1960s: there has been a significant decline in the number of marriages and, more important, a greater acceptance of alternative choices – later marriage, divorce, remaining single, and living alone or with other women.[3] Overall, women are now in a far better position than ever before to make independent choices about how and where they want to live.

Given these changes, one might well expect to find a greater number of women heads of households hiring architects to design or renovate their houses to suit a variety of new program requirements. Yet this is not the case, and the reasons are primarily economic.[4] In the United States real wages decreased by 19 percent for both men and women between 1973 and 1989; this decline, combined with a steep rise in the cost of education and housing, has made it far more difficult for most people – men *and* women – to even consider home ownership,

Conclusion:

The 1980s and 1990s

let alone new construction. According to a national survey conducted by the Chicago Title and Trust Company, the proportion of single-income families owning houses dropped from 47 percent in 1976 to 21 percent in 1989.[5] Although over 50 percent of women now work outside the home, the situation is not much better for double-income households: the high cost of living, particularly in cities and suburbs, has substantially decreased the ability of most couples to save the capital needed to buy a home. Women heads of households face even greater obstacles.

Changes in the American family have put additional pressures on women.[6] Women may have greater freedom to make choices about work and family than they had a generation ago, but they also bear heavier financial burdens. The combination of the decline in the marriage rate and the astronomical rise in the rate of divorce has meant that there are more women supporting themselves and their families than ever before: at present, one in five women is raising children alone.[7] Many of these women are poor: fully 40 percent of households headed by white women and 60 percent of those headed by black women fall below the poverty line (defined as roughly $10,000 a year for a family of three).[8] Middle-class and professional women also face a significant gap in earnings compared with men: although they are paid higher salaries than other working women, their wages and benefits have not kept pace with those of men performing similar jobs. Moreover, despite far-reaching changes in attitudes toward women and family life in Europe and America, women of all classes still have more responsibility than men for child care and housework; the cost of providing these services – a cost paid in both time and money – has had a significant impact on women's ability to provide shelter for themselves and their families, much less to afford architect-designed homes.[9]

In the face of these economic and demographic pressures, some women have turned to collective housing, focusing their attention on formulating creative design alternatives and financing strategies; in the process, the history of feminist housing has been rediscovered, and many innovative projects have been built over the past twenty years in Europe and the United States, including a number of successful co-housing communities and group homes.[10] Moreover, since the 1970s a small but significant number of women have designed and built their own homes in rural locations, exploring a range of alternatives for single people, groups, and families in extremely low cost projects. Building primarily in wood, these women have produced original new designs by altering the spatial arrangements of familiar vernacular house types – small single-family homes, cottages, and even log cabins.[11] Such collective and low-cost alternatives are the clearest reflection of the influence of the women's movement in architecture and planning.

Although women still commission architect-designed, single-family homes, they do so in numbers that are no greater than in previous generations. In the 1990s most women and their families continue to live in single-family homes and apartments designed for people with very different lives from their own. There is still much to be learned about the ways in which contemporary households – single people, groups of adults, working couples, people with and without children, single parents, or intergenerational families – change their homes, by reconfiguring spaces, tearing down walls, and attaching additions to older houses.[12] One emerging trend suggests that living rooms and dining rooms in existing single-family homes – spaces designed for formal entertaining but now rarely even entered – are being adapted for use as home offices, studios, and extra bedrooms.[13] These rooms in older housing stock can also provide a usable core of enclosed spaces to which open, communal areas might be added through renovation or new construction, as we shall see in the case of Venice III, the Bergren House.

The Bergren and Drager Houses

Two recent houses built for women clients suggest some of the ways in which architects and clients have interpreted new, postfeminist domestic programs. Both were designed for professional single mothers and their children. They share many of the characteristics discussed in the preceding chapters, but also reveal elements not previously explored in designs for women: redefinition of the relationship between parent and child or children to foster greater independence through spatial parity; enlargement and subdivision of private space to accommodate a variety of uses – study, reading, writing, listening to music, or other leisure pursuits – and to offer varying degrees of accessibility to the activities of children, visitors, and the outside world; elaboration of areas devoted to dressing, bathing, and relaxation.

The Bergren House (also called Venice III), built in 1985 in Venice, California (plates 1, 2; fig. 1), is a compact, multilevel addition to a 1920s bungalow designed by Thom Mayne and Michael Rotondi of Morphosis for Ann Bergren, a single mother and a professor of classics at U.C.L.A.[14] The program called for a new library, study, living area, bathroom, bedroom, and deck; these spaces were intended primarily for the use of Bergren herself, while the rooms in the existing house – including small bedrooms, a living room, kitchen, and dining area – would become common space and a bedroom and playroom for Bergren's young son.[15]

The site, a small backyard in an urban neighborhood of densely packed houses, offered very little room to build and no views at all, except over the roof of the bungalow to a busy street. The budget was also tight: new construction had to be limited, and costs were kept to a minimum. Since Mayne and Rotondi had a number of large-scale projects under way at the time, they could afford to view Bergren's modest addition as a learning experience in which to try out new ideas.[16] This case follows the pattern established by other small projects for women clients discussed in this book: like Truus Schröder, Edith Farnsworth, and Constance Perkins, Bergren took part in the creative process and encouraged the architects to experiment with alternative designs. Rotondi described the architects' approach to the project:

It allowed us to explore sequential movement in a way that we hadn't before. It was very processional. It allowed us to deal with the relationship between a visual axis and an organizational axis (as opposed to one of movement), which had to do with the rational ordering systems that we lay on the world in order to comprehend the world, but then beyond that, the circumstance of everyday life.[17]

Although such a statement seems to have more to do with design theory than with the program of a house for a single mother, it is in fact an extremely revealing distillation of the fundamental goals of the client: to provide a series of linked spaces for work and leisure that enhance and order the daily activities of the individual and household.

Using thresholds and boundaries to mark points of transition, the interior reveals itself as a sequence of distinct spatial environments. An axial, processional path leads from the common space of the old house directly into the center of the entrance lobby; from here one can view the open living area and library in the addition, and the stair and bathroom beyond (plate 3; fig. 2). At this point the path of movement shifts from the center to the perimeter of the room, but the path of sight continues on axis; the two paths are thus first conjoined and then separated, calling attention to the passage from a more public to a more private area of the house. At the back of the large room, the stairwell articulates the complexities of access in a similar way: it is a vertical slot of space, screened by a floating rectilinear grid yet traversed by the diagonal stairway, which moves up through and across it.

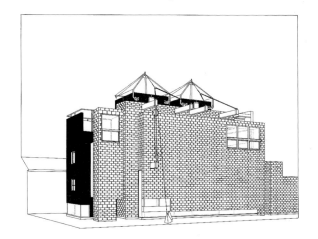

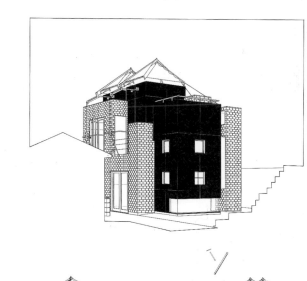

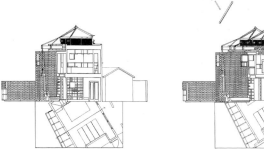

FIGURE 1

Morphosis. Bergren House,
Venice, California, perspectives,
sections, and plans. 1985.
Courtesy of Morphosis, Santa
Monica

PLATE 2

Bergren House, partial view of
front elevation

Conclusion

PLATE 3

Bergren House, view of living
area with stair and bathroom
beyond. The entrance to the
below-ground study is visible
just above the sofa

The stairs provide entry to a stack of ancillary spaces devoted to mind, body, and nature: a below-ground study, surrounded by windows on three sides; a light-filled bath with a window on axis with the door and landing (the toilet is in a small extruded space beyond, visible through the window wall of the library); and an open terrace at the top of the house. Here again, visual axes intersect with organizational and processional axes, creating a series of overlapping movements, vistas, paths, and rest points.

These architectural devices have the effect of framing the activities of family and individual, expressing Bergren's role as both mother and scholar, and highlighting the integration of mind and body. The complexity of the program and its expression in the sequence of separate but linked spaces reflects the changes in women's roles since the 1970s by balancing work, leisure, and family life within the home. While in this design there are clearly elements of Le Corbusier (particularly in the processional route) and of Mies (in the imposition of the grid, and in the notion of the domestic realm as a space of contemplation), the synthesis of these parts in a project for a woman client is new.

The Bergren House is not, however, simply an inward-looking retreat: in the bedroom and dressing area at the top of the stairs, the space opens up again and becomes more formal and axial, focusing attention on the relationship between the individual, the ordered environment, and the outside world. Doors and a balcony overlook the garden, windows open onto the street, and a pyramidal tent of white "sails" floats and flutters above the skylighted ceiling. Located between earth and sky, the bed at the center of the room is like a ceremonial platform, mediating between nature, the self, and the city beyond. The room, like the house itself, thus becomes a place of liberation from the social realm, a private space of deep contemplation and aesthetic pleasure that is nevertheless linked to the world beyond the home.

FIGURE 2

Bergren described her own awareness of the overlay of physical, intellectual, and compositional structure in an article entitled "Interplay of Opposites": "I, too, work with form, ambiguity, and the interrelations of old and new. I combine the traditional skills of philology with post-structuralist literary theory to study early Greek thought – especially about how language works through the instability of opposition like inside/outside, fixed/mobile, truth/imitation of truth."[18] Work and pleasure – like mind and body, individual and family, parent and child – are integrated but also delineated, providing each with shape and definition as constituent parts of a modern life. Bergren summed this up: "Here I realize what I've learned from Los Angeles and from ancient Greek architecture – that intellectual concentration is promoted best by relaxation, the relaxation of living in beautiful form animated by natural light. In this building, Morphosis has overcome for me the opposition between vacation and work."[19]

Conclusion

FIGURE 3

Franklin D. Israel. Drager House, Berkeley, California, plans. From upper left: a. second floor b. third floor c. fourth floor d. roof. 1994. Courtesy of Israel, Callas, Shortridge, Architects, Los Angeles

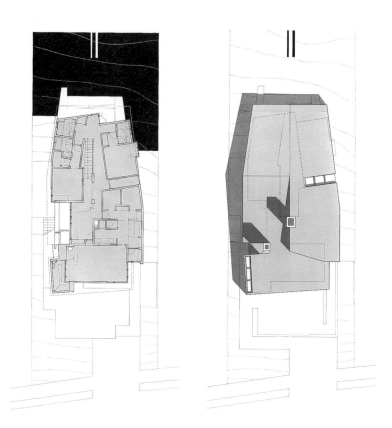

PLATE 4

Franklin D. Israel. Drager House, Berkeley, California, front elevation. 1994

PLATE 5
Drager House, view from the
southwest. 1994

In Franklin D. Israel's house for Sharon Drager, built in 1994 in Berkeley, California (plates 4, 5; fig. 3), some of the same concerns and devices became evident, despite the fact that the house is much larger and was far more expensive to build. For Drager, a vascular surgeon and mother of two teenage children, the home is not a place for work but for family life, leisure, and relaxation; nevertheless, like Bergren, she emphasizes the need for careful programming of linked spaces to accommodate a variety of activities, and for balance between individual privacy and family life.[20] Conceived and designed in the aftermath of the Berkeley fire of 1991, the Drager House is a resplendent phoenix, a tall, defiant, copper-clad symbol of continuity that literally rises from the ruined foundations of the modest wood-frame home that burned to the ground.[21] Although a recent article quoted Drager as saying, "The house looks like me.... It's an edgy house for an edgy owner,"[22] its sharp angles and folded planes belie the sense of stability and order that its complex forms and spaces express. Here, as at the Bergren House, the meaning of the domestic realm unfolds along a processional route, and this linking of diverse elements gives the Drager House its character as a modern home and as a work of contemporary architecture. As such, it follows in a long line of luxurious, architect-designed houses – the Villa Stein–de Monzie comes immediately to mind – which despite their size and ample budgets nevertheless contain lessons about domestic planning for more modest projects.

For Sharon Drager the starting point was an idea about her relationship with her children. Having divorced soon after the project began, she worked closely with the project manager, Barbara Callas, and project architect, Annie Chu, to develop the program as an alternative domestic environment, elaborating the project's dimensions as a feminist essay on architecture and domesticity. The design of the house carries with it remnants of its original concept as a "traditional" home – large, formal living and dining rooms occupy most of the main floor – but the way the house is currently used, these spaces seem somewhat vestigial and empty. By contrast, the family room, kitchen, breakfast nook, children's rooms, and Drager's own study and bedroom at the top of the house feel alive with daily activity and with their connection to one another. The integration of these areas is expressed by the dramatic stairway that traverses the interior space from front to back and top to bottom of the steep site.

Drager described the ideas that were important to her as a client:

I have very strong feelings about children's rooms....When I first started looking to buy a house when my kids were babies, I was appalled at some of the VERY fancy houses I saw with tiny children's rooms. They were almost after-thoughts in homes with very grand public spaces and very sybaritic master suites. I had to share a room with my sister when we were kids and I LONGED for my own room. I bought the house that burned down because it had great light, big closets, and two wonderful large bedrooms for the kids.[23]

Her comments reveal her awareness of children as people with a need for privacy: "One of the worst things about the house I rented after the fire was the fact that the kids' rooms were the size of monks' cells. True, kids' rooms are often messy, but they are also places to dream dreams, to try out fantasies and learn to be comfortable with yourself."[24] It was Israel who persuaded her to provide each child with a small bathroom en suite with a large bedroom, a decision she considers one of the successes of the project. Each of the children's rooms, which flank the stair on either side of the upper floor, is thus like a good-sized room in a hotel, complete with its own bath and enough space to accommodate a wide range of activities as well as storage of books, clothes, and so on. For Israel, an architect with a strong connection to Los Angeles architecture, the model for a house made up of self-enclosed studio/living rooms clustered around a

common space may have been R. M. Schindler's Elizabeth
Van Patten House (discussed in the introduction), a residence for three women that also sits on a steep site.[25]

Drager's private living area is on the same floor as
the children's rooms but removed from them by a long,
open hallway (fig. 4). Here the balance between family
and individual is most clearly articulated. Drager's study
(plate 6) is located in an open space outside the doorway
of her bedroom, an "extended threshold" of her private
space that allows her to be in several places at once.[26]
The client had strong feelings about the programming
of this area as well:

The idea of having my study "in the middle of everything"
was mine. I liked the idea of being able to "monitor" the
comings and goings from my space. I wanted to know if
someone came in the door or if the kids were in their rooms.
This was not snooping – just being in the center. I think
many women view the kitchen as that sort of space…but
cooking is not an important activity for me.[27]

With the many views that it provides, the study functions
like the central point in a panopticon: sitting at her desk,

Drager can look down at the front door, across to the
stairs and children's rooms, and out at the view, and monitor access to her own bedroom. Like the kitchen, the
open study (there is also an enclosed home-office next to
the entrance) also works as a transitional space within
the home: both are places where the children can "check
in" – notably while she is occupied with a task of her
own – and then move along. The stair and hallway, too,
function as places for spontaneous, informal meetings;
thus the house is like a city traversed by a busy thor-
oughfare, on which people meet and talk casually before
going their separate ways.[28]

With its threshold study, Drager's bedroom suite at
the top of the house is the signal spatial and programmatic event in the home. The bedroom itself, with a
fireplace, television, and built-in desk for working on jig-
saw puzzles, is a self-contained retreat. Like Bergren's
bedroom, it takes advantage of the view from the front
and side of the house, yet it is also inward looking, a
place for privacy and reflection, for mind and body.
Here, too, the space of private retreat extends into the
recesses of the house: in the large bathroom and bathing
area, muted colors, textured surfaces, and natural light
create an environment of physical awareness and aesthetic pleasure – Drager calls it "Frank's gift to me."[29]
This is not a place of vanity or glamour, but rather one
of sentience and calm.[30] A large shower room with a
three-quarter-length window opens onto a view across
the valley. Toilet, sink, shower, and dressing rooms (there
are two of them) are in separate areas. Thus washing and
bathing become a daily, choreographed ritual, a series of

FIGURE 4

Drager House, the stair
and hallway leading to the
threshold study

PLATE 6

Drager House, threshold study

distinct moments in which awareness of the body and its movements creates a reciprocal consciousness of objects and spaces. Drager understands this well after several years of use:

There are two doors, one from the bedroom and one from the hallway. The door from the bedroom is a pocket door – sort of like opening into a secret place. In the morning, I progress from my private sleeping space into the bathroom to the shower, sink and toilet, then to the closet, and finally dressed and fully "armed" I leave by the more public, official door to the hallway and the day.[31]

Comments such as this confirm the success of the house as a work of architecture and as a home. Like Bergren, Drager viewed her collaboration with the architects as positive, and she recognized that they not only enhanced the program as she defined it, but also reconfigured domestic space in a way that clarified and enlarged the experience of domestic life.[32]

Conclusion

Implications for Future Design

Ultimately, the significance of the Bergren and Drager houses, like that of the other projects discussed in this book, stems from their ability to integrate program and design in a meaningful synthesis of form, function, and symbolism. As houses built for women clients, they go further: in interpreting the needs of women and their households, both projects exceed the requirements of use to suggest new approaches to domestic planning – narratives of balanced integration among disparate parts – responsive to complex programs. By making and sustaining new connections through spatial organization, architecture goes beyond mere form to act as a cultural force for change.

The most successful projects are those that provide users with choices, offering a variety of spatial and social environments. Architectural experience is not simply physical and aesthetic but also cultural, and it is through the culturally constructed body that the mind and spirit of an individual are reached. This is why gender matters to architectural design, and why houses built for women who defied convention teach us important lessons about the power of architecture.

The Bergren and Drager houses suggest a number of lessons for domestic design, not only in the case of single-family houses but for multi-unit projects as well.[33] The innovative approaches taken in these houses need not be tied to budget or scale but can be applied to a variety of domestic conditions. First, it is evident from the comments of the architects and clients in both examples that these houses were viewed as collaborative projects from the start. Sustained and detailed discussion of the program requirements – and of the symbolic and psychological dimensions of each client's vision of the new house – ensured that the strong foundations of the collaboration were laid early. Further, these conversations were an opportunity for architects and clients to exchange ideas; such a process is grounded in the recognition that each participant has a role to play in the project as it develops. This is a crucial point: on the architect's side, there is an acknowledgment of the client's vision and experience, and, equally important, on the client's side, an affirmation that the architect not only satisfies the functional requirements of the program but adds to and enhances it through design. This, after all, is the bitter lesson of the Farnsworth House: ultimately, architect and client failed to come to terms with each other's vision, goals, and experience.

Second, the two projects suggest new approaches to design for nontraditional households. In each case the balance between public and private space is shifted to offer a wider range of choices for individual and group activities. Points of overlap between zones (the entrance lobby of the Bergren House, and the stairway and threshold study in the Drager House) become meeting places for household members. Communal spaces can thus be reduced in size relative to areas where adults and children can work or relax in private (the vestigial quality of the living and dining rooms in the Drager House confirm this point). Moreover, by expanding and elaborating private spaces, both houses acknowledge the complex lives of the adults and children who live in them, providing places to "dream dreams," as Drager put it. It is important to emphasize that projects such as these need not be large. It is not size but circulation and sequence that are critical, as is evident from the realization of how much is accomplished in the 800-square-foot addition at the Bergren House.

Third, both houses emphasize the importance of domestic ritual and meaningful daily contact with well-designed built form. Windows, vistas, furniture, and materials call attention to repeated actions, creating a storehouse of familiar experiences and memories over time. Moreover, the delineation of paths of movement and sight highlights specific actions and points of connection, making the work of architecture an active participant in shaping daily experience. Such connections help focus on what Bergren called "the interplay of opposites" – old and new parts of the house, work and relaxation, individual and family – and thus create coherence among the disparate parts of everyday life at home. Many good buildings offer such rich environments, but these examples, as houses designed for single women and children, underline the importance of respecting – and representing – the experience of a range of users.

Fourth, these two examples focus attention on the boundaries and connections between individuals not only within the household, but also between the home and the outside world. Windows offer views of the street and the city, terraces provide access to sky and air, and checkpoints within the house allow monitoring of entrances and exits, both interior and exterior. These devices anchor the home in its surroundings, offering the sort of connection to the wider community that the interior streets and paths offer to household members. As single-family homes, these houses represent individual, private solutions, yet they contain ideas that can be expanded and developed to create community and broaden connections between households.

Like all good buildings, the Bergren and Drager houses confirm architecture's ability to transform lives. By providing users with choices, and with contexts in which to order daily activities, they create an awareness of individual experience and of the lives of others.

I began this book with the voice of Frank Lloyd Wright, and it is only appropriate that I end it with that of Virginia Woolf, the person with whom the notion of "a room of one's own" is most closely associated. Though many readers may be familiar with the phrase, fewer will have read the text in which it appears. In her essay Woolf makes clear that it is not simply physical space but also money, freedom, and courage that are needed if women

are to create great works of literature or to become the equals of men in any field. For her, all these things were necessary if women were to put aside the expectations of society – to free themselves from the "common sitting-room," as she put it, of gender stereotype – and experience life and art more fully. Thus she spoke to her audience of women at Girton College, Cambridge, in October 1929 about Shakespeare's sister – that fictitious, frustrated woman poet "who never wrote a word" – and about how her spirit lived on, not only in each of them but "in many other women who are not here tonight" because they are at home "washing up the dishes and putting the children to bed."[34] With "five hundred [pounds] a year each of us and rooms of our own," she explained, she and the women around her could bring Shakespeare's sister back to life through their own work. But many things would have to change:

If we have the habit of freedom and the courage to write exactly what we think; if we escape a little from the common sitting-room and see human beings not always in relation to each other but in relation to reality; and the sky too, and the trees or whatever it may be in themselves…if we face the fact, for it is a fact, that there is no arm to cling to, but that we go alone and that our relation is to the world of reality and not to the world of men and women, then the opportunity will come and the dead poet who was Shakespeare's sister will put on the body which she has so often laid down. Drawing her life from the lives of the unknown who were her forerunners, as her brother did before her, she will be born.[35]

Like all the women in this book, Woolf knew well that with the money to live and a room of one's own, courage, independence, and creativity would follow. But the houses designed for these women teach us a further lesson: that if the room is not just a room but a home that gives pleasure, order, and meaning to life, then these things might come sooner.

1 See Rosalind Rosenberg, *Divided Lives: American Women in the Twentieth Century* (New York: Hill and Wang, 1992), and Claudia Dale Goldin, *Understanding the Gender Gap: An Economic History of American Women* (New York: Oxford University Press, 1990).

2 For a survey of changes in women's lives in the United States, see John d'Emilio and Estelle Freedman, *Intimate Matters: A History of Sexuality in America* (New York: Harper and Row, 1988); for Europe, see Drude Dahlerup, ed., *The New Women's Movement: Feminism and Political Power in Europe and the USA* (London: Sage, 1986), and Jane Rendell, *The Origins of Modern Feminism: Women in Britain, France and the United States* (New York: Schocken, 1984).

3 D'Emilio and Freedman, *Intimate Matters*, 331; Rosenberg, *Divided Lives*, 195–209.

4 For an overview of the effects of recent social and economic trends on women's lives, see Rosenberg, *Divided Lives*, 235–52.

5 Ibid., 236.

6 For a survey of recent changes in the American family, see Steven Mintz and Susan Kellogg, *Domestic Revolutions: A Social History of American Life* (New York: Free Press), 202–52.

7 For a summary of data relating to this point, see Sherry Ahrentzen, "Overview of Housing for Single-Parent Households," in Karen A. Franck and Sherry Ahrentzen, eds., *New Households, New Housing* (New York: Van Nostrand Reinhold, 1991), 143–60. On working women, see Arlie Russell Hochschild, *Second Shift: Working Parents and the Revolution at Home* (New York: Viking Press, 1989).

8 Rosenberg, *Divided Lives*, 247–48.

9 Ahrentzen, "Overview," 145–56. On women and housework, see also Susan Strasser, *Never Done: A History of American Housework* (New York: Pantheon, 1982).

10 For feminist housing alternatives, see Dolores Hayden, *The Grand Domestic Revolution: A History of Feminist Designs for American Homes, Neighborhoods and Cities* (Cambridge, Mass.: MIT Press, 1981), and her *Redesigning the American Dream: The Future of Housing, Work and Family Life* (Cambridge, Mass.: MIT Press, 1984). Further discussion of contemporary alternatives is in Franck and Ahrentzen, *New Households, New Housing*, esp. parts 1, 2. For collective living in apartments, see Elizabeth Cromley, *Alone Together: A History of Early New York Apartments* (Ithaca, N.Y.: Cornell University Press, 1989).

11 This movement is described in Janice Goldfrank, *Making Ourselves at Home: Women Builders and Designers* (Watsonville, Calif.: Papier-Mache Press, 1995).

12 For some recent alternatives, see K. Michael Hays et al., eds., *Assemblage* 24, issue entitled "House Rules" (1994). This type of work dominates the practice of many young architects.

13 The evidence for this observation comes from over one hundred "house histories" written by students in my courses on gender and domestic architecture at Wellesley College over the past twelve years.

14 For the Bergren House, see Peter Cook and George Rand, *Morphosis: Buildings and Projects* (New York: Rizzoli, 1989), 100–111; a full bibliography for the firm's work is included. See also Ann Bergren, "Interplay of Opposites," *House and Garden* (Jan. 1986), 126–33, and Dana Cuff, *Architecture: The Story of Practice* (Cambridge, Mass.: MIT Press, 1991), 199–209.

15 Ann Bergren and Taylor Bergren-Chrisman, interview with Alice Friedman, May 24, 1996.

16 Cuff, *Architecture*, 199–203.

17 Ibid., 203 (from an interview conducted in Feb. 1988).

18 Bergren, "Interplay of Opposites," 127–28.

19 Ibid., 174.

20 For the Drager House, see Diana Ketchum, "An Architect Conjures Up History from the Ashes," *New York Times*, Aug. 17, 1995, B: 1, 4, and Aaron Betsky, *Drager House: Franklin D. Israel* (London: Phaidon, 1996). For the work of Franklin D. Israel, see Franklin D. Israel et al., *Franklin D. Israel: Buildings and Projects* (New York: Rizzoli, 1992), esp. Frank O. Gehry's introduction, Israel's essay, "Cities Within," and Thomas Hines's essay, "Takeoff: The Journey of Frank Israel." See also James Steele, ed., *Franklin D. Israel* (London: Academy Editions, 1994).

21 Annie Chu, interview with Alice Friedman, Mar. 29, 1996.

22 David L. Kirp, "There Goes the Neighborhood," *Harpers Magazine* 294 (Mar. 1997), 52.

23 Sharon Drager, E-mail letter to Alice Friedman, May 4, 1996.

24 Ibid.

25 For Israel's debt to Schindler, see Hines, "Takeoff," 212.

26 The phrase is Annie Chu's; interview with Friedman.

27 Drager, E-mail letter to Friedman.

28 Sharon Drager, interview with Alice Friedman, Mar. 26, 1996, and Chu, interview with Friedman.

29 Drager, E-mail letter to Friedman.

30 For example, compare this bath to that in Israel's Strick House, Hollywood, Calif., of 1993, a room filled with smooth, reflective surfaces, glass partitions, and featuring a view over the rooftops of Hollywood from the spa bath itself; illustrated in Steele, *Franklin D. Israel*, 138–43.

31 Drager, E-mail letter to Friedman.

32 The Drager House was only the second house built by Frank Israel and, tragically, his last; he died in June 1996 at the age of fifty.

33 I am indebted here to the approach offered by Ghislaine Hermanuz in her essay "Housing for a Postmodern World," in Diana Agrest, Patricia Conway, and Leslie Kanes Weisman, eds., *The Sex of Architecture* (New York: Abrams, 1996), 233–40.

34 Virginia Woolf, *A Room of One's Own* (New York: Harcourt Brace, 1989), 113 (originally published in 1929).

35 Woolf, *A Room of One's Own*, 114.

Acknowledgments

Many people and institutions have helped make this book possible. As I was embarking on the project I was awarded a fellowship at the Bunting Institute, Radcliffe College, and I am very grateful to the former director, Florence Ladd, and to my "sister fellows" at the institute for helping me clarify the ideas and focus the questions from which my research developed. Special thanks are due to Eve Blau, Wini Breines, Karen Hansen, and Salem Mekuria for their advice and encouragement. At every stage my work has been supported by grants from Wellesley College, for which I am deeply grateful. The final phase of research and writing was completed with the aid of generous grants from the National Endowment for the Humanities and the John Simon Guggenheim Memorial Foundation. I want to thank these institutions for their support, which enabled me to take time off from teaching at a critical point in the project.

Throughout this endeavor I have relied on the expertise and generosity of specialists whose knowledge of the architects and houses discussed in the book helped me find my way. In my work on Frank Lloyd Wright and Hollyhock House, I benefitted enormously from the guidance and good counsel of Kathryn Smith, whose research forms the foundation for any study of the subject. I am also grateful to Neil Levine, Jack Quinan, and Virginia Kazor for their assistance and advice on numerous occasions. In the Department of Special Collections, Getty Center for the History of Art and the Humanities, I consulted microfiche copies of materials from the Frank Lloyd Wright Archive at Taliesin West; the Getty library staff was very helpful. A one-month grant from the Huntington Library and Art Gallery enabled me to carry out research on the arts in Southern California; during this period, as at other times, I made use of the Huntington's rich collections, and I want to acknowledge the assistance of the librarians and curators there. I also wish to thank my friend Jill Finsten of the J. Paul Getty Museum for her hospitality and for making my many visits to Los Angeles so pleasant.

My work on Truus Schröder and my research in
Holland would have been impossible without the collaboration of Maristella Casciato. An expert in Dutch architecture, she was the ideal guide and teacher; her patience,
generosity, and good humor sustained us both during our
campaigns of research in Utrecht and Amsterdam. A faculty grant from Wellesley College enabled us to travel
and work together. I also wish to thank Jaap Oosterhoff,
curator of the Rietveld-Schröder Archive at the Centraal
Museum, Utrecht, for his advice and encouragement.
Many others, including Lenneke Büller, Corrie Nagtegaal,
Frank den Oudsten, Pieter Singelenberg, Nancy Stieber,
Susana Torre, and Nancy Troy, contributed in various
ways. The staffs of the International Information Center
and the Archives for the Women's Movement in Amsterdam, and of the Netherlands Architecture Institute in
Rotterdam, were also very generous with their time.

In my study of the Villa Stein–de Monzie I have relied
on numerous people for guidance and advice. Mardges
Bacon helped direct my research at the Fondation Le
Corbusier in Paris and offered many invaluable suggestions. I am also grateful to Albert Bennett, Daniel and
Betty Stein, and Brenda Wineapple, all of whom kindly
shared their knowledge of the Stein–de Monzie household with me; special thanks are due to Mr. Bennett for
allowing me to study the letters and photographs in his
collection. With the help of a one-month fellowship at
the Beinecke Rare Book and Manuscript Library, Yale
University, I consulted materials in the Gertrude and Leo
Stein Collections, and I am very grateful for the assistance and hospitality of members of the staff. I conducted
additional research on the Steins and their circle at the
Bancroft Library, University of California at Berkeley.

My research on Edith Farnsworth began with a telephone call to her nephew Fairbank Carpenter, who
graciously donated the manuscripts and photographs in
his possession to the Newberry Library in Chicago. I am
grateful to the Newberry for a fellowship that made it
possible for me to consult these materials. I would also
like to thank Pierre Adler, curator of the Mies van der Rohe
Archive at The Museum of Modern Art, New York, for
making the documents and drawings in his care available
to me. A Travel to Collections Grant from the National
Endowment for the Humanities supported my work in
New York and at the Library of Congress, which holds
the Mies van der Rohe Papers. Conversations with Kevin
Harrington, Mary McLeod, and Christopher Reed helped
me in various ways, and I thank them for their support.
I would also like to thank Stanford Anderson and Mark
Jarzombek for inviting me to present the material on
Philip Johnson at M.I.T., and for their comments at a
critical stage in my work. Gigi Fernandez of the office of
Philip Johnson, Ritchie, and Fiore, New York, worked
tirelessly to obtain photographs on my behalf.

I was introduced to Constance Perkins by Susan
Danly, former curator of American art at the Huntington
Library and Art Gallery, and I greatly appreciate her
encouragement and interest. Conversations with Robert
Winter after Perkins's death helped enormously; I am
also grateful to Dion Neutra for discussing his father's
work with me. My research in Pasadena was supported
by a Robert Wark Fellowship at the Huntington, which
now owns and maintains the Perkins House; I was very
fortunate to have had the opportunity to stay at the
house during this time, and I would like to thank the
Huntington for extending that privilege to me. Perkins's
papers are now held by the Archives of American Art,
and I want to express my particular appreciation to the
staffs of both the San Marino and the Washington offices
for assisting me with my research. I extend my thanks as
well to the Department of Special Collections, University
of California at Los Angeles, which holds the Richard
Neutra Collection, and to the Architectural Drawings
Collection, University of California at Santa Barbara.

Special acknowledgment is due to Robert Venturi for taking the time to talk with me about his mother's house; my work on that chapter could not have gone forward without his support. Denise Scott Brown, Deborah Fausch, Liselotte Freed, John Izenour, and Susan Scanlon also offered advice, information, and guidance.

I am especially grateful to Ann Bergren and Sharon Drager for their willingness to be interviewed and for allowing me to visit their homes. Their expertise and insight contributed to the project in many ways. While I was working on the Drager House I learned a great deal from my conversations with Frank Israel and Annie Chu; Janet Sager of Morphosis was also extremely generous with her time and knowledge.

Many other people helped make this book possible. Donald Hallmark and Richard S. Taylor shared their expertise on the Dana-Thomas House; Nancy Gruskin, Lisa Reitzes, and Mary Daniels, librarian in the Department of Special Collections, Loeb Library, Harvard Graduate School of Design, assisted me with my research on Eleanor Raymond. At Wellesley College the staff of the Art Department, Art Library, and Visual Resources Collection, especially Marie Companion, Avalee Jenkins, and Jeanne Hablanian, patiently endured my many requests for help in locating photographs, books, and articles over the years; I am deeply grateful to all of them for their support and friendship. My research assistant, Lori Pavese, was always helpful and thorough, and she offered useful advice and encouragement along the way. Denise Decastro also assisted with the research.

Many colleagues in the Art Department at Wellesley took the time to discuss the project or offered their support in other ways. I gratefully acknowledge the contributions of Rebecca Bedell, Judith Black, Margaret Carroll, Anne Higonnet, and especially James O'Gorman, whose friendship and support have been important to me throughout my career and this project. I am indebted to Martin Brody, Zeynep Çelik, Ginna Donovan, Kathleen Harleman, Katharine Park, Geeta Patel, John Rhodes, Paul Robertson, and David Stang for their encouragement and advice throughout the process of research, writing, and revision. Patricia Berman read and commented on every chapter, sometimes more than once; I have relied heavily on her enormous talents as a scholar and specialist in twentieth-century art, and I thank her for her sound judgment, generosity, and good humor over the years.

Diana Murphy, my editor at Abrams, has stood behind the project from the very beginning. I have depended on her for many things, and she has been a constant friend and skillful collaborator. It is a pleasure to acknowledge her contribution here. I also wish to thank Elizabeth Robbins and Judy Hudson at Abrams for their efforts in making the book possible.

My greatest debt is to Lena Sorensen. She has contributed to every part of this undertaking, visiting each of the houses, discussing every chapter, helping with the research, and enduring the many challenges of living with this project and with me. No one could ask for a better collaborator and companion, and it is with the deepest gratitude and love that I dedicate this book to her.

Cambridge, Massachusetts
December 1997

Index

Page numbers in *italic* refer to illustrations.

Photograph credits